Globalisation and Labour Market Adjustment

Also by David Greenaway:

Paul Collier, Norman Gemmell, David Greenaway and David Bevan (eds)
TRADE AND FISCAL ADJUSTMENT IN AFRICA

David Greenaway and Rajan Dabee (eds)
THE MAURITIAN ECONOMY
A Reader

David Greenaway, Holger Görg and Richard Kneller (eds)
GLOBALISATION AND PRODUCTIVITY GROWTH
Theory and Evidence

David Greenaway, Robert C. Hine, Anthony P. O'Brien and Robert J.
Thornton (eds)
GLOBAL PROTECTIONISM

Ademola Oyejide, Benno Ndulu and David Greenaway (eds)
REGIONAL INTEGRATION AND TRADE LIBERALIZATION IN
SUBSAHARAN AFRICA
Volume 4: Synthesis and Review

Globalisation and Labour Market Adjustment

Edited by

David Greenaway
Leverhulme Centre for Research on Globalisation and Economic Policy,
University of Nottingham

Richard Upward
Leverhulme Centre for Research on Globalisation and Economic Policy,
University of Nottingham

Peter Wright
Leverhulme Centre for Research on Globalisation and Economic Policy,
University of Nottingham

First published 2008 by
PALGRAVE MACMILLAN
Houndmills, Basingstoke, Hampshire RG21 6XS and
175 Fifth Avenue, New York, N.Y. 10010
Companies and representatives throughout the world

PALGRAVE MACMILLAN is the global academic imprint of the Palgrave Macmillan division of St. Martin's Press, LLC and of Palgrave Macmillan Ltd. Macmillan®is a registered trademark in the United States, United Kingdom and other countries. Palgrave is a registered trademark in the European Union and other countries.

ISBN-13: 978–0–230–00493–1   hardback
ISBN-10: 0–230–00493–8   hardback

This book is printed on paper suitable for recycling and made from fully managed and sustained forest sources. Logging, pulping and manufacturing processes are expected to conform to the environmental regulations of the country of origin.

A catalogue record for this book is available from the British Library.

Library of Congress Cataloging-in-Publication Data

Globalisation and labour market adjustment / edited by David
  Greenaway, Richard Upward, Peter Wright.
      p. cm.
  Includes bibliographical references and index.
  ISBN 0–230–00493–8 (alk. paper)
  1. Labor market.   2. International trade.   3. International economic
  integration.   I. Greenaway, David.   II. Upward, Richard.   III.
  Wright, Peter, 1967-
  HD5706.G55 2008
  331.13—dc22
                                                                    2007052957

10   9   8   7   6   5   4   3   2   1
17   16   15   14   13   12   11   10   09   08

Printed and bound in Great Britain by
CPI Antony Rowe, Chippenham and Eastbourne

Contents

List of Tables

List of Figures

Acknowledgements

The work in this volume was completed at the Leverhulme Centre for Research on Globalisation and Economic Policy at the University of Nottingham and supported by funding from the Leverhulme Trust under Programme Grant F114/BF. The editors and authors gratefully acknowledge that financial support.

Notes on Contributors

Paulo Bastos is an economic analyst at the European Commission and External Research Fellow, Leverhulme Centre for Research on Globalisation and Economic Policy, University of Nottingham.

Carl Davidson is Professor of Economics, Michigan State University.

Barbara Dluhosch is Professor of Economics, Helmut-Schmidt University.

Rod Falvey is Professor of International Economics, University of Nottingham.

Ingo Geishecker is Researcher at the Chair of Wolfram Schrettl, Department of Economics and Institute of East-European Studies, Freie Universität.

Holger Görg is Associate Professor and Reader in International Economics, University of Nottingham. He is Programme Co-ordinator for Globalisation, Productivity and Technology at the Leverhulme Centre for Research on Globalisation and Economic Policy, University of Nottingham.

David Greenaway is Professor of Economics and Director of the Leverhulme Centre for Research on Globalisation and Economic Policy, University of Nottingham.

Alexander Hijzen is an Economist in the Employment Analysis and Policy Division of the OECD.

Udo Kreickemeier is Associate Professor in Economics, University of Nottingham.

Sara Maioli is Lecturer in Economics, Newcastle University Business School.

Steve J. Matusz is Professor of Economics, Michigan State University.

Douglas Nelson is Professor of Economics, Murphy Institute of Political Economy, Tulane University.

Joana Silva is an economist at the World Bank and Policy Associate, Leverhulme Centre for Research on Globalisation and Economic Policy, University of Nottingham.

Richard Upward is Associate Professor in Economics, University of Nottingham.

Niven Winchester is Lecturer in Economics, University of Otago.

Peter Wright is Associate Professor and Reader in Labour Economics, University of Nottingham. He is Programme Co-ordinator for Globalisation and Labour Markets at the Leverhulme Centre for Research on Globalisation and Economic Policy, University of Nottingham.

1
Introduction and Overview

David Greenaway, Richard Upward and Peter Wright

It has been argued that recent developments in international integration are historically large and have unprecedented characteristics (OECD, 2007). While the value of international trade in goods and cross-border investment has continued to grow somewhat faster than global GDP, three key developments distinguish this episode of globalisation from those observed in the past. First, the entry of China and India into the world economy has had a huge impact on the potential global supply of labour. Second, rapid developments in information and communications technology have allowed firms to trade more intermediate inputs and hence 'fragment' their production process. This fragmentation of production has also allowed the trade in a vast range of services which were previously regarded as non-tradable. Third, migration into almost all OECD economies has increased, with migrants making up a significantly larger proportion of the working-age population.

Economists would naturally point to the benefits of this process. The gains from specialisation and exchange from increased integration should lead to an increase in output and aggregate welfare. Although economists have long recognised that there will be adjustment costs in the short-run, and that there will be winners and losers in the long-run, the consensus is that the benefits outweigh the costs, and that therefore the losers can be compensated.

However, the popular perception of the impact of globalisation is far more pessimistic. In particular, the labour market consequences of globalisation are a source of genuine anxiety for many workers. Globalisation appears to have made workers feel less secure about their labour market position and raised a number of fears. First, there is a common perception that the advanced industrialised economies will be unable to compete with imports produced by cheap foreign labour. As a result,

1

there will be downward pressure on wages and increases in unemployment. Second, there is a widespread fear that 'offshoring' will destroy large numbers of jobs in developed economies. Moreover, the jobs which are at risk are not just those in traditional manufacturing industries or those which require low-skilled labour. Because firms can now trade many services as well as goods, many more jobs are thought to be under threat, such as those in research and development, customer services or IT support. Workers in these jobs may have previously felt relatively insulated from the effects of globalisation. Third, migrants are frequently viewed as a threat to domestic workers, by out-competing indigenous workers for jobs and forcing down the wages of those that remain in employment.

Until recently, a common view amongst academic economists was that these concerns were simply misguided. Academic studies which measured the impact of globalisation suggested that any employment effects would be small, and that the estimated gains from trade liberalisation dwarfed any costs of adjustment. This viewpoint was reflected in the theoretical modelling, where the Heckscher–Ohlin–Samuelson (HOS) model, in common with almost all models of trade, assumed that if workers lost their jobs then they would be re-employed immediately at the market wage.

Recently, these beliefs have come under increasing scrutiny. Economists have begun to take seriously the popular concerns regarding the adjustment costs of globalisation and to evaluate whether these concerns are warranted. This was one of the primary motivations for the Globalisation and Labour Markets (GLM) Programme within the Leverhulme Centre for Globalisation and Economic Policy at the University of Nottingham. The GLM programme examines the extent to which labour market adjustment is caused by increased globalisation, and the consequences of this adjustment for labour market structures and outcomes. Labour market adjustment is identified with differential rates of job creation and destruction between firms, sectors, occupations, regions or countries. This can cause quantity or price adjustments in the labour market as workers change jobs, suffer unemployment or experience wage changes. This volume seeks to bring together recent work in this important and rapidly expanding area.

The volume begins with the chapter by Carl Davidson and Steve Matusz, who expand on the themes outlined above and critically evaluate the traditional view that the adjustment costs of trade adjustment are likely to be outweighed by the aggregate gains. They then discuss a number of new theoretical developments which link globalisation to labour market turnover and suggest why existing trade models may need to be modified in order to explain recent labour market developments and to address the concerns raised. They also emphasise how introducing microeconomic models of firm behaviour and of labour market adjustment into trade models can enrich our understanding of both the drivers of globalisation and its likely impact. The new models allow an examination not just of relative wage rates but also of job security.

In Chapter 3, Paulo Bastos and Joana Silva examine the impact of increased international trade on workers' earnings more generally. They consider both the effects on the distribution of wages in the long-run (the 'winners and losers') and the effects on workers while adjustment is taking place. Their analysis of the long-run focuses on the role played by labour market rigidities and imperfections, such as imperfect factor mobility, minimum wages and collective bargaining institutions, in shaping the impact of trade liberalisation on the labour market. Their analysis on the short-run focuses on the wage and unemployment impact of workers who lose their jobs due to increased international competition. This chapter enriches both the theoretical and empirical modelling by introducing institutional detail, and is of crucial importance in understanding the differential response of industries and countries to trade liberalisation.

An alternative approach to the analysis of the effect of globalisation on labour markets is to use Computable General Equilibrium (CGE) models. In Chapter 4, Niven Winchester summarises the research that uses CGE models which examine the impact of trade liberalisation on wage inequality. Although the majority of CGE are essentially HOS in character, minor changes in the underlying assumptions can lead to large changes in the predictions regarding the impact of trade.

In Chapter 5, Udo Kreickemeier examines the impact of international integration in models where the wage does not fall to allow full employment. In these models, globalisation can affect not only relative wages, but also aggregate employment and the relative employment of different groups of workers. In light of the large employment differentials between skilled and unskilled workers which have arisen in many European countries (which themselves have relatively rigid wages), this seems a very relevant approach. In contrast to the standard HOS model, this chapter shows that, as an economy opens up to international trade, the number of employed workers alters, the effort that these workers exert alters and the wage differential between sectors changes.

Another commonly criticised feature of the standard HOS model is that it divides the workforce into a limited number of discrete skill categories, e.g. skilled and unskilled, with workers being treated as homogeneous within skill groups. However, an obvious characteristic of workers is that, although they are born with certain innate talents and abilities, many of their skills are learnt. Since the HOS framework suggests that changing trade patterns will lead to changes in the relative return to skilled labour, this will have implications for an individual's decision to acquire skills or to retrain. In Chapter 6, Rod Falvey, David Greenaway and Joana Silva model this process explicitly and examine the consequences of increased economic integration for the formation of this 'human capital' by examining the impact of a tariff reduction on both formal education and training. This provides a much richer account of the adjustment process following trade liberalisation, and differentiates the impact for workers of different ages and experience.

Whilst the chapter by Falvey, Greenaway and Silva examines the worker's decision to acquire human capital, Chapter 7, by Richard Upward and Peter Wright, examines the role of firms in the shift towards a more skill-intensive workforce in response to trade shocks. They outline a model in which workers have 'careers' which are affected not only by their own decisions but also by the decisions of firms. Trade shocks may disrupt career paths but also provide job opportunities for workers that were previously unavailable. The impact of trade shocks on workers' welfare is therefore more subtle than is commonly assumed, and represents a double-edged sword in terms of career prospects. Empirical evidence for this characterisation of the labour market is also presented.

Traditionally economists have focused on the impact of trade on labour market outcomes. However, as noted, the current phase of globalisation has witnessed an increase in the trade in intermediate goods that has outpaced the trade in final goods. The most commonly cited reason for this phenomenon is the attempt by firms to outsource the most labour-intensive parts of their production process from high wage to low wage countries in order to cut costs. This is frequently offered as a reason for the deteriorating employment prospects of low skilled workers in the OECD. However, the labour market implications of outsourcing may be even more wide-reaching. First, more managers may be required to co-ordinate a production process which is now geographically dislocated. Second, if fragmentation is associated with increasing returns to scale, then outsourcing of production from one industrialised country to another may be facilitated resulting in an increase in intra-industry trade. Barbara Dluhosch reviews these developments in Chapter 8, and theoretically examines the labour market implications of fragmentation under imperfect competition.

In Chapter 9, Ingo Geishecker, Holger Görg and Sara Maioli examine the empirical evidence for the labour market impact of international outsourcing. They begin by discussing the inherent difficulties in measuring outsourcing and discuss how these relate to the theoretical constructs. They then assess the strengths and weaknesses of the empirical work based on industry and worker level data. They conclude that there is evidence that international outsourcing leads to shifts in the relative demand for different types of labour, and this has implications for relative wages.

The final chapter by Alexander Hijzen and Doug Nelson considers the impact of immigration on the labour market, an area of continuing political and economic controversy. Hijzen and Nelson critically evaluate the empirical work that has attempted to measure the impact of immigration. They argue that, in contrast to popular perception, the great weight of the empirical evidence suggests that the labour market effects of migration are likely to be small for indigenous labour.

References

OECD (2007). *Policy Brief: Globalisation, Jobs and Wages*. Paris: Organisation of Economic Co-operation and Development.

2
Globalisation and Turnover
Carl Davidson and Steven J. Matusz

2.1 Introduction

There seems to be a common perception, both in the public and in the media, that increased exposure to international trade has profound implications for the rates of job creation and job destruction within an economy. The common view is summarised rather well by Paul Krugman in his 1993 *AER* paper 'What Do Undergrads Need to Know About Trade?' who wrote:

> One thing that both friends and foes of free trade seem to agree on is that the central issue is employment. George Bush declared the objective of his ill-starred trip to Japan to be 'jobs, jobs, jobs'; both sides in the debate over the North American Free Trade Agreement try to make their case in terms of job creation. And an astonishing number of free-traders think that the reason protectionism is bad is that it causes depressions. (Krugman, 1993: 25)

Recent survey evidence provides an indication of just how widespread such concerns are. In the United States, Scheve and Slaughter (2001a, 2001b) find that globalisation has made workers feel less secure about their labour market position. These workers seem to be concerned that increased competition from low wage countries might lead to a reduction in their wages, or, perhaps more importantly, result in them losing their jobs. Surprisingly, they find that roughly two-thirds of Americans think that international trade has been a principal cause of a decline in US living standards. Other survey evidence indicates that low skilled workers in a wide variety of countries are concerned that freer trade might cost them their jobs or lower their incomes (O'Rourke and Sinnott, 2001; Baker, 2005; Mayda and Rodrik, 2005; Beaulieu et al., 2005).

Yet, until recently, the common perception among academic economists seems to have been that concerns about trade's impact on job creation and destruction are unwarranted and misguided. For example, in the paragraph that *immediately follows* the quote given above, Krugman (1993:25) argues that:

> It should be possible to emphasize to students that the level of employment is a macroeconomic issue, depending in the short run on aggregate demand and depending in the long run on the natural rate of unemployment, with microeconomic policies like tariffs having little net effect. Trade policy should be debated in terms of its impact on efficiency, not in terms of phoney numbers about jobs created or lost.

As a result of attitudes such as this one, almost all of the attention of academic economists interested in the impact of trade on an economy has focused on the wage effects. In fact, most of the theoretical analysis has continued to assume that labour markets are perfectly competitive, so that job destruction rates are virtually irrelevant – workers do not care about losing their jobs if they can immediately find new ones at the market wage.

This attitude now seems to be changing. In recent years, several theories have developed that link globalisation and the rates at which jobs are created and destroyed. While some of these theories continue to employ models with perfectly competitive labour markets and full employment, others have broadened their focus to allow for equilibria consistent with non-trivial spells of unemployment. As a result, some surprising new insights have emerged. For example, it has been suggested that the link between turnover rates and trade may go in an unexpected direction with turnover rates influencing the pattern of trade.

The purpose of this chapter is to review several theories that link globalisation to worker turnover. These theories vary widely both in the nature of the link that is emphasised and the questions that are being addressed by the researchers. And, somewhat surprisingly, most of these theories are still in their very early forms. Thus, at the end of the chapter, we suggest several ways in which (we think) these theories need to be extended and refined in the future.

The remainder of the chapter divides into six sections. In the next section, we review the traditional theory linking trade to turnover. This theory posits that increased exposure to trade causes a reduction in domestic production and employment in import-competing industries and an expansion of production and employment opportunities in export-oriented industries. This suggests that trade increases job destruction in some industries while increasing job creation in others. Thus, trade reallocates employment across sectors, with the total effect on employment ambiguous.

In Section 2.3 we turn to a new theory suggested by Jagdish Bhagwati and Vivek Dehejia which argues that increased exposure to international trade makes industries 'footloose' in the sense that small shifts in costs can cause comparative advantage to shift from one country to another. This makes trade riskier in the sense that trade patterns are more likely to be altered by small changes in policy or exogenous shocks. Thus, globalisation leads to what they call 'kaleidoscopic' comparative advantage. This theory, which was developed to explain recent shifts in the distribution of income, links globalisation, labour market turnover, human capital accumulation and wages, with the primary emphasis on the joint role of turnover and trade in determining rates of skill acquisition and wage rates.

In Section 2.4 we turn to a theory that has recently emerged from the literature on trade and productivity which argues that a change in openness reallocates factors within an industry. For example, this theory predicts that in export-oriented markets, liberalisation results in the most efficient firms expanding while the most inefficient firms either contract or exit the industry. This means that jobs are reallocated within the industry with increased job creation at some firms and increased job destruction at other firms within the same industry.

Section 2.5 is devoted to a recent theory put forward by Kenneth Scheve and Matthew Slaughter (2004) that emphasises the link between foreign direct investment (FDI) and worker turnover. They argue that worker insecurity stemming from globalisation may be tied to the recent increase in FDI by multinational enterprises (MNEs). By operating multiple production facilities in different countries, MNEs can effectively play labour in one country off against labour in other countries. As a result, the elasticity of labour demand rises and labour's bargaining power is eroded.[1]

In Section 2.6 we turn to our own work on trade with imperfectly competitive labour markets. According to this theory, when labour markets are imperfect, equilibrium turnover generates uncertainty about future income streams. In industries with a great deal of turnover, firms must therefore pay compensating differentials to attract and retain workers. These wage premia push up autarkic prices and influence the pattern of trade. Briefly, countries tend to have a comparative advantage in industries in which turnover is low relative to the turnover in the same industry in other countries. Note that according to this theory, equilibrium turnover influences trade patterns with high rates of job destruction in a particular industry, making it difficult for a country to compete internationally in that market. We argue that this theory is consistent with a wide variety of models of trade with imperfect labour markets (search, efficiency wages, minimum wages) and that it is consistent with data on job and worker turnover in US manufacturing sectors since the 1970s.

We conclude the chapter in Section 2.7 where we suggest ways in which the insights from these five strands of literature can be integrated. We also discuss several avenues for future research.

2.2 The traditional view

Every economist would agree that international trade reallocates factors of production across sectors. In fact, one could easily argue that a quick and dirty summary of the basic message of trade theory over the past 200 years has been that trade is good because it reallocates a fixed amount of resources in a way that yields greater output. If there are disagreements within the field, they tend to be about which sectors might expand or contract, the rates at which factors will be reallocated, the importance of the costs of adjustment, and/or the manner and the magnitude of the impact of trade on factor rewards.

The Heckscher–Ohlin–Samuelson (HOS) model of trade is perhaps the most well known theory of how trade reallocates factors. According to this theory, different countries use the same technology to produce identical goods, but the countries differ in their factor endowments. These differences in factor endowments translate into differences in autarkic factor rewards, which then influence the pattern of trade. As an example, consider a situation in which one country has a relative abundance of some factor, say, labour. Then, in the absence of trade, labour would be relatively cheap in this country and these relatively low wages would imply that this country would be able to produce goods that use relatively labour intensive technologies more cheaply than other countries. In equilibrium, the low cost of production translates into low autarkic prices and gives this country a comparative advantage in that good. Thus, this country would tend to export goods that intensively use its abundant factor (labour) and import those goods that intensively use its scarce factor (say, capital).

In terms of worker turnover, this theory predicts that increased openness should create jobs in industries that make intensive use of its relatively abundant factor and it should destroy jobs that are tied to industries that make intensive use of its relatively scarce factor. Because of the conventional assumption that the labour market is frictionless and perfectly competitive, the net impact on jobs is zero. Other theories yield similar predictions about turnover, although they often point to a different set of factors as the determinants of an industry's trade position (for example, the Ricardian model relies on differences in technologies across countries as the main determinant of trade flows). Very little attention has been paid to this set of predictions, however, for a variety of reasons. To begin with, the HOS model, as is the case with almost all trade models, assumes that if workers lose their jobs they are assured of immediate re-employment at the market wage. Thus, all that these workers really care about is how trade affects the market wage, an issue that *does* receive considerable attention.

Another reason for this lack of attention has to do with the outcome of early attempts to measure the adjustment costs associated with trade reform. One of the best examples of this is the paper by Baldwin, Mutti and Richardson (1980: 411) in which they attempt to measure the aggregate employment effects on the US economy of a large multilateral tariff reduction. To do so, they explicitly assume that there exists a given level of unemployment 'due either to natural forces (e.g. normal quit-and-search behaviour) or to government choice (e.g. for anti-inflationary reasons)'. In the first stage of their analysis, they econometrically estimate the expected duration of unemployment for each worker based on that worker's demographic characteristics. This information is then used to estimate employment changes for 367 industries assuming a 50 per cent multilateral cut in tariffs. The duration of unemployment for a worker in a contracting industry was estimated by inserting the industry's demographic characteristics into the econometric model of unemployment duration. In the end, they predict that the effect of the tariff reduction would be quite small: roughly 135,000 jobs would be created in export-oriented industries and 150,000 jobs would be lost in import-related industries. A variety of other studies using similar (or less sophisticated) techniques reach a similar conclusion – the net impact of trade liberalisation on job creation and destruction is likely to be small (see Matusz and Tarr, 2000). These results lend credence to the Krugman (1993: 25) view that 'employment is a macroeconomic issue, depending in the short run on aggregate demand and depending in the long run on the natural rate of unemployment, with microeconomic policies like tariffs having little net effect.'

However, there are reasons to be sceptical about these results since they all make assumptions that tend to minimise employment changes and adjustment costs. For example, one of the basic assumptions underlying the Baldwin, Mutti and Richardson analysis is that liberalisation does not change the natural rate of unemployment. This implies that all employment effects are transitory and that the net effect on employment cannot be large. Other shortcomings of the analysis include a failure to take into account search and training costs that may be imposed on workers dislocated due to changes in trade patterns.

The Baldwin, Mutti and Richardson results are also inconsistent with a variety of studies from the 1980s and 1990s that found a significant link between international competition and domestic employment. For example, Branson and Love (1988) and Revenga (1992) both found that trade led to a loss of about 1 million manufacturing jobs in the US in the early 1980s.[2] Recent work by Trefler (2004) and Davidson and Matusz (2004a) makes one even more sceptical. Trefler presents evidence that NAFTA led to significant employment changes in several Canadian industries; whereas Davidson and Matusz's study, which explicitly allows for equilibrium unemployment and takes into account search and training costs, suggests that previous studies may significantly underestimate the true costs of adjustment.

In summary then, the traditional view is that changes in trade patterns caused by globalisation and/or changes in trade policy reallocate labour across sectors within an economy. This creates jobs in some industries while destroying jobs in other industries, so that globalisation *causes* turnover, but the changes are swift, so there is no notable impact on unemployment. A brief description of recent empirical work aimed at testing this theory, and distinguishing it from others, is provided at the end of Section 2.6.

2.3 The Bhagwati–Dehejia hypothesis

Over the past thirty years the distribution of income in most OECD countries has changed dramatically, with the rich getting richer and the poor getting relatively poorer. This stylised fact applies not only across industries, but within industries as well. At the same time, there has also been a dramatic increase in imports from developing countries. This has led to an intense debate about the reasons for the shift in the income distribution and the possible role played by globalisation. Many have focused on whether or not well-understood Stolper–Samuelson forces could have caused a decline in the incomes of low wage workers. Many seem to conclude that the data do not support such a claim (see, for example, Lawrence and Slaughter, 1993),[3] while others point out that even if

Stolper–Samuelson *could* explain changes in the income distribution in industrialised countries, a puzzle still remains since developing countries have experienced similar changes in their income distributions, a result that is at odds with Stolper–Samuelson predictions. This has led many to conclude that skill biased technical change is the main reason for the changes in inequality.

Over the last ten years or so, Bhagwati and Dehejia have argued that globalisation could have caused the change in inequality through a different channel (see, for example, Bhagwati and Dehejia, 1994). Their argument takes for granted that changes in the pattern of trade cause turnover (what we have referred to as the 'traditional view'). According to their hypothesis, globalisation implies an increase in international competition, which leads to razor-thin profit margins. As a result, firms that are able to compete internationally today might be driven from the market tomorrow by small changes in costs (production or transportation), productivity, and/or trade policy. This leads to what they call 'kaleidoscopic comparative advantage' with the pattern of trade changing constantly and labour market turnover increasing accordingly.

To link the increase in turnover to changes in inequality, Bhagwati and Dehejia point out that with reductions in job-security, workers face lower incentives to acquire job-specific human capital. They also argue that this reduction will be greater for low wage workers, whose skills do not transfer across jobs as easily or completely as do the skills of high wage workers. This leads them to conclude that globalisation will lead to a change in the pattern of skills acquired by workers. High wage workers will largely be unaffected, since their skills transfer easily across jobs, whereas low wage workers will acquire fewer skills and face flatter wage profiles over their careers.

While certainly intriguing, it is still too early to know just what to make of the Bhagwati–Dehejia hypothesis. There are reasons to be sceptical of its claims, but there are also some initial findings that tend to lend support to key parts of their story. In terms of scepticism, we begin by pointing out that although there is *some* evidence that labour market turnover has increased over the past thirty years (see, for example, Diebold, Neumark and Polsky, 1997 for low wage workers in the US, Heisz, 1996 and Beaulieu, Dehejia and Zakhilwal, 2004 for Canada), we know of no evidence that this increase is linked to globalisation. Moreover, others have called into question the very notion that job stability has declined at all (see, for example, Jaeger and Stevens, 1999). Second, a key step in their argument is that high wage workers tend to acquire skills that are more easily transferable across jobs than skills acquired by their low wage counterparts. While we would tend to agree with such an assessment (and have made similar assumptions in some of our work),[4] there are others who have argued that this is not the case. For example, if one tends to think of auto-workers as high wage workers, it is not at all clear that the skills they acquire in the auto industry are of much use in other high wage sectors of the economy. Since we know of no empirical work on this issue, whether this key assumption is valid remains an open question.

On the other hand, if one accepts the key components of their argument, then the argument seems compelling. In addition, recent theoretical and empirical research tends to provide some support for the theory. In models that explicitly allow for skill acquisition and equilibrium unemployment, Davidson and Matusz (2002) and Beaulieu, Dehejia and Zakhilwal (2004) have formalised the argument mathematically and shown that incentives shift in a manner consistent with the Bhagwati–Dehejia predictions. Moreover, the Beaulieu, Dehejia and Zakhilwal paper goes further and investigates whether recent trends in Canadian wages are more in line with Stolper–Samuelson forces or the Bhagwati–Dehejia hypothesis. They find that during the mid-1990s trade benefited both low and high skilled workers by increasing their wages. However, skilled workers experienced wage gains four times as great as those of low skilled workers. Since the wage gains of the high skilled workers did not come at the expense of low skilled workers, Beaulieu, Dehejia and Zakhilwal conclude that such changes are inconsistent with a Stolper–Samuelson explanation. They then go on to examine the impact of trade on labour market turnover in Canada during the same time period and conclude that job turnover rates increased in almost all sectors. These findings, which are consistent with similar studies of Canadian labour markets (see, for example, Heisz, 1996 and Baldwin and Rafiquzzaman, 1998), suggest that the wage gains are broadly consistent with the Bhagwati–Dehejia hypothesis. However, there is a caveat in that the authors find mixed evidence when trying to test the claim that increases in turnover have slowed down skill accumulation by low skilled workers by more than that of high skilled workers. Of course, since this claim plays a central role in the Bhagwati–Dehejia hypothesis, further empirical work along these lines is warranted.

2.4 Globalisation and job reallocation within industries

One of the fastest growing literatures in international economics over the past decade has been the empirical literature on firm and plant level adjustment to globalisation. Research in this area has uncovered several surprising stylised facts about the links between globalisation and productivity both at the firm and the industry level. Attempts to provide theoretical explanations for these stylised facts have led to important new developments in the way in which we think about trade's impact on an industry. Although most of the papers do not emphasise it, they all have implications for the manner in which globalisation affects worker turnover.

The stylised facts that we are concerned with can be found in two related strands of the literature. First, these studies establish that there are significant differences between firms that export and those that do not. Exporting firms are typically larger, more capital intensive, more productive and pay higher wages than their counterparts (Bernard and Jensen, 1999a). Second, related studies have focused on the impact of openness (or globalisation) on productivity at the firm and industry levels. One key finding is that openness tends to enhance productivity, although it is unclear why.[5] At least three possible explanations have been offered. First, openness may allow exporting firms to take advantage of scale effects as they expand. Second, there may be increases in total factor productivity at the firm level, perhaps due to 'learning-by-exporting'. Third, since more efficient firms tend to export, liberalisation may lead to a reallocation of market shares away from the least productive firms, resulting in higher aggregate productivity. Note that in the latter case, there are no within-firm productivity gains, only an increase in average productivity at the industry level.

Empirical studies do not offer much support for the scale effect explanation (Tybout, 2003), and provide mixed findings for the two other theories. Aggregate productivity gains in export-oriented industries are largely attributed to the fact that: firstly, it is the relatively efficient firms that choose to export; secondly, openness seems to trigger a reallocation in market shares in favour of these firms (Bernard and Jensen, 1999b; Pavcnik, 2002). It has been difficult to find evidence of within-firm productivity gains in export markets (Clerides, Lach and Tybout, 1998; Bernard and Jensen, 1999a, 1999b; Aw, Chung and Roberts, 2000).[6] On the other hand, there is evidence of within-firm productivity gains in *import-competing* markets (Pavcnik, 2002; Fernandes, 2007; Topalova, 2004).

The key theoretical papers that offer explanations for these findings are Melitz (2003) and Bernard et al. (2003). Both papers attempt to explain why exporting firms are different from their counterparts, and generate aggregate productivity gains as the result of market share reallocations.

This is accomplished by assuming that firms within each industry are heterogeneous, with productivity determined by a random draw; and that any firm that wishes to engage in international trade must pay a fixed cost associated with exporting. Firms make their exporting decision after learning their productivity, and it is the high productivity firms that face the strongest incentive to export. This follows from the fact that it is the high productivity firms that gain the most from selling their goods on world markets (where the world price exceeds the domestic price) and therefore they have an easier time covering the fixed cost associated with exporting. Openness (or globalisation), which is modelled as a reduction in trade costs, then leads to a reallocation of market shares towards high productivity firms and results in some low productivity firms exiting the market.[7] In terms of turnover, the implication is clear: globalisation reallocates labour *within* the sector. As trade costs fall and international markets become more integrated, we should see more job creation by high productivity firms and job destruction by the least efficient, weakest firms in the industry.

Although both the Melitz (2003) and the Bernard et al. (2003) papers use general equilibrium models, they both focus exclusively on the impact of openness on a single sector. The Melitz paper has recently been extended in an important manner by Bernard, Redding and Schott (2007) who merge Melitz's model of firm heterogeneity and trade costs with the standard HOS trade model. In their model, all sectors of the economy have the basic Melitz structure and trade across countries is driven by HOS forces: differences in factor endowments. This requires adding another sector and another factor to the Melitz model and extending the HOS model to allow for monopolistic competition (as in Helpman and Krugman, 1985). Firms within a given sector use the same basic technology, regardless of which country they operate in, but there is a productivity parameter that is determined randomly which affects variable costs. Due to the firm heterogeneity and trade costs, the model possesses Melitz's feature that only the most productive firms within an industry export. However, a new feature is that high productivity firms in *import-competing industries* also export their goods since there is demand for their unique variety abroad and they can afford to pay the trade cost. This result follows directly from the monopolistically competitive framework – we get two-way trade in all industries.

For our purposes though, the most interesting features of this model are tied to the predictions about globalisation and turnover. Because of its HOS structure, the model predicts that each country will be a *net* exporter of the good that makes intensive use of its abundant factor and a *net* importer of the good that makes intensive use of its scarce factor. As a result, just as in the HOS model, trade should result in *net* job creation in export-oriented industries and *net* job destruction in import-competing industries – that is, trade should reallocate labour *across* industries. Moreover, trade should reallocate factors *within* each industry as well. As market shares are reallocated in favour of the most productive firms, high productivity firms create jobs as they expand and low productivity firms destroy jobs as they are driven from the market. Surprisingly, trade has a *larger* impact on turnover in export-oriented industries, with greater job destruction and greater job creation taking place.[8] The implication is that workers in *all* sectors may feel less secure about their jobs as international markets become more open, consistent with Scheve and Slaughter's (2001a) findings, and that it may actually be the workers in export markets that have the most to fear if they are employed by relatively low productivity firms.

The Bernard, Redding and Schott (2007) paper is clearly important in that it begins to merge the new trade literature, which investigates the impact of trade on economies at a very disaggregated level (by focusing on the adjustment at the firm and plant level), with the conventional trade model that views the industry as the appropriate unit of measure. The focus on the impact of openness on job turnover is also non-standard and, in our opinion, long overdue. There is, however, at least one important extension of the model that needs to be undertaken. Since Bernard, Redding and Schott (2007) assume that labour markets are frictionless and perfectly competitive, equilibrium is characterised by full employment and there is no reason for any worker to be concerned about job security. Any worker who loses a job because their employer is driven from the market can easily find re-employment at an expanding firm. Thus, all workers are really concerned with is the impact of globalisation on the market wage. We return to this issue and suggest ways to deal with it in Section 2.7 below.

2.5   Globalisation, FDI and insecurity

Globalisation is a complex process that often involves more than just a reduction in trade barriers. Over the last thirty years, this process has led to significant changes in the manner in which firms produce and market their products. For example, Scheve and Slaughter (2004) point out that, in recent decades, cross-border flows of foreign direct investment (FDI) have grown at a much faster rate than have the cross-border flows of goods and services. In addition, the recent furore over the outsourcing of production can be attributed to the fact that globalisation and important advances in technology have provided firms with greater access to foreign labour markets and this has resulted in the 'fragmentation' of the production process. Scheve and Slaughter emphasise that it is this 'multinationalisation of production' that makes this recent phase of globalisation fundamentally different from previous phases (see also Bordo, Eichengreen and Irwin, 1999).

Scheve and Slaughter (2004) argue that it is the change in the way production occurs that holds the real key to understanding why globalisation makes workers feel less secure about their labour market position. As with most of the other theories we have surveyed, the argument is remarkably simple and can be illustrated by considering a vertically integrated firm that produces a product using several stages. Suppose, initially, that this firm completes each stage of the production process using local labour, so that all of its output is produced domestically. Now, suppose that globalisation allows this firm greater access to foreign labour markets and that the firm responds by opening several production facilities in other countries. This allows the firm to produce some of its intermediate inputs abroad where labour may be cheaper. It also erodes the bargaining power of domestic labour. During negotiations with domestic workers, if domestic workers seek a wage increase, the new production facilities provide the firm with a credible threat that they can move more operations abroad, resulting in lower domestic employment. In addition, random changes in foreign labour markets will now filter through to the domestic labour market by affecting the manner in which the firm structures the production process across its plants. This, of course, has important implications for domestic employment and wage rates. The bottom line is that the fragmentation of the production process increases the elasticity of labour demand for domestic workers. This makes domestic wage increases harder to secure and leads to greater volatility in domestic employment and wages. In terms of turnover, the implication is that increases in FDI ought to lead to greater equilibrium turnover in labour markets.

The Scheve and Slaughter hypothesis that increases in FDI lead to greater economic insecurity is important because it emphasises the fact that globalisation has substantially altered the manner in which multinational corporations produce their products. While others in the profession have noted this change and begun to explore its implications (see, for example, the literatures on fragmentation, e.g. Jones, 2000 or Jones and Kierzkowski, 2001; and imperfect contracting, e.g. Grossman and Helpman, 2002, 2005), Scheve and Slaughter are the first to make an explicit link to the uneasiness with which workers view the current globalisation process. Of course, there is much work left to be done here, with the theory needing to be fleshed out a bit more (it has not been formalised mathematically). Also, the explicit link between globalisation and rates of job creation and destruction when production is fragmented has not been explored at all.

2.6   Does turnover cause trade?

Over the past twenty years, much of our research has focused on extending traditional trade models to allow for imperfectly competitive labour markets. Our main goal is twofold: firstly, we are interested in investigating the extent to which well established results that have been obtained in full employment models need to be modified when labour markets are characterised by equilibrium unemployment; second, we wish to develop a framework in which the concerns that the public seems to have about links between trade and jobs can be examined using rigorous models. To us, it is simply not enough to dismiss such concerns as misguided without first investigating them using an appropriate framework.

Along the way, our research has occasionally generated some unexpected results, one of which is that differences in equilibrium turnover rates across industries and across countries can cause trade. The argument is really rather simple, and, in retrospect, perhaps we should have never been surprised by this finding. To understand the link, imagine a model in which it takes time and effort for unemployed workers and firms with vacancies to meet and establish a relationship. The time it takes to establish such a relationship depends upon a variety of factors including, but not limited to, the nature of the production process (its complexity and the skill mix of labour required), the nature of the search process (in terms of the matching function and the amount of information available), the composition of the labour force in the region, and the degree of competition in the local labour market. It is easy to imagine that vacancies in some industries, where jobs require no particular skills or experience, might be quite easy to fill. In contrast, vacancies in other industries with complex production processes might be difficult to fill because the matching process is harder to solve. Firms in the latter industries might hire and fire several workers before finally finding an employee that fits their particular needs. Finally, to complete our description of the setting we have in mind, assume that even once the firm and worker establish a relationship, the length of the subsequent employment relationship is uncertain (this could be due to, say, random fluctuations in demand).

In such a model, workers cycle between periods of employment and unemployment and may very well face non-trivial spells of unemployment after losing a job. The implication is that choosing an occupation is equivalent to choosing a risky income stream, with low turnover sectors offering a less risky alternative. Utility maximising agents take such risk into account and this affects the wage rates that firms must offer in order to attract and retain employees. Briefly, firms in industries with high turnover (i.e. sectors in which jobs are difficult to find and not very durable) will have to pay compensating differentials in order to convince workers that such jobs are worth seeking.[9] These compensating differentials push up the cost of production, affect autarkic prices and thus influence the pattern of trade. In particular, when job turnover rates are both sector- and country-specific, a decrease in the rate at which jobs are created or an increase in the rate at which jobs break up in a particular sector–country pair raises the cost of producing that good, increasing its autarkic price and reducing a country's comparative advantage in that good (or aggravates its comparative disadvantage). It follows that, with search generated unemployment, labour market turnover rates can be an independent determinant of comparative advantage. In other words, turnover can cause trade.

There are two points worth making about this result. First, the intuition underlying it is based on one of the main lessons from general equilibrium trade theory – that comparative advantage is the result of the interaction of inter-sectoral differences with cross-country differences. In the Ricardian model, comparative advantage arises because cross-sector differences in labour productivity vary across countries. Comparative advantage in the HOS model is the result of cross-sector differences in factor intensities combined with cross-country differences in factor supplies. According to our model, it is differences in labour market turnover across industries and countries that drive trade patterns. The fact that labour market structures vary dramatically across countries, and turnover rates vary significantly across industries, suggests that these differences may be enough to have a significant influence on the pattern of comparative advantage.

The second point worth emphasising has to do with the generality of this result. Although we originally established the link between turnover and trade using a model with search generated unemployment in Davidson, Martin and Matusz (1999), in our recent monograph (Davidson and Matusz, 2004b), we showed that a similar link exists in almost any model which includes an equilibrium rate of unemployment. For example, if unemployment is driven by efficiency wage concerns, then the rates of job creation and job destruction influence the wage rate that firms must offer to motivate effort.

We investigated the nature of the link in our monograph by providing four different models of unemployment based on search theory, efficiency wages, and minimum wage laws. In all four, we showed that turnover rates affect autarkic prices and the pattern of trade in qualitatively similar ways. We believe that the reason that these results are so robust is that the logic behind them is compelling. All jobs are risky. When a worker chooses an occupation, they must take into account the eventual difficulty that they will face in finding employment once their education and training are complete. In addition, they must consider the likelihood that at some point they may lose their job and have to search for re-employment. Thus, the average duration of unemployment and employment associated with each occupation should affect workers' decisions. All else equal, the easier it is to find a job, or the longer that job is expected to last, the more appealing that job will appear to be. It follows that, if a particular occupation is characterised by a relatively long expected duration of unemployment or a relatively short expected duration of employment, compensation in that sector will have to be relatively high to induce workers to search for those jobs. This extra compensation pushes up the price of the good produced in that sector and a higher domestic price makes it more likely that the consumers in that country will turn to international markets where the good may be offered at a lower price. This logic should carry through in any model in which workers randomly cycle between employment and unemployment, regardless of the underlying cause of the unemployment.

In Davidson and Matusz (2005) we attempted to test our theory that turnover and trade are linked, while at the same time trying to sort out whether the evidence provided any clues about the direction of causation: Does trade cause turnover or does turnover cause trade? Or, is it possible that the evidence supports both theories? To do so, we needed data on worker turnover and trade by industry. For trade, we relied on the NBER US trade data compiled by Robert Feenstra. For turnover, we relied on two sources. First, we made use of the Davis, Haltiwanger and Schuh (1996) data on job turnover in US manufacturing sectors. The advantage of this dataset is that it covers a rather long time horizon, 1973–86, and provides turnover rates for 447 4-digit SIC industries. The main disadvantage is that the DHS data measure *job* turnover whereas our theory about employment risk and compensating differentials refers to *worker* turnover. Therefore, we also carried out our analysis using measures of worker accessions and separations from the Bureau of Labor Statistics covering 106 4-digit SIC industries from 1978 to 1981 (the BLS stopped collecting the data in 1981). Unfortunately, neither the DHS measure of job creation nor the BLS measure of worker accessions really measures what we have in mind when we refer to 'the rate at which jobs are found' in our theoretical model, since neither takes into account the number of workers seeking jobs in a given industry. Thus, we focus our attention on the link between the job destruction rate and each industry's trade position.

Our theory predicts that, all else equal, the US should have a comparative advantage in industries with relatively low job destruction rates.[10] This suggests that we should look for a negative correlation between the industry-specific job destruction rate and our measure of net exports associated with the industry. To explore this issue, we regressed our trade measure on job destruction and several control variables (capital per worker, a measure of the skill mix of workers, a measure of industry size, and the value of the dollar measured as a trade-weighted index). For the DHS data, we ran the regression for each year and for the pooled sample. The results were striking. In each case, with the exception of 1976, the coefficient on job destruction had the predicted sign and in almost all cases they are statistically significant at the 5 per cent (or better) level. Remarkably similar results held for the BLS data.

Of course, both theories that we have discussed could explain this relationship – turnover rates could be influencing trade patterns *or* changes in trade patterns could be driving turnover. According to the latter theory, a surge of imports could be destroying domestic jobs and increasing job destruction. There are, however, important distinctions between these two theories that can be exploited to shed some light on the direction of causation. In our theory, workers choose an occupation based, in part, on the turnover rates associated with each industry. In making such a decision it is likely that the worker focuses on the average turnover rate in each sector, ignoring short run fluctuations in turnover rates that might be caused by temporary shocks. In contrast, the 'trade causes turnover' theory is consistent with short run fluctuations (caused by sudden changes in the pattern of trade) driving turnover rates.

We therefore regressed our trade measure on the average job destruction rate in each industry over the sample period, the per cent deviation of the job destruction rate from its long run average rate in industry i in year t, and the other controls listed above. The idea is that if turnover causes trade, the average job destruction rate should be significant; whereas, if trade causes turnover, then the deviation of the job destruction rate from its average value should be significant. Once again, the results were striking. Using the pooled data from DHS we found that the coefficient on the industry's average job destruction rate had the correct sign and was strongly significant. In contrast, the trade causes turnover theory did not fare as well. While the coefficient on the deviation of job destruction from its average had the right sign, the estimated coefficient was not statistically different from zero. Remarkably similar results were obtained when we used the BLS data.[11]

We close this section by addressing one important weakness in the empirical evidence. Our theory about trade and turnover is one of comparative advantage – a country has a comparative advantage in a good because workers in that industry face *relatively* high job acquisition rates and/or *relatively* low job break-up rates. As with any theory of comparative advantage, the term 'relative' refers to the rest of the world. It is not possible to test such a theory with data from just one country. But, the empirical results discussed above were generated using only US data. These results are, at best, indicative. A proper test of the theory requires a cross-country analysis of inter-sectoral differences in labour market turnover and trade patterns. This is not an easy task. While it is true that there is a great deal of data now available on turnover for a wide variety of countries, there are many serious obstacles to carrying out such an analysis. In particular, there is the issue of industry concordance. Fortunately, we were able to offer an initial analysis along these lines that yielded promising results. We did so by making use of data on US and Canadian labour market turnover provided in Baldwin, Dunne and Haltiwanger (1998). In that paper, the authors report average job creation and job destruction rates for 1974–92 for nineteen 2-digit SIC industries. We combined this data with data on bilateral trade between the US and Canada to get a better test of our theory. If our theory is correct, then, all else equal, US exports to Canada should be highest in industries in which US job destruction rates are lowest relative to those in Canada.

The Baldwin, Dunne and Haltiwanger (1998) data provide us with 399 observations of job destruction rates and our measure of bilateral trade (for details on the latter, see Davidson and Matusz, 2005). Regressing our trade measure against the ratio of job destruction rates yielded an estimated coefficient that was negative, as predicted by the theory, and highly significant. The simple bivariate regression line also fits the data rather well, with differences in turnover explaining approximately 30 per cent of the variation in trade. We conclude that the limited amount of data available tends to provide further support for our theory linking labour market turnover rates to trade patterns.

It is also worth noting that the results reported by Baldwin, Dunne and Haltiwanger (1998) do not seem to be consistent with the theory that changes in trade patterns cause turnover. One of their main findings (1998: 347) is that 'the Canadian and U.S. industry level job creation and destruction data are remarkably similar'. This is not at all what one would expect to see if trade causes turnover. After all, trade is a much more important component of the overall economy in Canada than it is in the US – for the US, the combined values of imports and exports make up less than 30 per cent of GDP, whereas the comparable figure for Canada is close to 80 per cent! If exposure to international trade really causes labour market turnover, we would expect to see much more turnover in Canada than we see in the US. But, as Baldwin, Dunne and Haltiwanger (1998) emphasise, this is not the case.

2.7 Future avenues to explore

As we noted in the introduction, four of the five theories that we surveyed in this chapter are quite new, having emerged in the past two decades. This recent interest in the link between globalisation and turnover marks a significant change from the traditional view that has dominated international economics for so long, which is that the main labour market effect from globalisation is tied to its effect on wage rates. In our opinion, this subtle shift of focus is welcome and long overdue. Survey evidence clearly indicates that workers are worried that globalisation makes them less secure with respect to their labour market position. Moreover, recent surveys on the economics of happiness make it clear that workers view job dislocation as a far more serious setback than a reduction in their annual income (see, for example, Winkelmann and Winkelmann, 1998, Helliwell, 2002 or Di Tella, MacCulloch and Oswald, 2001). It is time for international trade economists to take concerns about globalisation and labour market turnover seriously and to develop frameworks in which these concerns can be investigated rigorously.

In terms of the immediate future, there are several avenues of research that seem warranted. To begin with, in our opinion, the empirical work showing a clear link between trade and job destruction warrants further attention. As we pointed out in Section 2.6, the theory which implies that differences in labour market structures across countries and differences in turnover across sectors can influence the pattern of trade should be tested using data from more than one country. The initial findings based on US and Canadian data are encouraging, but further work along these lines, using more countries and better data, would be worthwhile.

Further work aimed at pinning down the direction of causation would also be useful. Although the tests run by Davidson and Matusz (2005) seem to lend more support to the 'turnover causes trade' theory than to the 'trade causes turnover' theory, there are probably more sophisticated ways to go about differentiating between these two stories. The ideal way to handle this issue would be to instrument for turnover. Unfortunately, there is a serious problem with this approach in that, as far as we know, all known correlates of turnover are also variables that presumably have some impact on trade.

One way of exploring more deeply the issue of cause and effect would be to develop a multi-country model where steady-state differences in turnover create comparative advantage, but also allowing country-specific shocks to technology, endowments and preferences to impact turnover in the trading partner. This sort of model might point towards a more complete empirical investigation that captures forces that jointly determine the pattern of trade and turnover.

Further empirical work aimed at testing the predictions of the Bhagwati–Dehejia hypothesis is also warranted. There are several approaches that could be taken to do so. To begin with, the basic premise of the Bhagwati–Dehejia story needs to be examined more closely. Is there ample evidence that labour market turnover has increased dramatically due to changes in trade patterns? And, if so, has this led to a change in the pattern of skill acquisition across workers in the manner that they suggest? Neither question has a straightforward answer. In terms of labour market turnover, the evidence is mixed. As we noted above, some authors have found evidence of increased turnover while others have argued that there has been little or no change in job stability. Moreover, even if turnover *has* increased, the increase has not yet been convincingly linked to globalisation. Others have made a more basic claim – that globalisation has increased the risk associated with the labour market (see, for example, Rodrik, 1997); but, again, others have argued that drawing such conclusions from the data is unwarranted (see, for example, Iversen and Cusack, 2000). As for the impact of globalisation on skill acquisition, this is an area that is virtually untouched.

Although we view these empirical projects as important, in our opinion, the most important avenues for future research lie in the development of general equilibrium models of trade that allow for imperfect labour markets along with heterogeneity across firms and workers. The Bernard, Redding and Schott (2007) paper represents an important step in this direction, since it embeds the new trade models with heterogeneous firms within the traditional HOS framework. However, their model still assumes perfect competition in the labour market so that there is no reason for workers to fear losing their jobs. In a recent paper (Davidson, Matusz and Shevchenko, 2005), we develop a model in which workers with different skill levels search across firms for a job while initially identical firms must choose the type of technology to adopt. In equilibrium, some firms adopt a basic technology, employ relatively low skilled workers and pay low wages, whereas others adopt a more advanced technology, employ high skilled workers and pay high wages. Thus, equilibrium is characterised by heterogeneity across both firms and workers and the trading frictions that force workers to search for jobs generate equilibrium unemployment. We believe that extending the Bernard, Redding and Schott (2007) model to allow for a richer depiction of the labour market along these lines would aid our understanding of the manner in which trade alters labour market outcomes. After all, the new trade theory emphasises that in order to understand the response and behaviour of firms to changes in openness, we must acknowledge the importance of heterogeneity across firms. We anticipate that, in order to understand the link between trade, turnover and wages, it will be necessary to allow for equilibrium unemployment and heterogeneity across labour as well.

Finally, as emphasised by Scheve and Slaughter (2004), we believe that our models of trade must be extended to allow for more complex production processes in which several components must be produced and assembled before the product is complete. This will allow us to tackle more complex issues such as 'what role does the outsourcing of stages of the production process play in the link between trade and labour market outcomes?' There is substantial research that has begun on this issue, for example the literatures on fragmentation (e.g., Jones, 2000 or Jones and Kierzkowski, 2001) and imperfect contracting (e.g., Grossman and Helpman, 2002, 2005), but so far most of this work ignores the issue of globalisation and turnover and has adopted the conventional approach of looking at the link between trade and wages.

Notes

1. There is a sixth theory which links turnover and trade through fluctuations in exchange rates: see Klein et al. (2003).
2. For additional empirical work on trade and employment or trade and job flows see Sachs and Shatz (1994), Kletzer (1998), Levinsohn (1999), Bentivogli and Pagano (1999) and Gourinchas (1999).

3. One important issue is that, for trade to affect wages through the traditional Stolper–Samuelson channel there must be changes in goods prices driving the changes in inequality. There seems to be little or no evidence supporting this.

4. We tend to think of low-wage jobs as undesirable jobs that require few, if any, skills – the type of jobs that workers hold when first entering the labour force. In addition, if there are skills to be acquired, they are often very job-specific. For example, a low-wage worker might need to learn how to stock shelves or prepare fast food, but, knowing how to perform such tasks does not facilitate the acquisition of other job-specific skills.

5. For a survey of this literature see Tybout (2003).

6. This is actually quite a complex issue. Many papers report increases in productivity just before a firm starts to export that persist and grow after exporting starts. Since the initial increase in productivity comes *before* the firm starts to export, papers such as those cited in the text view this as something other than 'learning-by-exporting'. However, others such as Castellani (2002), Baldwin and Gu (2003, 2004), Blalock and Gertler (2004), Girma, Greenaway and Kneller (2004), Van Biesbroeck (2005) and Greenaway and Kneller (2007) point to the productivity gains *after* exporting begins and conclude that there is evidence of learning-by-exporting.

7. See also Yeaple (2005) in which the heterogeneity across firms arises endogenously: initially identical firms make technology choices with the knowledge that different choices allow them to employ different types of workers.

8. This is a prediction of the model that one should be able to test using Davis, Haltiwanger and Schuh's (1996) data on job creation and job destruction along with data on trade patterns by industry.

9. Abowd and Ashenfelter (1981) find empirical support for the proposition that inter-industry wage differentials compensate for differences across industries in the risk of unemployment. In their work, they assume that a worker can choose to accept a job in a sector where there is no constraint on labour supply, or accept employment in a sector where labour supply is constrained. They assume that the expected value of the constraint is known, but the actual constraint is random. In equilibrium, worker indifference between the two sectors implies that the constrained sector must pay a higher wage. The authors use data from the Panel Study of Income Dynamics (1967–75) to estimate the effect of unemployment uncertainty on the wage differential. They conclude that the compensating differentials ranged from less than 1 per cent in industries where there was relatively little anticipated unemployment, to as much as 14 per cent in industries where there was a relatively large amount of anticipated unemployment.

10. Of course, the key word here is 'relative' – we really need to compare the turnover rates in the US with those in similar industries in other countries. We return to this issue at the end of this section.

11. We also tried three other tests aimed at uncovering the direction of causation. These three tests yielded similar predictions in that the 'turnover causes trade' theory performed relatively well. Interested readers should refer to Davidson and Matusz (2005) for details.

References

Abowd, J. and Ashenfelter, O. (1981). 'Anticipated Unemployment, Temporary Layoffs, and Compensating Wage Differentials', in S. Rosen, ed., *Studies in Labor Markets*. Chicago: University of Chicago Press.

Aw, B. Y., Chung, S. and Roberts, M. (2000). 'Productivity and Turnover in the Export Market. Micro-Level Evidence from the Republic of Korea and Taiwan (China)', *World Bank Economic Review*, Vol. 14, 1, pp. 65–90.

Baker, A. (2005). 'Who Wants to Globalize? Consumer Tastes and Labor Markets in a Theory of Trade Policy Beliefs', *American Journal of Political Science*, Vol. 49, 4, pp. 924–38.

Baldwin, J., Dunne, T. and Haltiwanger, J. (1998). 'A Comparison of Job Creation and Job Destruction in Canada and the United States', *Review of Economics and Statistics*, Vol. 80, pp. 347–56.

Baldwin, J. and Gu, W. (2003). 'Export Market Participation and Productivity Performance in Canadian Manufacturing', *Canadian Journal of Economics*, Vol. 36, pp. 634–57.

Baldwin, J. and Gu, W. (2004). 'Trade Liberalization: Export-Market Participation, Productivity Growth and Innovation', *Oxford Review of Economic Policy*, Vol. 20, pp. 372–92.

Baldwin, R., Mutti, J. and Richardson, D. (1980). 'Welfare Effects on the United States of a Significant Multilateral Tariff Reduction', *Journal of International Economics*, Vol. 10, pp. 405–23.

Baldwin, J. and Rafiquzzaman, M. (1998). 'The Effect of Technology and Trade on Wage Differentials between Non-production and Production Workers in Canadian Manufacturing', Research Paper Series No. 92, Analytical Studies Branch, Statistics Canada.

Beaulieu, E., Dehejia, V. and Zakhilwal, H. (2004). 'International Trade, Labour Turnover, and the Wage Premium: Testing the Bhagwati–Dehejia Hypothesis for Canada', CESifo Working Paper No. 1149, CESifo, Munich, Germany.

Beaulieu, E., Yatawara, R. and Wang, W. (2005). 'Who Supports Free Trade in Latin America?' *World Economy*, Vol. 28, 7, pp. 941–58.

Bentivogli, C. and Pagano, P. (1999). 'Trade, Job Destruction and Job Creation in European Manufacturing', *Open Economies Review*, Vol. 78, pp. 165–84.

Bernard, A., Eaton, J., Jensen, J. B. and Kortum, S. (2003). 'Plants and Productivity in International Trade', *American Economic Review,* Vol. 94, pp. 1265–90.

Bernard, A. and Jensen, J. B. (1999a). 'Exceptional Exporter Performance: Cause, Effect or Both?' *Journal of International Economics*, Vol. 47, 1, pp. 1–25.

Bernard, A. and Jensen, J. B. (1999b). 'Exporting and Productivity', NBER Working Paper No. 7135.

Bernard, A., Redding, S. and Schott, P. (2007). 'Comparative Advantage and Heterogeneous Firms', *Review of Economic Studies*, 74, 1, pp. 31–66.

Bhagwati, J. and Dehejia, V. (1994). 'Free Trade and Wages of the Unskilled – Is Marx Striking Again?' in J. Bhagwati and M. Kosters, eds, *Trade and Wages: Leveling Wages Down?* Washington, D.C.: AEI Press, pp. 36–75.

Blalock, G. and Gertler, P. (2004). 'Learning from Exporting Revisited in Less Developed Settings', *Journal of Development Economics*, Vol. 75, pp. 397–416.

Bordo, M., Eichengreen, B. and Irwin, D. (1999). 'Is Globalisation Today Really Different from Globalisation a Hundred Years Ago?' in D. Rodrik and S. Collins, eds, *Brookings Trade Forum 1999*. Washington, D.C.: Brookings Institution Press, pp. 1–50.

Branson, W. and Love, J. (1988). 'United States Manufacturing and the Real Exchange Rate', in R. Mastson, ed., *Misalignment of Exchange Rates: Effects on Trade and Industry*. Chicago: University of Chicago Press.

Castellani, D. (2002). 'Export Behavior and Productivity Growth: Evidence from Italian Manufacturing Firms', *Weltwirtschaftliches Archiv*, Vol. 138, pp. 605–28.

Clerides, S., Lach, S. and Tybout, J. (1998). 'Is Learning by Exporting Important? Micro-dynamic Evidence from Columbia, Mexico, and Morocco', *Quarterly Journal of Economics*, Vol. 113, 3, pp. 903–47.

Davidson, C., Martin, L. and Matusz, S. (1999). 'Trade and Search Generated Unemployment', *Journal of International Economics*, Vol. 48, pp. 271–99.

Davidson, C. and Matusz, S. (2002). 'Globalisation, Employment and Income: Analyzing the Adjustment Process', in D. Greenaway, R. Upward and K. Wakelin, eds, *Trade, Investment, Migration and Labour Market Adjustment*, IEA Conference Volume No. 35. New York: Palgrave Macmillan.

Davidson, C. and Matusz, S. (2004a). 'Should Policy Makers be Concerned About Adjustment Costs?' in D. Mitra and A. Panagariya, eds, *The Political Economy of Trade, Aid and Foreign Investment Policies*. Amsterdam: Elsevier.

Davidson, C. and Matusz, S. (2004b). *International Trade and Labor Markets: Theory, Evidence and Policy Implications*. Kalamazoo: W. E. Upjohn Press.

Davidson, C. and Matusz, S. (2005). 'Trade and Turnover: Theory and Evidence', *Review of International Economics*, Vol. 13, 5, pp. 861–80.

Davidson, C., Matusz, S. and Shevchenko, A. (2005). 'Globalisation and Firm Level Adjustment with Imperfect Labor Markets', Michigan State University Working Paper.

Davis, S., Haltiwanger, J. and Schuh, S. (1996). *Job Creation and Job Destruction*. Cambridge, MA: MIT Press.

Diebold, F., Neumark, D. and Polsky, D. (1997). 'Job Stability in the United States', *Journal of Labor Economics*, Vol. 15, pp. 206–33.

Di Tella, R., MacCulloch, R. and Oswald, A. (2001). 'Preferences Over Inflation and Unemployment: Evidence from Surveys of Happiness', *American Economic Review*, Vol. 91, 1, pp. 335–41.

Feenstra, R. C. http://cid.econ.ucdavis.edu/

Fernandes, A. (2007). 'Trade Policy, Trade Volumes and Plant-level Productivity in Columbian Manufacturing Industries', *Journal of International Economics*, Vol. 71, pp. 52–71.

Girma, S., Greenaway, D. and Kneller, R. (2004). 'Does Exporting Increase Productivity? A Microeconomic Analysis of Matched Firms', *Review of International Economics*, Vol. 12, pp. 855–66.

Gourinchas, P. (1999). 'Exchange Rates Do Matter: French Job Reallocation and Exchange Rate Turbulence, 1984–1992', *European Economic Review*, Vol. 43, pp. 1279–1316.

Greenaway, D. and Kneller, R. (2007). 'Exporting, Productivity and Agglomeration: a Difference in Difference Analysis of Matched Firms', *European Economic Review*.

Grossman, G. and Helpman, E. (2002). 'Integration Versus Outsourcing in Industry Equilibrium', *Quarterly Journal of Economics*, Vol. 117, pp. 85–120.

Grossman, G. and Helpman, E. (2005). 'Outsourcing in a Global Economy', *Review of Economic Studies*, Vol. 72, pp. 135–59.

Heisz, A. (1996). 'Changes in Job Tenure and Job Stability in Canada', Research Paper Series No. 95, Analytical Studies Branch, Statistics Canada.

Helliwell, J. (2002). 'How's Life? Combining Individual and National Variables to Explain Subjective Well-being', NBER Working Paper 9065.

Helpman, E. and Krugman, P. (1985). *Market Structure and Foreign Trade*. Cambridge, MA: MIT Press.

Iversen, T. and Cusack, T. (2000). 'The Causes of Welfare State Expansion', *World Politics*, Vol. 52, pp. 313–49.

Jaeger, D. and Stevens, A. H. (1999). 'Is Job Stability in the United States Falling? Reconciling Trends in the Current Population Survey and Panel Study of Income Dynamics', *Journal of Labor Economics*, Vol. 17, 4, pp. 1–28.

Jones, R. (2000). *Globalisation and the Theory of Input Trade*. Cambridge, MA: MIT Press.

Jones, R. and Kierzkowski, H. (2001). 'A Framework for Fragmentation', in Sven Arndt and Henry Kierzkowski, eds, *Fragmentation: New Production Patterns in the World Economy*. Oxford: Oxford University Press, pp. 17–34.

Klein, M. W., Schuh, S. and Triest, R. K. (2003). 'Job Creation, Job Destruction, and the Real Exchange Rate', *Journal of International Economics*, Elsevier, Vol. 59, 2, March, pp. 239–65.

Kletzer, L. (1998). 'International Trade and Job Loss in US Manufacturing, 1979–91', in Susan Collins, ed., *Imports, Exports and the American Worker*. Washington, D.C.: Brookings Institution, pp. 423–72.

Krugman, P. (1993). 'What Do Undergrads Need to Know About Trade?' *American Economic Review*, Vol. 83, pp. 23–6.

Lawrence, R. and Slaughter, M. (1993). 'Trade and US Wages in the 1980s: Giant Sucking Sound or Small Hiccup?' *Brookings Papers on Economic Activity (Microeconomics)*, pp. 161–210.

Levinsohn, J. (1999). 'Employment Responses to International Liberalization in Chile', *Journal of International Economics*, Vol. 47, pp. 321–44.

Matusz, S. and Tarr, D. (2000). 'Adjusting to Trade Policy Reform', in A. Krueger, ed., *Economic Policy Reform: the Second Stage*. Chicago: University of Chicago Press.

Mayda, A. M. and Rodrik, D. (2005). 'Why Are Some People More Protectionist Than Others?' *European Economic Review*, Vol. 49, 6, pp. 1393–1430.

Melitz, M. (2003). 'The Impact of Trade on Intra-industry Reallocations and Aggregate Industry Performance', *Econometrica*, Vol. 71, 6, pp. 1695–1726.

O'Rourke, K. and Sinnott, R. (2001). 'What Determines Attitudes Toward Protection? Some Cross-country Evidence', in Susan M. Collins, ed., *Brookings Trade Forum 2001*. Washington, D.C.: Brookings Institution Press.

Pavcnik, N. (2002). 'Trade Liberalization, Exit, and Productivity Improvements: Evidence from Chilean Plants', *Review of Economics Studies*, Vol. 69, pp. 245–76.

Revenga, A. (1992). 'Exporting Jobs? The Impact of Import Competition on Employment and Wages in US Manufacturing', *Quarterly Journal of Economics*, Vol. 107, pp. 255–84.

Rodrik, D. (1997). *Has Globalisation Gone Too Far?* Washington Institute for International Economics.

Sachs, J. and Shatz, H. (1994). 'Trade and Jobs in US Manufacturing', *Brookings Papers on Economic Activity 1994*, pp. 1–65.

Scheve, K. and Slaughter, M. (2001a). *Globalisation and the Perceptions of American Workers*. Washington, D.C.: Institute for International Economics.

Scheve, K. and Slaughter, M. (2001b). 'What Determines Individual Trade-Policy Preferences?' *Journal of International Economics*, Vol. 54, 2, pp. 267–92.

Scheve, K. and Slaughter, M. (2004). 'Economic Insecurity and the Globalisation of Production', *American Journal of Political Science*, Vol. 48, 4, pp. 662–74.

Topalova, P. (2004). 'Trade Liberalization and Firm Productivity: the Case of India', IMF Working Paper.

Trefler, D. (2004). 'The Long and Short of the Canada–US Free Trade Agreement', *American Economic Review*, Vol. 94, pp. 870–95.

Tybout, J. (2003). 'Plant- and Firm-level Evidence on "New" Trade Theories', in E. Kwan Choi and James Harrigan, eds, *Handbook of International Trade*. Oxford: Blackwell Publishers.

Van Biesebroeck, J. (2005). 'Exporting Raises Productivity in Sub-Saharan African Manufacturing Firms', *Journal of International Economics*, Vol. 67, pp. 373–91.

Winkelmann, L. and Winkelmann, R. (1998). 'Why Are the Unemployed so Unhappy? Evidence from Panel Data', *Economica*, Vol. 65, pp. 1–15.

Yeaple, S. (2005). 'A Simple Model of Firm Heterogeneity, International Trade and Wages', *Journal of International Economics*, Vol. 65, 1, pp. 1–20.

3
The Wage and Unemployment Impacts of Trade Adjustment

Paulo Bastos and Joana Silva

3.1 Introduction

In recent years the labour market consequences of trade liberalisation appear to have become a major source of anxiety. The spectre that freer trade leads to job josses and induces a 'race to the bottom' in wages appears to be widespread among the general public, and has frequently spilled over into the policy arena.[1] These concerns are not inconsequential. In the European Union, for example, negative perceptions towards globalisation were highlighted as one of the main reasons for the recent rejection of the European constitution by French and Dutch voters (Niblett, 2005). At the same time, opinion polls carried out in the older member states point to a rising anti-Europe attitude, partly reflecting fears that an enlarged Europe may be amplifying the threats of globalisation by opening borders to cheaper labour and products from the new member states (Dempsey, 2005).[2] Concerns about this issue are also evident in the US. In a speech made just before his visit to China in March 2007, Treasury Secretary Henry Paulson Jr. argued that:

> Despite our healthy economy and rising living standards, more and more Americans seem to doubt that trade brings greater benefits than costs. Some politicians from both parties, reflecting what they are hearing from their constituents, are moving further toward embracing protectionism. This is a worrisome trend. (...) We must make it a priority to help workers succeed in our rapidly changing and increasingly global economy, while maintaining our commitment to open markets and the benefits that come with them.[3]

There is now a sizeable body of academic research seeking, on the one hand, to uncover the key mechanisms whereby freer trade impacts on labour market outcomes and, on the other, to quantify the magnitude of the associated effects. In this chapter we discuss some of the main developments on the wage and employment impacts of trade liberalisation.

We start by reviewing three different strands of research on the long-run wage impacts of trade liberalisation. Section 3.2.1 discusses the literature on the link between trade liberalisation and wage inequality between skilled and unskilled workers in the context of the neo-classical trade model. The models reviewed in Section 3.2.2 show how industry wage premiums may arise in the presence of imperfect factor mobility across sectors, and provide insights on how they may respond to trade liberalisation. Section 3.2.3 is devoted to the literature examining the effects of trade liberalisation on wages when labour markets are unionised. In Section 3.3, we discuss the empirical evidence on the short-run adjustment costs inflicted on trade-displaced workers, both in terms of wages and spells of unemployment. Section 3.4 offers some concluding remarks and identifies some possible avenues for future research.

3.2   The long-run wage effects of freer trade

3.2.1   The effect of trade on returns to skill

Most trade models that examine the relationship between trade liberalisation and labour market adjustment focus on the rise in wage inequality between skilled and unskilled workers associated with labour reallocation between contracting and expanding industries. The standard Heckscher–Ohlin–Samuelson (HOS) model assumes full employment and perfect factor mobility between sectors. Since adjustment occurs through frictionless labour reallocation, there is no unemployment in this model. However, there are earnings losses. In response to product price changes, factor prices change; harming the scarce and benefiting the abundant factor. A rise in the relative price of a good will lead to a rise in the real return to that factor which is used most intensively in production, and a fall in the real return to the other factor (the Stolper–Samuelson Theorem). In skill-abundant countries, HOS predicts that liberalisation induces increased inequality between skilled and unskilled workers, and possibly poverty through decreases in unskilled workers' wages. In this context, earnings losses are homogeneous within each skill group: in developed countries all unskilled workers and in developing countries all skilled workers, are harmed, independent of whether they reallocate or not; displacement is not in itself a source of adjustment costs. Since trade liberalisation affects relative wages through its direct effect on relative domestic prices, empirical investigations closely linked to the HOS theory analyse the price of traded products and skilled and unskilled wage responses.

There is a large empirical literature on the effect of liberalisation on wage inequality between skilled and unskilled labour, with general agreement that liberalisation may have contributed to a rise in the skill premium in skill abundant countries, albeit playing a small role relative to skill biased technological change (Slaughter, 2000; Acemoglu, 2002; Machin, 2003).[4] However, the results for developing countries are more controversial. Studies on Mexico (Cragg and Epelbaum, 1996; Hanson and Harrison, 1999; Robertson, 2004), Chile (Beyer et al., 1999) and Argentina (Galiani and Sanguinetti, 2003) all show that these countries have experienced post-liberalisation increases in wage inequality. Trade-induced increases in wage inequality in unskilled-labour abundant countries goes against the predictions of the HOS framework. Modified versions have been developed, however, and the theoretical explanation that is closest is that of Davis (1996). He considers three countries, one located in a cone of diversification marked by relative abundance of skilled labour and the other two in a different, less skilled-labour abundant cone. The HOS distributional result does then apply to the two countries in the same cone – between these two, wage inequality will increase in the more skilled-labour abundant country. A competing view associates the rising skill premium with skill biased technological progress (see, for example, Wood, 1995; Acemoglu, 2002, 2003; Thoenig and Verdier, 2003).

A recent study investigating the role of trade liberalisation on relative earnings in Brazil (Gonzaga et al., 2006) obtains different results, however. Trade liberalisation seems to have played an important role in the decrease in the wage premium observed in Brazil, and this appears to have occurred through the conventional HOS mechanism. This study also provoked a methodological debate. In contrast to most of the previous literature on developing countries, it uses educational attainment rather than occupation as a proxy for skill. While this distinction does not appear to affect the results for the USA (see Krueger, 1997 and Slaughter, 2000), it does in Brazil. The authors argue that 'the occupation measure is specially problematic in developing countries, since, as unskilled wages in these countries tend to be low, firms are more likely to hire workers for non-production tasks that do not require skills, such as janitors and phone operators'(Gonzaga et al., 2006: 350).

Given the diversity in these empirical results, several issues invite further attention. A first is to disentangle the effects of trade reforms from other reforms and technological shocks that may also increase the relative demand for skilled labour. Unfortunately, trade reform is rarely undertaken in isolation. Second, to use appropriate measures of skill groups. Third, to investigate the causes of increases of within-group inequality (i.e. among similar workers with respect to their observable characteristics), which seem to account for much of the observed rise in wage inequality (see, for example, Autor et al., 2005).

3.2.2   Trade liberalisation and industry wage premiums

In trade models where factors are homogeneous and costlessly mobile between sectors, factors will reallocate until earnings are equalised across sectors. If we observe persistent wage differentials between sectors, it suggests that there is an absence of perfect factor mobility. If factors are not mobile across sectors, trade liberalisation may alter these industry wage differentials. Initial theoretical efforts along these lines examined the effects of changing the assumption of perfect mobility between sectors to complete immobility of at least one factor.[5] Specific-factors models were introduced by Samuelson (1971) and Jones (1971), and formalised by Mayer (1974), Mussa (1974) and Neary (1978). Equilibrium is consistent with different factor returns to the specific factors in each sector, but equal returns for the mobile specific factor. Factor returns respond to changes in output prices somewhat differently than in the HOS model. A higher relative price of the good which uses the abundant factor intensively will translate into higher (nominal and real) returns to the specific factor in the expanding export sector, and lower (nominal and real) returns to the factor specific to the import competing sector. Its effect on the real return to the mobile factor will depend on the consumption patterns of that factor.

Complete immobility between sectors is an extreme assumption. By developing a model where capital is partially but not totally mobile, Grossman (1983) shows that the degree of capital mobility is an important determinant of the response of factor prices and industry outputs to changes in commodity prices. In particular, the wage-price elasticity in the partially mobile model is a weighted average of the elasticities of the HOS and specific factor models. Moreover, if the industry whose relative output price increases is relatively labour intensive, then labour benefits from an increase in the degree of capital mobility.

Others studies assume a specific type of labour market imperfection. Neary (1982) investigates the consequences of sluggish wage adjustment where the wage rate is fixed in the short run and slow to respond to excess demand or supply. In contrast to the previous literature, in this setting income losses can arise as a consequence of temporary unemployment for workers of the contracting industry. Greenaway and Milner (1986) extend this analysis by considering the existence of constraints on workers' mobility between sectors. Imperfect inter-sectoral mobility of labour is also the focus of Leger and Gaisford (2001), who consider that imperfect labour mobility arises from different specifications of relocation costs. They examine the benefits and costs of working in a particular industrial sector in the face of trade liberalisation, both when the other factor is sector-specific and when it is perfectly mobile. Their general conclusion is that 'if the relocation activity is itself costly, or if agents are not identical, then the welfare effects of exogenous changes in world prices are not in general distributed equally across sectors' (Leger and Gaisford, 2001: 465). However, the size of the welfare change depends crucially on how relocation costs are specified: 'different specifications of relocation costs lead to very different welfare effects and policy prescriptions.' (Leger and Gaisford, 2001: 463).

3.2.3   Trade and wages in unionised labour markets

In a related strand of theoretical research, models with imperfectly competitive product markets and unionised labour markets seek to uncover the mechanisms whereby reductions in trade barriers affect the capacity of trade unions to influence collective wages. Motivated by the spectre that deeper international economic integration may induce trade unions to engage in a 'race to the bottom' in wages, a burgeoning body of academic research investigates this issue by nesting elements of various economics sub-disciplines (labour, industrial and international economics) into a single theoretical framework. The literature that has so far gained most popularity explores the impact of trade liberalisation on union wages by means of one-sector, two-country models, with oligopolistic competition in the product market and union wage setting in the labour market.

Initial theoretical efforts along these lines appear to bear out the 'race to the bottom' hypothesis: Huizinga (1993) and Sørensen (1993) both show that the wage level is lower under free trade than under autarky. This is because, although market expansion as a result of product market integration causes wages to rise, this is more than offset by the increased product market competition which serves to moderate wages. Naylor (1998, 1999) argues, however, that the conclusion that integration leads to wage reductions is a special case, and results from a comparison of polar ends of the possible range of trade regimes. To show this, Naylor considers the process of integration as a marginal reduction in trade costs.

He shows that the movement from autarky to two-way trade is triggered when the unions in the two countries find it optimal to abandon their previous high wage strategies, and instead lower their wage demands in order to allow their firms to compete internationally. This causes a discontinuity in the wage level, as union demands are adjusted downwards. However, the union gains from the rapid expansion in employment. As trade costs are reduced further, Naylor (1998) arrives at the striking conclusion that, within the context of two-way trade, integration induces greater labour demand (and more importantly, a smaller labour demand elasticity) which leads the monopoly unions to set higher wages. However, in Naylor's model, wages under free trade are always lower than those under autarky. The wage fall, as the union discretely moves from a high wage strategy to a low wage strategy, outweighs any subsequent expansion in wages.

Naylor's key result has been refined in several subsequent papers. Munch and Skaksen (2002) distinguish between fixed and variable trade costs when both labour markets are unionised. They conclude that, while a fall in fixed trade costs leads to an unambiguous fall in wages, the implication of a reduction in variable costs is ambiguous. Piperakis et al. (2003), unlike Naylor (1998), allow for asymmetry between the countries. They show that if the market size of the two countries differs widely, a reduction in trade costs can lead to decreases in wages, employment and welfare in the country with the larger market. This is because the larger economy has less to gain, relatively speaking, from the market expansion effect of integration. The paper by Lommerud et al. (2003) shows that, if one country is unionised while the other is not, a much wider range of trade regimes is possible.[6] Under autarky, all trade is prevented by the level of trade costs, and wages are set in isolation in each country. However, as trade costs fall, the ability of organised labour to obtain higher wages in the unionised country will be limited by the possibility that firms from the low wage (non-unionised) country will begin to export. This leads to what Lommerud et al. (2003) call the *import deterrence* regime. If liberalisation continues, eventually trade costs will fall to such an extent that trade begins and the foreign firm starts to export. One-way trade continues until trade costs fall to a level such that the unions find it in their best interests to adopt a low wage strategy in order to induce the domestic firm to export as well. Under two-way trade, the Naylor result prevails: further reductions in trade costs cause wages to rise.[7] As with the preceding papers, wages are shown to be higher in autarky compared with free trade.[8]

More recently, the paper by Bastos et al. (2007) uncovers a new mechanism whereby trade liberalisation affects the capacity of trade unions to influence union wages. They note that a common feature of the models reviewed above is the implicit assumption that the trade union is a 'closed shop' with 100 per cent level of membership. This assumption, however, contrasts with reality where 'open shop' arrangements, in which the union is recognised for bargaining purposes but represents only part of the workforce, are the dominant form of union organisation (OECD, 2004). Building on the well-established result that, by affecting the employer's disagreement payoff, the level of union density impacts on the bargained wage, they argue that trade liberalisation may also influence the outcome of collective bargaining via that route.

In order to make this point, Bastos et al. (2007) embed an open-shop union model of collective bargaining into the international oligopoly framework. Within this setting, the fall-back position of firms is no longer zero in the event of a dispute, as they may continue to operate with the non-union workers that they employ. This will impact on wage outcomes. In addition, since firms continue to operate in the event of a dispute, it is possible that lower trade protection will impact on the wage outcome via this route, even if no trade exists in equilibrium. Both of these features help to convey new insights into how trade liberalisation impacts on negotiated wages. Of particular interest in this regard is what the authors call the 'import threat regime'. In this situation, trade does not occur in equilibrium. However, the threat that the foreign firm will export to meet the shortfall in product supply in the event of a strike acts as an additional discipline on the firm and serves to help the union in the bargain. Thus, within this range, we may observe unionised wages rising with trade liberalisation. Their results also contrast with the earlier literature in that, with intermediate levels of union density, wages may be higher under free trade than in autarky. At low levels of density the union is only able to capture a small proportion of the relatively large surplus under autarky. Its position under free trade is stronger. Although the surplus to be bargained over is smaller, a strike not only causes disruption to production but also elicits a competitive response from the overseas firm. This reduces the firm's strike profits further and serves to bolster the position of the union. Hence, when workers are represented by open shop unions, wages need neither fall monotonically as trade liberalisation occurs, nor indeed fall in absolute terms as an economy moves from autarky to free trade.

An important advantage of the one-sector unionised international oligopoly model is that it allows one to explicitly highlight the strategic interactions between firms and unions within the same industry, and to investigate how these interactions change with closer product market integration. A potential shortcoming of this modelling approach, however, is that in contrast with a long-standing tradition in international trade theory the impact of trade liberalisation on wages is investigated within a partial equilibrium framework. In fact, the analysis focuses on a single industry, where imperfect competition in the product market generates oligopoly rents which organised labour seeks to capture in the form of higher wages. Although the models assume that unionised workers can always find employment in a non-unionised sector, the wage rate in that industry (which constitutes the reservation wage of union workers) is exogenously given and hence unaffected by trade liberalisation throughout the analysis. For this reason, this modelling approach does not provide any guidance as to how freer trade affects the interaction between unionised and non-unionised sectors in general equilibrium.

Bastos and Kreickemeier (2007) develop a model that seeks to overcome the major shortcomings of this modelling strategy, while preserving its main advantages. Building on a recent framework proposed by Neary (2002, 2003), they develop a two-country, multi-sector model of oligopolistic competition, in which unionised and non-unionised sectors interact in general equilibrium. The model nests the contributions of Brander (1981) and Naylor (1998, 1999) into a single general equilibrium framework, thereby allowing examination not only of interactions between unions and firms within each sector, but also the interactions between unionised and non-unionised sectors. In addition, within this framework it is possible to analyse how these interactions change as national product markets become integrated. One of the main insights of this model is that, within a context of two-way trade, further product market integration impacts on union wages through a 'general equilibrium' channel. Product market integration causes an increase in labour demand. This leads to a rise in the reservation wage of union workers, thereby inducing a rise in union wages. Because of this general equilibrium effect, union wages may actually be higher under free trade than in autarky. The model also indicates that, within a context of industry-level union wage setting, the impact of changes in the degree of competition within each industry on union wages depends on the trade regime. Under autarky, union wages unambiguously increase with the number of firms operating in each sector. Although firm entry does not have any direct impact on the union wage bargain, higher competition within each sector increases labour demand. This leads to a rise in the competitive wage, and consequently to higher union wages. By contrast, with two-way trade in all sectors, the impact of an increase in the number of firms on union wages is ambiguous. Two opposite effects can be identified. First, higher competition within each sector increases the elasticity of labour demand. As a result, unions face a higher trade-off between wages and employment, and hence set lower wages. Second, increased competition increases the demand for labour, and hence the competitive wage. This, in turn, induces a rise in union wages. The overall impact on the wages of unionised workers is therefore ambiguous. Independent of the effect on union wages, however, the union wage premium falls as competition increases.

The implications of freer trade for unionised labour markets have also received growing empirical scrutiny in recent years. In this regard, the increased availability of large-scale datasets combining longitudinal information on workers and/or firms with industry data on trade protection has opened the door to a deeper empirical examination of testable theoretical hypotheses. Despite increased empirical examination, however, the impact of closer integration on the wages of workers covered by collective agreements remains unsettled. In fact, the signs and the statistical significance of the coefficients of interest in the wage regressions vary considerably across studies. A study by Gaston and Trefler (1995), based on US data, finds that lower tariffs are associated with higher wages of unionised workers. In a study for Mexico, Revenga (1997) reaches the opposite conclusion: tariff reductions appear to induce a fall in wages. By contrast, Feliciano (2001), also for Mexico, does not find a statistical association between wages and tariff reductions. Goldberg and Pavcnik (2005), for Colombia, find that tariff reductions are associated with declines in industry wages. By contrast, Mishra and Kumar (2005), for India, find a negative relationship between changes in tariffs and changes in wages: sectors with the greatest liberalisation have the largest increase in wages. Lastly, Pavcnik et al. (2004), for Brazil, do not find any statistical association between wages and trade liberalisation.

Given the differing country experiences, further research is needed on issues such as the importance of the degree of pre-existing distortions and their distribution among industries dependent on comparative advantage. Additional research is also required in order to investigate the role of the institutional design of the collective bargaining system (such as the degree of centralisation at which bargaining takes place), and its interaction with other market forces, in shaping the response of wages to trade liberalisation.

A recent study by Bastos (2007) seeks to make some progress along these lines. He starts by noting that a well-established strand of labour economics research shows that, in countries where collective bargaining takes place at the industry-level, collective wages are frequently supplemented by firm-specific arrangements; see Flanagan (1999) for a literature survey. In spite of compelling evidence that the magnitude of these mark-ups is far from trivial, previous literature on the impact of trade on wages does not distinguish between these two stages of the wage determination process. Making use of a particularly rich longitudinal matched worker–firm dataset for Portuguese manufacturing, Bastos (2007) models both components, thereby identifying the specific route via which trade expansion impacts on actual worker compensation. The empirical results suggest that within-industry changes in openness have a (small) positive impact on industry-level contractual wages, and indeed on actual wages. The positive association between openness and contractual wages seems to reflect the role of the export share. However, no evidence is found that changes in export share actually influence the final worker compensation. Additionally, the estimates do not support the hypothesis that increased import penetration has a negative impact on wages. To account for potential endogeneity of these indicators, Bastos then proceeds by exploiting a sharp appreciation of the Portuguese currency as well as pre-existing differences in openness across sectors to identify an exogenous change in the degree of international competition. The results of this quasi-natural experiment suggest that increased international competition does indeed lead to reductions in actual wages, and that this negative effect operates both via collective bargaining and through firm-specific arrangements.

3.3   Trade and labour market adjustment in the short run

In the analysis of the adjustment costs inflicted on workers by trade expansion, empirical research on trade-displaced workers using micro-level data plays a central role. This line of research has focused on a number of key questions which attempt to uncover the short-run labour market adjustment costs induced by trade expansion. How can one identify trade-displaced workers? Which workers are more likely to be displaced by trade? How large are the wage losses imposed by displacement? Are losses greater for trade-displaced workers? How long does it take for workers to become re-employed? Are trade-displaced workers jobless for longer periods? In the following sub-sections, we review some of the main contributions which provide answers to each of these questions.

3.3.1 How can one identify trade-displaced workers?

A frequently used method for classifying workers as trade displaced is to identify displaced workers from a sample of industries increasingly exposed to international competition – see, for example, Kletzer (1998, 2001, 2004) and OECD (2005a).[9] This classification has also been used by policy-makers: the Trade Adjustment Assistance (TAA) programme of the United States uses displacement from an industry facing increased import competition as an eligibility criterion.[10]

This approach builds on three important premises. First, that it is possible to identify the industries that are most affected by increased international competition. Second, that increased foreign competition is an important cause of job loss. Third, that trade-displaced workers are sufficiently over-represented in industries facing increased international competition. With regard to the first of these premises, most studies on trade-induced displacement rely on changes in indicators of openness (such as industry import penetration ratios and export shares) to identify which industries faced a significant increase in the degree of international competition in a given time period. Kletzer (1998, 2001), for instance, ranks industries by increases in import penetration ratios and identifies workers displaced from industries in the top quartile of this ranking as trade-displaced workers. The study by OECD (2005a) adopts a related approach by identifying trade-displaced workers as those displaced in the manufacturing industries where the net imports ratio rose more strongly over the period of analysis.[11]

To argue in favour of the legitimacy of this method it is necessary, though perhaps not sufficient, to examine whether increased international competition (as measured by these indicators) is indeed an important cause of job loss. In recent years this hypothesis has attracted significant attention within the research community, and the empirical results seem to support the view that changes in these indicators are indeed associated with net job loss and a larger incidence of displacement – see, for example, Revenga (1992), Haveman (1998), Kletzer (2001, 2002) and Scott (2005). However, other determinants of displacement (such as technological change and demand shifts) may be also relatively more prevalent in those industries which face stronger foreign competition, thereby contaminating the selected sample of trade-displaced workers. This potential pitfall is acknowledged by OECD (2005a), who nonetheless argue that even though measuring trade displacement in this way entails obvious inaccuracies, the analysis of this sample should provide an indication of differences between trade-displaced workers

and other job losers, provided that trade-displaced workers are sufficiently over-represented in high-international-competition industries.
Testing this assumption remains an open challenge, and warrants further
attention.

3.3.2   Which workers are more likely to be displaced by trade?

The studies by Kletzer (2001), for the USA, and OECD (2005a), for the EU,
compare the characteristics of import-competing displaced workers with
other manufacturing workers, and with workers displaced from other sectors of the economy. They find that the average displaced worker from
high import-competing industries is a production worker in his 40s, with
a low level of formal education. In the EU, around 15 per cent of trade-
displaced workers are between 55 and 64 years old and the average age
at the time of displacement is 41. In the US, the share of trade-displaced
workers in this age group is smaller (10 per cent), but they are still slightly
older than other displaced manufacturing workers. The average tenure
in both countries groups is seven years and a significant proportion
(32 per cent in the EU, and 22 per cent in the US) have been in the job at
least ten years. More than two-thirds are blue collar. In the US, only 14.8
per cent of workers displaced in high import competition industries had
a college degree.

In the US, these average characteristics are also common to other
workers displaced from manufacturing industries. However, in the EU
there are differences in the share of older and more experienced workers,
both being higher in import-competing industries. In the US the more
significant difference is that women represent a larger share of import-
competing job losses. Conversely, in the EU the share of women is higher
in other manufacturing industries. The contrast between manufacturing
and non-manufacturing displaced workers is much sharper. The latter
tend to be younger, have lower job tenure, higher formal education and
be much less likely to be employed in blue-collar jobs.

3.3.3   How large are the wage losses imposed by displacement?
Are losses greater for trade-displaced workers?

There is now a sizeable body of academic research which estimates the
earnings loss imposed by displacement. Most initial efforts along these
lines utilise US data. The influential paper by Jacobson et al. (1993)
makes use of a longitudinal administrative dataset for Pennsylvania
that comprises information on high-tenure displaced and non-displaced
workers. They estimate the wage effects of displacement through

a difference-in-differences approach and their estimates point to a size-able and long-lasting wage loss: six years after displacement, wages of the treatment group are still 25 per cent lower than those of the control group.[12] Importantly, they also find that the wage loss is not caused by higher rates of unemployment, and that the largest difference in patterns of losses between workers of different birth cohorts is the rate of recovery, which is higher for younger workers. A subsequent study by Schoeni and Dardia (1996) obtains estimates of similar magnitude using a larger dataset for California, for a different time period. In addition, they confirm the Jacobson et al. (1993) result that the earnings loss is not due to higher rates of unemployment. More recently, Hildreth et al. (2005) supplement state administrative data with information from DWS, which provides direct data on displacement and thereby enables them to correct for measurement error. Compared to previous US studies, they estimate a significant smaller loss of displacement: 12 to 16 per cent of the pre-displacement wage.

Several papers provide estimates for other OECD countries. In the light of considerable differences in labour market institutions and social security systems between economies, a cross-country comparison of this sort may be particularly informative. The study by Hijzen et al. (2005) provides the first direct estimates of the earnings losses due to firm closure in the UK. In order to do so, they link a 1 per cent random sample of workers to a large panel of firms spanning the 1994–2003 period. These longitudinal matched employer–employee data allow them to base the definition of displacement on observed firm closure rather than self-reported job loss. Additionally, the relatively large time-series dimension of the data enables them to track workers' earnings for several years after displacement. Moreover, their paper also improves upon the existing literature on the methodological dimension, by implementing propensity score matching methods to explicitly compare the earnings of displaced workers with the unobserved counterfactual of displaced workers had they not been displaced. Their results indicate that earnings losses associated with firm closure in the UK are primarily caused by periods of non-employment rather than with falls in wages for those who are re-employed, a result that contrasts sharply with previous findings for the US. In addition, they find that earnings losses do not appear to be particularly long-lived. After controlling for observable characteristics displaced workers' earnings are not lower than non-displaced workers' five years after displacement. These findings are consistent with the idea that wages are less flexible in the UK than in the US.

More generally, these findings suggest that, in the face of important institutional differences across countries, particular care should be taken when relying on experiences of other labour markets to draw policy lessons about earnings losses associated with displacement. The evidence reported in studies for other European countries appears indeed to support this view. In effect, studies using large longitudinal datasets for Austria, Finland, France, Germany, Netherlands, Portugal and Sweden tend to report lower wage losses of displacement than those obtained in studies for the US.[13] Some of these studies also suggest, however, that the size of the earnings losses is contingent on worker characteristics and macroeconomic conditions. The paper by Eliason and Storrie (2006), for instance, indicates that the size of the wage loss depends critically on the state of the macroeconomy, the reason being that recently displaced workers are more at risk from subsequent shocks. Another important finding is that workers who return to employment in a different industry tend to have higher wage losses than workers who return to the same industry (e.g. OECD, 2005a; Carneiro and Portugal, 2006).

Evidence for developing countries is much more scant. Recent studies by Kaplan et al. (2005), for Mexico, and Menezes-Filho (2006), for Brazil, are therefore particularly welcome. Kaplan et al. (2005) focus on differences in institutions, inequality, and labour market conditions between regions, to explain differences in time and space in the earnings trajectory of individuals who relocate. They find large, negative, and lasting effects of displacement on wages for workers who are displaced during times of high unemployment and in less economically active regions. Menezes-Filho (2006) combines information on workers' education and earnings trajectories with information about their firms to estimate the costs of job displacement in Brazil. He finds that high-tenure workers displaced from their firms during mass lay-offs suffer a long-term loss in monthly wages of about 20 per cent per year, and reports that this result is driven by the losses suffered by more educated individuals working in large firms at the time of displacement.

An important question from a policy perspective is whether wage losses of trade-displaced workers are larger than for other displaced workers. Arguably, this might provide a ground for tailoring specific adjustment assistance for trade-displaced workers. Descriptive statistics provided by OECD (2005a) suggest that this may indeed be the case, both in the US and in the EU. However, the evidence points to a relatively small difference, which may well be explained by the fact that trade-displaced workers tend to have characteristics associated with larger earnings losses. Previous results from regression analysis appear indeed to point in that direction. Using a before and after comparison to investigate the change in (log real) weekly earnings between pre- and post-displacement weekly earnings, Kletzer (2001, 2002) finds no evidence that being displaced in a high import-competition industry is a significant determinant of earnings losses, when controlling for other worker characteristics.[14]

3.3.4 How long does it take for workers to become re-employed? Are trade-displaced workers jobless for longer periods?

Whereas wage cuts after re-employment appear to be an important source of earnings losses in the US, long-term joblessness seems to play a more important role in the EU. The study by OECD (2005a) indicates that in the EU, two years after displacement, 48.2 per cent of displaced workers from high import-competition industries are jobless, compared to 43 per cent of other manufacturing industries and services workers. The same study suggests that trade-displaced workers in the US are more rapidly re-employed, and that workers displaced in high international-competition industries are moderately more likely to be jobless (37 per cent) than displaced workers from other manufacturing industries (33 per cent). Importantly, the finding that the employment effects of displacement tend to be larger in Europe is also generally confirmed in the country-specific econometric studies on the effects of displacement mentioned in the previous sub-section.

An important complement to this analysis is the analysis of how worker characteristics are related to post-displacement employment possibilities. Kletzer (2001) estimates a logit model, including a set of worker characteristics as explanatory variables (age at displacement, educational attainment, job tenure, gender, years since displacement, marital status and minority status). She finds that age, gender, education level and belonging to a minority are significantly associated with the likelihood of re-employment. Relative to 45- to 64-year-old workers, those who are 25 to 34 or 35 to 44 years old are about 11 percentage points more likely to be re-employed.[15] Relative to high-school dropouts, workers who completed a college degree or more are 25 percentage points more likely to be re-employed (high-school graduates 10, and workers with some college experience 14 percentage points respectively). Displaced workers from a minority are 10 percentage points less likely to find a job and so are females relative to males. Differences in job tenure have a lower but statistically significant impact.[16] Workers with more than ten years' tenure when they lost their jobs are less likely to be re-employed than workers with lower tenure (2 to 4 percentage points).[17]

Kletzer (2001) also analyses explicitly whether being a trade-displaced worker matters for the probability of being re-employed in subsequent periods, but finds no evidence of an independent effect of having been displaced by trade. While she reports some evidence that trade-displaced workers tend to suffer higher average unemployment spells following displacement, this appears to reflect the fact that trade-displaced workers possess characteristics that are typically associated with longer periods of non-employment. In fact, when controlling for all workers' characteristics, the estimates do not support the view that workers displaced in high international-competition industries are less likely to find a new job.

3.4   Concluding comments

As is clear from this review, the academic literature on the wage and employment effects of trade liberalisation has evolved significantly over the past recent decades, in terms of both its size and scope. From a theoretical perspective, several efforts have been made to develop frameworks capable of conveying insights on the role of labour market rigidities and imperfections (such as imperfect factor mobility across sectors, minimum wages and collective bargaining institutions) in shaping the response of wages and employment to trade liberalisation. These developments are, in our view, particularly welcome and deserve further exploration. In this respect, and given the prevalence of important institutional differences across countries, we feel that more research is warranted in order to investigate the role of the institutional design of the collective bargaining system (such as the degree of centralisation at which bargaining takes place), and its interaction with other labour market institutions, in moulding the impact of trade liberalisation on wages and unemployment.

With regard to the empirical literature, several important developments deserve to be pointed out. Firstly, the analysis relies increasingly on very rich datasets, matching longitudinal data on workers and/or firms with information on trade flows and protection. Second, there is a greater focus on the role of labour market institutions in shaping the response of wages and unemployment to trade liberalisation. Lastly, there is increasing empirical evidence for developing countries, many of which have undertaken significant trade reforms under the period of analysis.

There are, however, several tasks that invite further attention. Firstly, while most of the literature on wage inequality focuses on skilled versus unskilled workers, recent contributions (e.g. Autor et al., 2005) seem to suggest that increases in within-group inequality (i.e. among similar workers with respect to their observable characteristics) seem to account for much of the observed rise in wage inequality. In this regard, the recent work of Egger and Kreickemeier (2006) provides an insightful theoretical framework that, by combining firm heterogeneity and fair wages, yields interesting predictions on the link between trade liberalisation and within-group inequality. These predictions warrant, in our opinion, further exploration by empirical research.

Secondly, there are two issues that require further attention in the literature on the adjustment costs imposed on trade-displaced workers. On the one hand, some progress is required in order to better identify trade-displaced workers at the micro-level. This might be achieved by integrating into a single analysis the literature on globalisation and firm survival (e.g. Bernard et al., 2006; Greenaway et al., 2005) and the studies on the earnings losses imposed by firm closure (e.g. Jacobson et al., 1993; Hijzen et al., 2005). In order to do so, it would be particularly important to resort to longitudinal data, matching information on workers and firms with data on protection and/or trade flows. On the other hand, the existence of differing country experiences suggests that it would be interesting to explicitly analyse the importance of changes in social security systems in a given economy in determining the magnitude of earnings losses and spells of non-employment imposed by displacement. This would allow us to make stronger claims on how the institutional design of the social security system impacts on the earnings losses and unemployment spells of displaced workers than simple cross-country comparisons.

Notes

1. These concerns are apparent in recent publications of the OECD (2004, 2005a, 2005b) and the European Commission (2005).
2. Additionally, a Special Eurobarometer on the 'Future of Europe' undertaken by the European Commission (2006) indicates that a (relative) majority of Europeans (47 per cent of interviewees) consider first and foremost that globalisation is a threat to employment and companies in their country (compared with 37 per cent who see it as a good opportunity for companies in their country). Perhaps more importantly, a comparison of these results with those from a similar survey carried out in 2003 indicates that negative perceptions towards globalisation have risen sharply in most of the older member states.
3. The full speech can be found at http://www.treas.gov/press/releases/hp285.htm.
4. For recent surveys of literature on trade and inequality see Greenaway and Nelson (2002), Feenstra and Hanson (2003), Goldberg and Pavcnik (2007) and Bardhan (2005).

5. While continuing to assume competitive and undistorted markets with flexible factor prices and full employment.

6. Brander and Spencer (1988) develop a model in which a unionised domestic firm competes against a foreign firm that operates in a perfectly competitive labour market, with the home country wage being the outcome of a Nash bargain between the union and the firm. They show that tariff protection permits the union to bargain for higher wages.

7. In Naylor (1998) the market expansion effect is stronger as the wages of the unions in each country are strategic complements.

8. Lommerud et al. (2003) then examine how wage setting impacts on the location decisions of multinational firms. They argue that if the firm has plants located in both countries then this would serve to simplify the wage schedules, since the union no longer gains by adopting a low wage strategy in order to induce its plant to export. Thus wages fall continuously from autarky to free trade. More generally, the option of locating abroad serves to weaken the position of the union.

9. Job displacement is commonly understood as involuntary termination of employment (layoff) based on employers' downsizing.

10. The 2002 reforms of TAA extended the scope of this programme to all workers displaced from industries facing shifts in production to countries with bilateral free trade agreements with the US and where there has been or is likely to be an increase in imports, and to workers who lose their jobs from plants producing inputs into goods that face significant import competition (secondary workers); see Kletzer and Rosen (2005).

11. To identify displaced workers in the US data on recipients of TAA, Mass Layoffs Statistics (MLS) or Displaced Worker Survey (DWS) can be used. The majority of the studies opted for using the DWS. This household survey covers adults (20 years or older) that had lost a job in the preceding five-year period due to a plant or company closing or moving, or a layoff from which the workers were not recalled. The displacements are job displacements. Kletzer (2001) finds that the incidence of trade-related adjustment in the sample is 14 per cent. MSL is administrative data on job loss resulting from mass layoffs that also reports what has been, in the perception of the manager, the economic reason for job losses including imports and overseas relocation as possible choices. MSL and TAA tend to underestimate the incidence of trade-related job loss; see OECD (2005a).

12. A number of other studies for the US investigate this question by comparing earnings before and after displacement using DWS data; see, for example, Addison and Portugal (1989), Gibbons and Katz (1991) and Farber (2003). An important shortcoming of the data, however, is that it only contains information on displaced workers, and therefore an explicit control group is not available.

13. The papers by Bender et al. (1999), Burda and Mertens (2001) and Margolis (1999) provide estimates for France and Germany. Abbring et al. (2002) compare the estimates for the US and the Netherlands. Ichino et al. (2006), Huttunen et al. (2006), Carneiro and Portugal (2006) and Eliason and Storrie (2006) provide estimates for, inter alia, Austria, Finland, Portugal and Sweden.

14. It is worth noting, however, that Kletzer uses a simple before-and-after methodology rather than difference-in-differences, and therefore does not account for a counterfactual.
15. However, it is important to note that workers more than 55 years old are more likely to move into retirement (out of the labour force).
16. However, it is important to note that tenure is highly correlated with age and the model controls for the latter.
17. Farber (2003) undertakes a related study using data from the 1984–2002 DWS. For each survey date (three-year periods), he estimates separate linear probability models of the probability of being re-employed at the subsequent survey date. This allows him to draw conclusions on whether the characteristics differential acts cyclically or counter-cyclically on the re-employment probability. He concludes that whereas the education differential acts counter-cyclically, the racial differential is clearly cyclical. An important result of this study is that re-employment takes time: relative to workers who lost their job in the calendar year immediately prior to the survey date, workers displaced two or three years prior to that date are 15 to 25 percentage points more likely to be re-employed.

References

Abbring, J., van den Berg, G., Gautier, P., Lomwel, A., van Ours, J. and Ruhm, C. (2002). 'Displaced Workers in the United States and the Netherlands', in P. Kuhn, ed., *Losing Work, Moving On: International Perspectives on Worker Displacement*. Kalamazoo: W. E. Upjohn Institute.

Acemoglu, D. (2002). 'Technical Change, Inequality, and the Labor Market', *Journal of Economic Literature*, Vol. 50, pp. 7–72.

Acemoglu, D. (2003). 'Patterns of Skill Premiums', *Review of Economic Studies*, Vol. 70, pp. 199–230.

Addison, J. and Portugal, P. (1989). 'Job Displacement, Relative Wage Changes and Duration of Unemployment', *Journal of Labor Economics*, Vol. 7, pp. 281–302.

Autor, D., Katz, L. and Kearney, M. (2005). 'Trends in US Wage Inequality: Re-assessing the Revisionists', NBER Working Paper No. 11627, Cambridge, Massachusetts.

Bardhan, P. (2005). 'Globalization, Inequality, and Poverty: an Overview', University of California at Berkeley, mimeo.

Bastos, P. (2007). 'Industry-level Wage Bargaining and International Trade: Evidence from Longitudinal Worker-Firm data', PhD thesis, Chapter 5, University of Nottingham.

Bastos, P. and Kreickemeier, U. (2007). 'Unions, Competition and International Trade in General Equilibrium', University of Nottingham, mimeo.

Bastos, P., Kreickemeier, U. and Wright, P. (2007). 'Oligopoly, Open Shop Unions and Trade Liberalisation', GEP Research Paper 07/30, University of Nottingham.

Bender, S., Dustmann, C., Margolis, D. and Meghir, C. (1999). 'Worker Displacement in France and Germany', IFS Working Paper 99/14.

Bernard, A., Jensen, J. and Schott, P. (2006), 'Survival of the Best Fit: Exposure to Low-wage Countries and the (Uneven) Growth of US Manufacturing Plants', *Journal of International Economics*, Vol. 68, pp. 219–37.

Beyer, H., Rojas, P. and Vergara, R. (1999). 'Trade Liberalization and Wage Inequality', *Journal of Development Economics*, Vol. 59, pp. 103–23.

Brander, J. (1981). 'Intra-Industry Trade in Identical Commodities', *Journal of International Economics*, Vol. 11, pp. 1–14.

Brander, J. and Spencer, B. (1988). 'Unionized Oligopoly and International Trade Policy', *Journal of International Economics*, Vol. 24, pp. 217–34.

Burda, M. and Mertens, A. (2001). 'Estimating Wage Losses of Displaced Workers in Germany', *Labour Economics*, Vol. 8, pp. 15–41.

Cameron, A. and Trivedi, P. (2005). *Microeconometrics: Methods and Applications.* Cambridge: Cambridge University Press.

Carneiro, A. and Portugal, P. (2006), 'Earnings Losses of Displaced Workers: Evidence From a Matched Employer–Employee Data Set', CETE Discussion Paper 2006–07, University of Porto.

Cragg, M. and Epelbaum, M. (1996). 'Why Has Wage Dispersion Grown in Mexico? Is It the Incidence of Reforms or the Growing Demand for Skills?', *Journal of Development Economics*, Vol. 51, pp. 99–116.

Davis, D. (1996). 'Trade Liberalization and Income Distribution', NBER Working Paper No. 5693, Cambridge, Massachusetts.

Dempsey, J. (2005). 'In Europe, Division Among Old and New', *International Herald Tribune*, 13 June.

Egger, H. and Kreickemeier, U. (2006). 'Firm Heterogeneity and the Labour Market Effects of Trade Liberalisation', GEP Research Paper 2006/26, University of Nottingham.

Eliason, M. and Storrie, D. (2006). 'Lasting or Latent Scars? Swedish Evidence on the Long-term Effects of Job Displacement', *Journal of Labor Economics*, Vol. 24, pp. 831–56.

European Commission (2005). 'The EU Economy 2005 Review', *European Economy*, Vol. 6, Luxembourg: Office for Official Publications of the EC.

European Commission (2006). 'The Future of Europe', Special Eurobarometer 251, European Commission.

Farber, H. (2003). 'Job Loss in the United States, 1981–2001', NBER Working Paper 9707, Cambridge, Massachusetts.

Feenstra, R. and Hanson, G. (2003). 'Global Production Sharing and Rising Inequality: a Survey of Trade and Wages', in K. Choi and J. Harrigan, eds, *Handbook of International Trade*. Oxford: Basil Blackwell, pp. 146–87.

Feliciano, Z. (2001). 'Workers and Trade Liberalization: the Impact of Trade Reform in Mexico on Wages and Employment', *Industrial and Labor Relations Review*, Vol. 55, pp. 95–115.

Flanagan, R. (1999). 'Macroeconomic Performance and Collective Bargaining: an International Perspective', *Journal of Economic Literature*, Vol. 37, pp. 1150–75.

Galiani, S. and Sanguinetti, P. (2003). 'The Impact of Trade Liberalization on Wage Inequality: Evidence from Argentina', *Journal of Development Economics*, Vol. 72, pp. 497–513.

Gaston, N. and Trefler, D. (1995). 'Union Wage Sensitivity to Trade and Protection: Theory and Evidence', *Journal of International Economics*, Vol. 39, pp. 1–25.

Gibbons, R. and Katz, L. (1991). 'Layoffs and Lemons', *Journal of Labor Economics*, Vol. 9, pp. 351–80.

Goldberg, P. and Pavcnik, N. (2005). 'Trade, Wages, and the Political Economy of Trade Protection: Evidence from the Colombian Trade Reforms', *Journal of International Economics*, Vol. pp. 75–105.

Goldberg, P. and Pavcnik, N. (2006). 'The Effects of Colombian Trade Liberalization on Urban Poverty', in A. Harrison, ed., *Globalization and Poverty*. Chicago: University of Chicago Press.

Goldberg, P. and Pavcnik, N. (2007). 'Distributional Effects of Globalization in Developing Countries', *Journal of Economic Literature*, Vol. 45, 1, March, pp. 39–82.

Gonzaga, G., Menezes-Filho, N. and Terra, C. (2006). 'Trade Liberalization and the Evolution of Skill Earnings Differentials in Brazil', *Journal of International Economics*, Vol. 68, pp. 345–67.

Greenaway, D., Gullstrand, J. and Kneller, R. (2005). 'Surviving Globalisation', GEP Research Paper 2005/19, University of Nottingham.

Greenaway, D. and Milner, C. (1986). 'Adjustment to Trade Expansion', in D. Greenaway and C. Milner, *The Economics of Intra-Industry Trade*. Oxford: Basil Blackwell.

Greenaway, D. and Nelson, D. (2002). 'The Assessment: Globalization and Labour-Market Adjustment', *Oxford Review of Economic Policy*, Vol. 16, pp. 1–11.

Grossman, G. (1983). 'Partially Mobile Capital: a General Approach to Two-Sector Trade Theory', *Journal of International Economics*, Vol. 15, pp. 1–17.

Hanson, G. and Harrison, A. (1999). 'Trade Liberalization and Wage Inequality in Mexico', *Industrial and Labor Relations Review*, Vol. 52, pp. 272–88.

Haveman, J. (1998). 'The Influence of Changing Trade Patterns on Displacements of Labor', *International Trade Journal*, Vol. 12, pp. 259–92.

Hijzen, A., Upward, R. and Wright, P. (2005). 'The Earnings Cost of Business Closure in the UK', GEP Research Paper 2005/31, University of Nottingham.

Hildreth, A., von Wachter, T. and Handwerker, E. (2005). 'Estimating the "True" Cost of Job Loss: Evidence Using Matched Data from California 1991–2000', University of California at Berkeley, mimeo.

Huizinga, H. (1993). 'International Market Integration and Union Wage Bargaining', *Scandinavian Journal of Economics*, Vol. 95, pp. 249–55.

Huttunen, K., Moen, J. and Salvanes, K. (2006). 'How Destructive is Creative Destruction? Investigating Long-term Effects of Worker Displacement', University of Helsinki, mimeo.

Ichino, A., Schwerdt, G., Winter-Ebmer, R. and Zweimuller, J. (2006). 'Too Old To Work, Too Young to Retire?', University of Bologna, mimeo.

Jacobson, L., LaLonde, R. and Sullivan, D. (1993). 'Earnings Losses of Displaced Workers', *American Economic Review*, Vol. 83, 4, pp. 685–709.

Jones, R. (1971). 'A Three-Factor Model in Theory, Trade, and History', in J. Bhagwati, R. Jones, R. Mundell and J. Vanek, eds, *Trade, Balance of Payments, and Growth: Essays in Honor of Charles P. Kindleberger*. Amsterdam: North-Holland.

Kaplan, D., Gonzalez, G. and Robertson, R. (2005). 'What Happens to Wages After Displacement', *Economia*, Spring, pp. 197–242.

Kletzer, L. (1998). 'Job Displacement', *Journal of Economic Perspectives*, Vol. 12, pp. 115–36.

Kletzer, L. (2000). 'Trade and Job Loss in US Manufacturing, 1979–94', in R. C. Feenstra, ed., *The Impact of International Trade on Wages*. Chicago: University of Chicago Press.

Kletzer, L. (2001). *Job Loss from Imports: Measuring the Costs*. Washington, D.C.: Institute for International Economics.

Kletzer, L. (2002). *Imports, Exports, and Jobs: What Does Trade Mean for Employment and Job Loss?* Kalamazoo, MI: W. E. Upjohn Institute for Employment Research.

Kletzer, L. (2004). 'Trade-related Job Loss and Wage Insurance: a Synthetic Review', *Review of International Economics*, Vol. 12, pp. 724–48.

Kletzer, L. and Fairlie, R. (2001). 'The Long-Term Costs of Job Displacement for Young Adult Workers', University of California at Santa Cruz, mimeo.

Kletzer, L. and Rosen, H. (2005). 'Easing the Adjustment Burden on US Workers', Chapter 10 in C. Bergsten, ed., *The United States and the World Economy: Foreign Economic Policy for the Next Decade*. Washington, D.C.: Institute for International Economics.

Krueger, A. (1997). 'Labor Market Shifts and the Price Puzzle Revisited', NBER Working Paper 5924.

Leger, L. and Gaisford, J. (2001). 'Imperfect Inter-sectoral Labour Mobility and Welfare in International Trade', *Journal of Economic Surveys*, Vol. 15, 4, pp. 463–90.

Lommerud, K., Meland, F. and Søgard, L. (2003). 'Unionised Oligopoly, Trade Liberalisation and Location Choice', *Economic Journal*, Vol. 113, pp. 782–800.

Machin, S. (2003). 'Wage Inequality Since 1975', in R. Dickens, P. Gregg and J. Wadsworth, eds., *The Labour Market under New Labour*. Basingstoke and New York: Palgrave Macmillan.

Margolis, D. (1999). 'Worker Displacement in France', CNRS TEAM Université Paris I, mimeo.

Mayer, W. (1974). 'Short-Run and Long-Run Equilibrium for a Small Open Economy', *Journal of Political Economy*, Vol. 82, pp. 955–67.

Menezes-Filho, N. (2006). 'The Cost of Displacement in Brazil', University of Sao Paulo, mimeo.

Mishra, P. and Kumar, U. (2005). 'Trade Liberalization and Wage Inequality: Evidence from India', IMF Working Paper 05/20.

Munch, J. and Skaksen, J. (2002). 'Product Market Integration and Wages in Unionized Countries', *Scandinavian Journal of Economics*, Vol. 104, pp. 289–99.

Mussa, M. (1974). 'Tariffs and the Distribution of Income: the Importance of Factor Specificity, Substitutability, and Intensity in the Short and Long Run', *Journal of Political Economy*, Vol. 82, pp. 1191–1204.

Naylor, R. (1998). 'International Trade and Economic Integration When Labour Markets are Generally Unionised', *European Economic Review*, Vol. 42, pp. 1251–67.

Naylor, R. (1999). 'Union Wage Strategies and International Trade', *Economic Journal*, Vol. 109, pp. 102–25.

Neary, P. (1978). 'Short-run Capital Specificity and the Pure Theory of International Trade', *Economic Journal*, Vol. 88, pp. 488–510.

Neary, P. (1982). 'Inter-sectoral Capital Mobility, Wage Stickiness, and the Case for Adjustment Assistance', in J. Bhagwati, ed., *Import Competition and Response*, Chicago: University of Chicago Press.

Neary, P. (2002). 'International Trade in General Oligopolistic Equilibrium', University College of Dublin, mimeo.

Neary, P. (2003). 'Globalization and Market Structure', *Journal of the European Economic Association*, Vol. 1, pp. 245–71.

Niblett, R. (2005). 'Shock Therapy', *CSIS Euro Focus*, Vol. 11, 3 June.

OECD (2004). 'Wage-setting Institutions and Outcomes', in *OECD Employment Outlook 2004 Edition*. Paris: Organisation for Economic Co-operation and Development.

OECD (2005a). 'Trade-adjustment Costs in OECD Labour Markets: a Mountain or a Molehill?' in *OECD Employment Outlook 2005 Edition*. Paris: Organisation for Economic Co-operation and Development.

OECD (2005b). 'Helping Workers to Navigate in "Globalised" Labour Markets', *Policy Brief*, June. Paris: Organisation for Economic Co-operation and Development.

Pavcnik, N., Blom, A., Goldberg, P. and Schady, N. (2004). 'Trade Liberalization and Industry Wage Structure: Evidence from Brazil', *The World Bank Economic Review*, Vol. 18, pp. 319–44.

Piperakis, A., Hine, R. and Wright, P. (2003). 'Market Size and Economic Integration when Labor Markets are Unionized', *Review of International Economics*, Vol. 11, pp. 483–94.

Revenga, A. (1992). 'Exporting Jobs? The Impact of Import Competition on Employment and Wages in US Manufacturing', *Quarterly Journal of Economics*, Vol. 107, pp. 255–84.

Revenga, A. (1997). 'Employment and Wage Effects of Trade Liberalization: the Case of Mexican Manufacturing', *Journal of Labour Economics*, Vol. 15, pp. S20–S43.

Robertson, R. (2004). 'Relative Prices and Wage Inequality: Evidence from Mexico', *Journal of International Economics*, Vol. 64, pp. 387–409.

Samuelson, P. (1971). 'Ohlin Was Right', *Swedish Journal of Economics*, Vol. 73, pp. 365–84.

Schoeni, R. and Dardia, M. (1996). 'Wage Losses of Displaced Workers in the 1990s', RAND, mimeo.

Scott, R. (2005). 'US–China Trade, 1989–2003: Impact on Jobs and Industries, Nationally and State-by-State', Economic Policy Institute Working Paper 270, Washington, D.C.

Slaughter, M. (2000). 'What Are the Results of Product-prices Studies and What Can We Learn From their Differences?' in R. Feenstra, ed., *The Impact of International Trade on Wages*, NBER Conference Report, Chicago: University of Chicago Press, pp. 129–70.

Sørensen, J. (1993). 'Integration of Product Markets When Labour Markets are Unionised', *Recherches Economiques de Louvain*, Vol. 59, pp. 485–502.

Thoenig, M. and Verdier, T. (2003). 'A Theory of Defensive Skill-Biased Innovation and Globalization', *American Economic Review*, Vol. 93, pp. 709–28.

Wood, A. (1995). 'How Trade Hurt Unskilled Workers', *Journal of Economic Perspectives*, Vol. 9, pp. 57–80.

4
Trade and Rising Wage Inequality: What Can We Learn from a Decade of Computable General Equilibrium Analysis?

Niven Winchester

4.1 Introduction

Increased North–South, or developed–developing, trade and rising skilled–unskilled relative wages (or skill premiums) in the North are linked via two propositions widely used by trade economists – the Heckscher–Ohlin (HO) and Stolper–Samuelson (SS) theorems. Specifically, if the global economy is HO, and skilled and unskilled labour the factors of production, the skill-abundant North will export the skill intensive good and the unskilled-abundant South will export the unskilled intensive commodity. If, as has occurred in recent decades, there is an increase in the relative economic size of the South and/or trade frictions are reduced, then the relative price of skill intensive products will rise in the North. This price movement, in accordance with the SS theorem, will increase the skilled wage and decrease the unskilled wage.

It is, therefore, quite natural that the HO and SS theorems are used as the starting point for most empirical analyses of the connection between trade and wages. Three strands of empirical research have emerged: product price studies; factor content of trade analyses; and computable general equilibrium (CGE) investigations. The first two approaches draw on HO and SS properties. Specifically, product price studies utilise simple general equilibrium relationships between changes in relative product prices and changes in relative factor prices that must hold under the zero profit condition of perfectly competitive models, and factor content of trade studies make use of the property that trade in goods is a substitute for trade in factors in the HO model.

CGE studies, on the other hand, build a theoretically consistent general equilibrium model, introduce shocks representative of trade changes, and compute a set of relative prices so that all markets are in equilibrium. CGE modellers typically introduce several modifications to the HO model so that their models are able to explain certain real world phenomena, such as intra-industry trade. However, these modifications compromise the clarity of the SS theorem. CGE modelling therefore serves an important role in settling the argument of when trade might affect wages. Indeed, François and Nelson (1998: 1483) note, 'when the issue at hand is the link between international trade and relative wages there is simply no substitute for general equilibrium analysis.'

Following more than a decade of CGE analysis concerning the link between trade and wages, this study takes stock of the current body of knowledge, outlines key findings in the literature, provides an analytical framework to explain the key results, and suggests how future research might proceed.

4.2   CGE studies of trade and wage inequality

CGE analyses of the link between trade and wages differ with respect to dimensionality, market structure and calibration. To make headway, we organise the literature into three categories: pioneering, illustrative and empirical studies. As their name suggests, pioneering studies were the first CGE studies to contribute to the trade and wages debate, and did so using models closely related to the HO framework. Illustrative studies typically provide insights into how departures from the HO model influence the link between trade and wages, identify a small number of industrial sectors, and/or are largely parameterised by 'guesstimates'. Empirical studies, on the other hand, are calibrated using real world data and usually employ a finer level of disaggregation than their illustrative counterparts. CGE studies contributing to the trade and wages debate are summarised in Table 4.1.

4.2.1   Pioneering studies

Krugman (1995) undertakes the simplest CGE analysis of the link between trade and wage inequality. Krugman's model represents the OECD as a 'standard' HO economy (two goods, two factors, perfect competition etc.) and uses an offer curve to represent newly industrialised economies (NIEs), which dictates that the OECD has substantial market power. Krugman asks the following question: 'how large a change in relative wages in the OECD might be associated with the emergence of NIE trade as actually seen?' The results reveal that increased OECD–NIE trade raised the relative wage of skilled labour in the OECD by less than

Table 4.1: Trade-wage CGE studies

Study	Modelling framework*	Key experiment(s)	Change in skilled–unskilled relative wage due to trade
Krugman (1995)	1-2-2, perfect competition, the OECD is able to influence world prices	Determines the change in relative wages associated with the observed increase in OECD–NIE trade	<3%
Lawrence and Evans (1996)	1-3-2, perfect competition, non-traded sector, exogenous world prices	Changes world relative prices so that US basic manufacturing is replaced by imports	Small
Cline (1997)	13-5-3, perfect competition, restrictions on sectoral imports and exports	Forward- and backward-looking experiments examining changes in transports costs and trade barriers	5%
Abrego and Whalley (2000 & 2003)	1-2-2, perfect competition, Armington assumption, exogenous world prices	Simulates observed changes in world prices for alternative Armington elasticities	Small
Tokarick (2005)	1-3-3, perfect competition, sector-specific capital, exogenous world prices	Simulates observed changes in the US trade deficit, import tariffs and the terms of trade	Negligible
De Santis (2002 & 2003)	1-2-2, perfect competition, differentiated capital goods which complement skilled labour, reduced trade costs stimulate the introduction of new foreign capital goods	Reduces trade costs so that the model replicates the observed change in the UK skilled–unskilled relative wage	N.A.

(Continued)

Table 4.1: (Continued)

Study	Modelling framework*	Key experiments(s)	Change in skilled–unskilled relative wage due to trade
Thierfelder and Robinson (2002)	1-12-6, perfect competition, Armington product differentiation	50% reduction in the world price of imports and a $200 billion increase in the US trade balance	1%
Cortes and Jean (1999)	3-13-3, imperfect competition in manufacturing, perfect competition elsewhere, Armington and Dixit–Stiglitz product differentiation	Doubles the size of emerging economies	1%
Jean and Bontout (2000)	1-9-3, perfect competition in services, imperfect competition elsewhere, Armington and Dixit–Stiglitz product differentiation	Simulates changes in French imports with and without trade-induced technical change	1% or 6%
Tyers and Yang (1997)	6-37-5, perfect competition, Armington product differentiation, GTAP framework with imperfect labour mobility	Forward- and backward-looking experiments examining changes in trade frictions and rapid RDE growth	<1%
Winchester, Greenaway and Reed (2006)	4-19-5, perfect competition, Armington product differentiation, GTAP framework	Removes changes in UK sectoral imports relative to GDP	1%
Winchester (2008)	4-7-7, perfect competition, Armington product differentiation, GTAP framework	Removes changes in New Zealand sectoral imports and exports relative to GDP	–27%

Note: * Dimensionality is represented regions-sectors-factors.

3 per cent. As the value of OECD imports from NIEs is only around 2 per cent of OECD GDP, Krugman attributes the small change in relative wages to a small trade volume effect.

Lawrence and Evans (1996) contribute to the debate using a framework similar to Krugman's, except that three sectors (high skilled and basic manufacturing, and non-tradables) are identified, and world prices are exogenous. The model is parameterised so as to represent the US economy in 1990 and Lawrence and Evans analyse the future impact of trade on wages by adjusting world prices so that US production of basic manufacturing is replaced by imports. This shock, which requires a fivefold increase in US imports of basic manufacturing, causes the skill premium to increase by 7.5 per cent. This is a relatively small increase, given the extreme nature of the shock, and can be attributed to the small decline (1.8 per cent) in the price of basic manufacturing required to eliminate domestic production and the small share (7 per cent) of these commodities in US output. Lawrence and Evans (1996: 18) conclude that 'if the impact of very large shifts in trade in the future is likely to be relatively small, it suggests that the much smaller growth in trade with developing countries over the past 15 years is unlikely to have had [a] major impact on labour markets.'

4.2.2 Illustrative studies

Cline (1997) contributes to the debate by constructing what he calls the 'trade and income distribution equilibrium' (TIDE) model. The TIDE model is perfectly competitive and identifies three factors (skilled labour, unskilled labour and capital), five sectors (three traded and two non-traded) and thirteen regions. Cline focuses on wage inequality in the US. An important feature of the TIDE model is that constraints are placed on trade flows for each commodity in each region so that imports cannot exceed half of domestic consumption and exports cannot exceed half of domestic production. This specification stops regions from specialising in a subset of goods and is an alternative to assuming that domestic and imported products are imperfect substitutes (as in the Armington approach). Additionally, production functions differ across regions with respect to technical efficiency. Cline calibrates the TIDE model using a mixture of empirically grounded and postulated estimates to benchmark the model to 1993.

Cline assesses the impact of trade on wages by comparing the results from a number of backward looking simulations to a baseline backcast, which is computed by simulating actual changes in factor endowments, transport costs and trade barriers. Due to the significant increase in the relative supply of skilled labour, the skill premium falls by 47 per cent between 1973 and 1993 in the baseline. Cline assesses the impact of increased trade by freezing transport costs and protection at their 1973 levels. The results indicate that the skill premium would have been 10 per cent lower than in the baseline of 1993 if trade frictions had not been reduced. In another counterfactual, Cline eliminates transport costs and tariffs from 1973 onwards. The simulation indicates that the removal of trade barriers would have increased the US skill premium by around 20 per cent in 1973 but only by 6.25 per cent in 1993, relative to the respective baselines. The smaller impact of the counterfactual in later years reflects falling transport costs and tariffs in the baseline. From this, Cline concludes that the world has moved a long way towards free trade over the last three decades, and any further decreases in transport costs and protection are likely to have only moderate effects.

In another experiment, Cline moves the TIDE model as close as possible to the HO model. The counterfactual removes non-tradable sectors, gets rid of the constraints on trade flows, and sets tariffs and transport costs equal to zero. In this simulation, the US wage ratio doubles and there is a trend towards global factor price equalisation, but US unskilled wages are still many times greater than those in developing countries.[1] Consequently, Cline concludes that the existence of non-tradable sectors and consumers' preferences for domestically produced goods over imports are natural barriers against large changes in factor prices due to trade.

Cline also assesses the likely impact of trade on wages in the future. He does this by creating a 2013 baseline (which incorporates estimates of changes in factor endowments, technical efficiency parameters, transport costs and trade distortions) and considering several forward looking scenarios. In one future scenario, Cline freezes transport costs and protection at 1993 levels. The US skill premium falls 5 per cent relative to the 2013 baseline in this experiment. Drawing on results from his forward and backward looking scenarios Cline (1997: 238) concludes that 'the results of the TIDE model simulations suggest that trade . . . [has] had a significant impact over the past decade in the observed rise of skilled wages relative to unskilled wages. In contrast, for the future the model suggests a much more benign outlook.'

Although the TIDE model is a productive workhorse for evaluating the channels through which trade influences relative wages, Cline's conclusion regarding the historical impact of trade is a little misleading. This is because Cline ignores the large difference between the observed increase in wage inequality and the change in wage inequality simulated in the

TIDE model. Specifically, results from Cline's backward looking analysis suggest that reduced transport costs and trade barriers increased the US skill premium by around 5 per cent and factor supply changes reduced the premium by 47 per cent between 1973 and 1993. Combined with Cline's assertion that the US skill premium increased by about 20 per cent over this period, these figures indicate that trade accounted for only 7.4 per cent of the total (factor) demand induced increase in the skill premium. The influence of trade, therefore, seems small relative to that of other factors.

Abrego and Whalley (2000, 2003) consider a small country HO model with a skilled–unskilled dichotomy, and a heterogeneous good variant of the model where imports and domestically produced importables are imperfect substitutes (the so-called Armington assumption). The model is calibrated to UK data for 1990 and the authors shock the model by imposing the observed increase in the world relative price of the skill intensive commodity. Like Lawrence and Evans (1996), Abrego and Whalley (2000) find that the trade shock eliminates domestic production of the unskilled intensive commodity when goods are homogeneous. For a relative price change that does not induce specialisation (a price change smaller than that observed) the authors report that trade accounts for around 50 per cent of the observed increase in wage inequality. This finding, however, is somewhat misleading as the authors do not consider the large increase in the relative supply of skilled labour. The proportion of increased wage inequality attributable to trade is, therefore, likely to be much less than 50 per cent. When imports and the domestic good are imperfect substitutes, Abrego and Whalley illustrate that there may be little or no transmission of international price shocks to relative wages and that simulated changes in relative wages can change sign, depending on whether the demand side substitution elasticity between domestic and foreign goods is greater or less than one.

Tokarick (2005) focuses on the role of non-traded goods. The model identifies three sectors (exportables, importables and non-tradables) and three factors (skilled labour, unskilled labour and capital). World prices for tradable goods are exogenous and the problem of specialisation is avoided by assuming that capital is sector-specific. Tokarick calibrates his model to US data for 1982 and conducts simulations under two alternative assumptions concerning non-tradables: firstly when adjustment of the non-traded sector is permitted; and secondly when it is not.

Tokarick shocks the model by implementing observed changes in trade variables (the trade deficit, import tariffs and the terms of trade) between 1982 and 1996. A small increase in the skill premium (0.2 per cent) is simulated in both variants of the model. Decomposition analysis, however, reveals that the movement in relative wages associated with each component of the trade shock changes sign for some components when the assumption regarding the adjustment of non-tradables is altered. For example, tariff cuts are associated with a decrease in wage inequality when the non-traded sector is able to adjust and an increase in the skill premium when it is not. This is because there is a decline in the price of (skill intensive) non-tradables when non-tradables adjustment is allowed, whereas, by design, there is no change in the price of non-tradables in the alternative scenario.

Tokarick also considers what would happen if the 1996 US economy had no opportunity to trade. When the non-traded sector is allowed to adjust, autarky results in output of exportables contracting, production of importables and non-tradables increasing, and a rise in the price of non-tradables. These changes are associated with a 2.2 per cent rise in the skill premium. Conversely, wage inequality falls by 6 per cent when there is no adjustment in the market for non-traded goods, as the only sectoral adjustments are a decrease in the production of exportables and an increase in importable output, which results in a decline in the relative price of exportables. Tokarick (2005: 858) concludes that 'changes in trade related variables has a negligible effect on relative wages' and, through interactions between the non-traded sector and the rest of the economy, expanding trade may have reduced wage inequality.

De Santis (2002, 2003) produces evidence that the influences of trade and technology on wages are not independent. The author models a small open economy that employs skilled and unskilled labour to produce two goods, unskilled intensive manufactures and skilled intensive services. De Santis refers to the unskilled intensive commodity as a capital good, as it is used as an intermediate input in both sectors. Services also employ a set of differentiated foreign capital goods, which are imperfect substitutes for the domestic variety. Manufactures are produced by a Cobb–Douglas production technology whereas there is relative complementarity between skilled labour and capital goods in services (the elasticity of substitution between skilled labour and capital is lower than that between unskilled labour and capital). De Santis (2002) also models imperfect inter-sectoral labour mobility by stipulating that aggregate quantities of skilled and unskilled labour are assigned to different sectors according to separate constant elasticity of transformation (CET) functions. To facilitate the analysis of two different technology shocks, two variants of the model are created. In the base model, the number of foreign capital goods, which are produced by monopolistic firms, is endogenous. The number of foreign capital goods is fixed in the alternative specification.

De Santis benchmarks his model to UK data for the late 1970s and attempts to explain the 18 per cent increase in the UK skill premium between 1979 and 1992 using two alternative technology shocks. In the variant where the number of capital goods is variable, a reduction in trade costs results in an increase in wage inequality as it fosters the development of new capital goods by foreign firms, which increases the marginal product of skilled labour relative to that of unskilled labour, due to the capital–skill complementarity assumption. De Santis's trade shock, therefore, involves an endogenous reduction in trade costs so that the model reproduces the observed change in UK wage inequality. In the author's second shock, the number of foreign capital goods is fixed and De Santis simulates the observed increase in wage inequality by introducing endogenous skilled labour augmenting technical change in both sectors. De Santis refers to the first shock as trade induced, sector biased technical change, and the second as skill biased technical change. Both variants of the model are able to explain the expansion in services and the contraction of manufacturing in the UK, but De Santis favours the variant of the model with trade induced technical change as it can also explain the large increase in UK imports of capital goods.

4.2.3 Empirical models

Thierfelder and Robinson (2002) analyse a fifteen-sector (twelve in manufacturing), six-factor (professional, technical support, semi-skilled labour, low skilled labour, land, and capital) model calibrated to the 1982 US economy. A 'double Armington' assumption is employed (for each good), so that imported and domestic varieties are imperfect substitutes, and there is imperfect substitution in production between exported and domestic varieties. Two shocks considered by Thierfelder and Robinson include a 50 per cent reduction in the world price of imports and a $200 billion increase in the trade balance. Combined, these shocks generate a 1.25 per cent increase in the professional to low skill relative wage. When labour is immobile, however, a 17.3 per cent increase in wage inequality is observed. Thierfelder and Robinson (2002: 24) conclude, 'trade is responsible for very little of the wage gap', but 'in the short term, when it is difficult for unskilled workers to move out of manufacturing sectors, trade shocks can have a strong impact on the wage ratio' (2002: 23).

Cortes and Jean (1999) analyse the impact of the expansion of developing countries on European wages by doubling the size of the emerging economies. The authors' model identifies three regions (the EU, emerging economies, and the rest of the world), three factors (skilled labour, unskilled labour and capital), and thirteen sectors (agriculture, services and eleven manufacturing sectors). Output is produced by a Leontief nest of intermediate inputs and a composite of primary factors. The primary factor nest is such that there is capital–skill complementarity. There is imperfect competition in manufacturing and perfect competition in other sectors. On the consumption side, goods produced by Europe and the rest of the world are imperfect substitutes for emerging country goods, and manufactures within each composite region are differentiated using a CES function as in the Dixit–Stiglitz approach.

The increase in the size of the emerging economies results in the share of emerging country imports in European final demand (import penetration) rising from 1.6 per cent to 3.0 per cent in manufacturing. As might be expected, increases in import penetration are greatest in manufacturing sectors with low fixed costs producing relatively undifferentiated products (e.g. textiles and clothing) and smallest in sectors producing highly differentiated goods that have high fixed costs (e.g. chemical products). These adjustments, and the associated changes in production, result in European wage inequality increasing by 0.8 per cent. From this, Cortes and Jean (1999: 117) deduce that 'the increased international integration of emerging countries in the world economy does not appear to be the main source of problems in the European labour market.'

Jean and Bontout (2000) employ a single country CGE model to analyse the causes of growing wage inequality in France between 1970 and 1992. Three primary factors (skilled labour, unskilled labour and capital) and nine sectors are identified. There is perfect competition in services, which are non-traded, and Cournot competition elsewhere. The production structure is the same as in Cortes and Jean (1999). Consumption is modelled using a series of CES nests. Imports from the North and South are differentiated using an Armington aggregation and a Dixit–Stiglitz approach is used to differentiate French varieties from each other.[2]

Jean and Bontout's trade shock involves changing relative import prices and Armington share coefficients, which results in an increase in the skill premium of 1 per cent. In another simulation, the authors assume that increased import penetration increases productivity and sectoral skilled–unskilled employment ratios. Although the skill premium increased by 5.5 per cent in this simulation, the authors conclude that, in the presence of significant downward pressure on wage inequality resulting from factor supply changes, trade did not have a significant effect on relative wages.

Tyers and Yang (1997) consider the effects of trade liberalisation, and the rapid development of several developing countries using a modified version of the standard Global Trade Analysis Project (GTAP) model (Hertel, 1999) and release 3 of the GTAP database (McDougall et al., 1998). The authors' aggregation of the database identifies North America, the EU, Australasia (which are collectively known as the 'Older Industrialised Countries' or OIEs), Japan, the 'Rapidly Developing Economies' (RDEs: China, Indonesia, Hong Kong, Malaysia, Singapore, Republic of Korea, Taiwan and Thailand), and the rest of the world. Five factors of production (skilled labour, unskilled labour, farm labour, land and capital) and thirty-two sectors are also recognised. Tyers and Yang's chosen model is a perfectly competitive representation of the global economy that captures both bilateral trade flows amongst regions and inter-sectoral linkages within regions. Imports are differentiated by country of origin using the Armington assumption. A non-standard feature of the model concerns the allocation of labour to different uses. Specifically, (aggregate) labour is allocated to either the farm or the urban labour market, and urban labour is distributed between the skilled and unskilled labour markets in a two-level CES nest.

Like Cline (1997), Tyers and Yang conduct both a backward and a forward looking analysis. The authors look back to examine the effects of the emergence (increased trade openness and dramatic expansion) of RDEs, and forward to evaluate the impact of a continuation of recent trends. The backward looking simulation focuses on the period 1970–92, and evaluates the impact of observed changes in the world economy by removing the dramatic growth and increased openness of RDEs. This is accomplished by shocking factor endowments and making tariffs endogenous to control for the level of RDE imports of each commodity. The results reveal that trade increased skilled–unskilled wage inequality by 0.2 per cent, 0.3 per cent and 0.9 per cent in North America, the EU and Australasia, respectively. Changes in the ratios of skilled to farm wages are more interesting. As RDEs are land scarce, this shock lowers wage inequality between skilled and farm labour by around 9 per cent in North America and Australasia, and by about 6 per cent in the EU.

Tyres and Yang then generate a 2010 baseline and simulate two counterfactuals in their forward looking analysis. In the first, tariff and export subsidy equivalents of trade distortions in agriculture and food processing are reduced by half and all other trade barriers are abolished. This simulation results in a contraction of unskilled intensive manufacturing sectors in OIEs and increases skilled–unskilled wage inequality by between 1 and 3 per cent relative to the 2010 baseline. There is also a decrease in urban–rural wage inequality in North America and Australasia. In the second forward looking counterfactual, in addition to the above trade reforms, voluntary export restraints are placed on RDE exports to OIEs so that domestic absorption of RDE imports in each product category is maintained at 1992 levels. This shock results in declines of the skilled to unskilled wage ratios in OIEs of less than 1 per cent. The authors close by noting that trade has only resulted in a small increase in the dispersion of skilled and unskilled wages and future changes in trade policy will not have a large impact on relative wages.

Other studies built on the GTAP framework include Winchester (2008) and Winchester et al. (2006). Winchester et al.'s contribution embodies a new labour classification. The classification observes wage and educational attainment data for 77 occupations in the UK and uses cluster analysis to determine both the composition and number of labour groups. Four labour types – highly skilled, skilled, semi-skilled and unskilled – are generated. Cost shares for these labour types are mapped onto the UK component of Version 6 of the GTAP database, which corresponds to the global economy in 2001. The aggregation of the database identifies four regions (the UK, other developed economies, RDEs and the rest of the world), and five factors of production (four labour types and capital). Two alternative sectoral aggregations are employed; one identifies five sectors and the other nineteen. The trade shock removes changes in UK sectoral imports relative to GDP between 1980 and 2001 by introducing a set of endogenous export taxes in other regions. The results are an increase in wage inequality between any pair of labour types, but the simulated changes in relative wages are small. For example, the largest movement in relative wages, which occurs for the highly skilled to unskilled wage, is 1.5 per cent. The authors conclude that trade is not the main driver of increased wage inequality in the UK.

Winchester (2008) focuses on New Zealand. The author begins by indicating that the impact of trade on wages in New Zealand should be greater than the impact of trade on US or UK wages since, relative to GDP, New Zealand imports more from RDEs than either the US or the UK. Winchester extends the New Zealand component of the GTAP database by including data for four labour types with different qualifications (degree, vocational, high school, and no qualification). The author's trade shock removes changes in New Zealand exports and imports relative to GDP between 1980 and 2001 by controlling import tariffs and export taxes in other regions. The results reveal that, as New Zealand has a comparative advantage in agriculture based products and these commodities make intensive use of unskilled labour, trade has caused a reduction in New Zealand wage inequality. The largest impact is to the ratio of wages for those with degrees relative to no qualifications, which falls by 3.46 per cent.

Decomposition of the impact of imports by commodity and region uncovers that imports from other developed nations and RDEs increased the degree to no qualification relative wage by 0.88 per cent and 0.53 per cent, respectively. These results not only suggest that trade cannot be responsible for increased wage inequality in New Zealand, but also that most of the downward pressure on unskilled wages due to imports results from trade with other developed nations.

Winchester also investigates the short run impact of trade on wages. The author does this by restricting the mobility of unqualified labour employed in unskilled intensive manufacturing, which he labels 'vulnerable' labour. When vulnerable labour is immobile, import changes increase the relative wage of workers with a degree to vulnerable labour by 13.6 per cent. This indicates that imports may have had a relatively large detrimental effect on this small subset of the population in the short run. However, a small degree of labour mobility softens this blow to unskilled labour considerably, and vulnerable labour accounts for only a small proportion of total unskilled labour. Hence, imports could not have driven the observed increase in New Zealand wage inequality.

4.3   Lessons from a decade of CGE analysis

The overwhelming conclusion from more than a decade of CGE analysis is that the impact of trade on wages via HO channels has been small relative to the role played by other factors. The skilled to unskilled wage ratio in both the US and UK has increased from 1.5 to 1.8 during the final decades of the twentieth century. The CGE literature indicates that this ratio would have been around 0.9 in both nations at the end of the century if factor supply changes had occurred in isolation (Cline, 1997; Winchester and Greenaway, 2007). These numbers suggest that demand side influences resulted in the relative wage rising by 0.9 (or 60 per cent of the 1980 skilled–unskilled wage ratio) over a twenty-year period. Studies surveyed in this chapter indicate that trade increased the skilled–unskilled wage by at most 5 per cent (or 0.075), which implies that the force of other factors was at least twelve times greater than that of trade. Moreover, several studies (Tyers and Yang, 1997; Tokarick, 2005; Winchester, 2008) indicate that increased trade may actually be associated with declining wage inequality.

To examine why the results from empirical modelling are at odds with the predictions of the Stolper–Samuelson theorem (SS), we consider a small HO economy where imports (M) are differentiated from domestically produced importables (D) in an Armington fashion but exportables (E) are not differentiated on global markets. Following Robinson and Thierfelder (1996), the proportional change in the skilled wage ($\hat{w}_S$) minus the corresponding change in the unskilled wage ($\hat{w}_L$) can be expressed as:

$$\hat{w}_S - \hat{w}_L = \frac{1}{(\theta_{SE} - \theta_{SD})} \frac{(\sigma_A - 1)}{(\sigma_A + \Omega)} (\hat{p}^E - \hat{p}^M) \qquad (4.1)$$

where θ_{SE} and θ_{SD} are, respectively, the cost shares of skilled labour in E and D and are less than one, σ_A is the elasticity of substitution between M and D, $\hat{p}^E$ and $\hat{p}^M$ are proportional changes in the world prices of E and M respectively, and Ω is the elasticity of transformation in production between E and M and is positive.[3]

This framework nests the standard HO model, which is obtained by setting σ_A equal to infinity. In this case (4.1) reduces to:

$$\hat{w}_S - \hat{w}_L = \frac{1}{(\theta_{SE} - \theta_{SD})} (\hat{p}^E - \hat{p}^M) \qquad (4.2)$$

If E uses skilled labour relatively intensively ($\theta_{SE} > \theta_{SD}$), and there is an increase in the relative price of E, it is possible to derive the following relationship between product and factor prices:

$$\hat{w}_S > \hat{p}^E > \hat{p}^M > \hat{w}_L \qquad (4.3)$$

This is the well-known magnification effect and demonstrates the SS theorem.

If M and D are not perfect substitutes, the relationship between factor and product prices depends crucially on the value of the Armington elasticity. When $1 < \sigma_A < \infty$ M and D are imperfect substitutes and, because the decline in the relative price of M has a smaller impact on the price of D, world prices have less influence on factor prices than in the HO case. Changes in international prices have no impact on domestic product or factor prices when σ_A is unity, as the Armington nest is Cobb–Douglas, so a change in the price of M is offset by a demand change of equal proportion. If $\sigma_A < 1$, M and D are gross complements, and the SS effect is reversed. That is, an increase in the relative price of E is associated with falling wage inequality. Therefore, as also demonstrated by Abrego and

Whalley (2000, 2003), the magnification effect is less likely to hold as the Armington elasticity decreases, since the impact of trade on wages is weakened considerably when the homogeneous goods assumption is relaxed.[4]

Dimensionality and specialisation are other reasons why the transmitted effect of product price changes is less than that predicted by the SS theorem. With respect to dimensionality, Ethier (1984) reveals that the SS theorem is replaced by the much weaker SS correlation when there are more than two commodities.[5] Turning to specialisation, as noted by Lawrence and Evans (1996), once there is complete specialisation, the SS theorem no longer holds and further trade will have a limited impact. If a country no longer produces the importable good, wages are determined in the domestic and exportable sectors. These results suggest that, although qualitative support for the SS theorem is provided by many CGE analyses, as in, for example, Winchester et al. (2006), real world modifications to the HO model (e.g. product differentiation) moderate the effect of changes in international prices.

Before closing, we investigate regional sources of relative wage change in developed nations, by extending the decomposition analysis of Winchester (2008). Our modelling framework is identical to the author's except that we employ a skilled–unskilled dichotomy and modify the region of focus. Specifically, we undertake additional simulations in which the UK and the US are the focus regions and other developed regions are included in a composite. The results are reported in Table 4.2 and reveal that, as New Zealand is more open than the UK or the US, movements in relative wages are larger than those in the other nations of interest. As might also be expected, an increase in skill intensive exports reinforces the effect of imports on the skilled–unskilled wage ratio in the UK and US. For example, although changes in US imports over the 1980–2001 period increased the relative wage of skilled labour by 0.19 per cent,

Table 4.2: Percentage changes in the skilled–unskilled relative wage, 1980–2001

Due to change in:	*New Zealand*	*UK*	*US*
Imports and exports	−2.26	1.08	0.60
Imports	0.93	0.66	0.19
Unskilled-manufacturing imports	0.56	0.71	0.41
Imports from developed nations	0.51	0.36	0.11

Source: Model simulations described in the text.

the combined impact of rising imports and exports pushed up this ratio by 0.60 per cent. Nevertheless, simulated changes in wage inequality remain small.

Another anticipated result is that changes in unskilled intensive manufacturing imports generate large increases in wage inequality relative to the total amount of wage inequality provoked by changes in import volumes. The most striking result, which is located in the final row of Table 4.2, is that over half of the import induced increase in wage inequality (in all three countries) results from increased trade with other developed nations. These findings provide further support that trade has not significantly influenced wage inequality in the North through HO channels.

A substantial caveat regarding our conclusions should be noted. Specifically, our discussion does not eliminate the possibility that trade from low wage economies has influenced the wage distribution in developed nations via mechanisms other than HO and SS forces. Wood (1994) argues that increased competition from low wage countries may induce producers of importables in developed nations to adopt new, unskilled-labour saving technologies. As noted earlier, Jean and Bontout (2000) illustrate that, although the impact of trade on wages is larger when imports (partially) drive skill biased technical change, the usual conclusion is not overturned. This result does not, however, rule out the possibility that the threat of import competition may induce a larger shift in skill biased technical change.

In general, skill biased technical change has been poorly captured by CGE modellers. Typically, the impact of skill biased technical change is determined residually as the proportion of the increase in relative wages unexplained by trade, and production function parameters or other variables are adjusted so that the model simulates the desired change in relative wages (Cline, 1997; Tyers and Yang, 1997; Abrego and Whalley, 2000, 2003; De Santis, 2002, 2003). One exception is Winchester and Greenaway (2007), who estimate changes in three capital assets and show that changes in the skill premium can be explained by the fall in the effective price of high-tech equipment when capital equipment complements skilled labour. The authors' framework is, however, silent on the source of the decline in the price of high-tech equipment and, therefore, cannot determine what proportion of the price decline results from trade pressures. Conversely, De Santis (2002, 2003) provides a useful illustration of the channels through which the interaction of trade and technology can influence relative wages, though the author employs a highly aggregated model and determines technical change residually.

In particular, De Santis notes that the fall in transport costs required for his model to generate the observed increase in UK wage inequality is plausible, but a much larger decrease in transport costs would have been required if he had also considered the increase in the relative supply of skilled labour. Determining the role of trade induced technical change is an area requiring further research.

4.4   Conclusions

This chapter has surveyed CGE contributions to the trade and wages debate. Despite the strong link between trade and wages in a simple and well-known general equilibrium model, this literature provides an avalanche of support for the consensus in the wider empirical literature that the impact of trade on relative wages has been minor. The reason for this conflict is that CGE models soften the link between product and factor prices, in order to mould the HO framework into a more accurate representation of the real world. Moreover, some studies show that trade may be associated with falling wage inequality and/or reveal that North–North trade is responsible for a greater proportion of the increase in northern wage inequality than North–South trade. A caveat concerning this conclusion, however, is that CGE analysis has little to say about how trade influences wages via non-HO channels. In particular, the role of trade induced technical change has not been examined in detail.

Notes

1. Factor price equalisation does not occur because all regions do not continue to produce all commodities and differences in technologies across regions are maintained.
2. The authors' empirical framework is unable to model the large increase in unemployment over the sample period. Instead, Jean and Bontout assume that there was full employment in 1970 and account for the observed increase in structural unemployment by calculating an underlying full employment equilibrium by adjusting relative wages.
3. See Robinson and Thierfelder (1996) for the arguments of Ω.
4. Other restrictions on the substitutability between imports and domestic production, such as Dixit–Stiglitz product differentiation and the restrictions in Cline's (1997) model, also reduce the impact of changes in foreign prices on the domestic economy.
5. The Stolper–Samuelson correlation says 'there is a tendency for changes in relative commodity prices to be accompanied by increases in the rewards of factors employed most intensively by those goods whose prices have relatively risen the most and employed least intensively by those goods whose prices have fallen the most' (Ethier, 1984: 164).

References

Abrego, L. and Whalley, J. (2000). 'The Choice of Structural Model in Trade-Wages Decompositions', *Review of International Economics*, Vol. 8, 3, pp. 462–77.

Abrego, L. and Whalley, J. (2003). 'Goods Market Responses to Trade Shocks and Trade and Wages Decompositions', *Canadian Journal of Economics*, Vol. 36, 3, pp. 747–57.

Cline, W. R. (1997). *Trade and Income Distribution*. Washington, D.C.: Institute for International Economics.

Cortes, O. and Jean, S. (1999). 'Does Competition from Emerging Countries Threaten Unskilled Labour in Europe? An Applied General Equilibrium Approach', in P. Brenton and L. Pelkmann, eds, *Global Trade and European Workers*. Basingstoke: Macmillan, pp. 96–122.

De Santis, R. A. (2002). 'Wage Inequality Between and Within Groups: Trade-Induced or Skill-Bias Technical Change? Alternative AGE Models for the UK', *Economic Modelling*, Vol. 19, 5, pp. 725–46.

De Santis R. A. (2003). 'Wage Inequality in the United Kingdom: Trade or/and Technology', *The World Economy*, Vol. 26, 6, pp. 893–910.

Ethier, W. F. (1984). 'Higher Dimensional Issues in Trade Theory', in E. W. Jones and P. B. Kenen, eds, *Handbook of International Economics, Vol. I*. Amsterdam: North-Holland, pp. 131–84.

François, J. F. and Nelson, D. (1998). 'Trade, Technology and Wages: General Equilibrium Mechanics', *Economic Journal*, Vol. 108 (September), pp. 1483–99.

Hertel, T. W., ed. (1999). *Global Trade Analysis: Modeling and Applications*. Cambridge: Cambridge University Press.

Jean, S. and Bontout, O. (2000). 'What Drove Relative Wages in France? Structural Decomposition Analysis in a General Equilibrium Framework, 1970–1992', Centre for Research on Globalisation and Labour Markets Working Paper 2000/8, University of Nottingham.

Krugman, P. (1995). 'Growing World Trade: Causes and Consequences', *Brookings Papers*, 1, pp. 327–77.

Lawrence, R. Z. and Evans, C. L. (1996). 'Trade and Wages: Insights from the Crystal Ball', National Bureau of Economic Research Working Paper 5633.

McDougall, R. A., Elbehri, A. and Truong, T. P. (1998). *Global Trade Assistance and Protection: the GTAP 3 Data Base*. Center for Global Trade Analysis, Purdue University.

Robinson, S. and Thierfelder, K. (1996). 'The Trade-Wage Debate in a Model with Non-traded Goods: Making Room for Labor Economists in Trade Theory', International Food Policy Research Institute, Discussion Paper 9.

Thierfelder, K. and Robinson, S. (2002). 'Trade and the Skilled–Unskilled Wage Gap in a Model with Differentiated Goods', International Food Policy Research Institute, Discussion Paper 96.

Tokarick, S. (2005). 'Quantifying the Impact of Trade on Wages: the Role of Non-traded Goods', *Review of International Economics*, Vol. 13, 5, pp. 841–60.

Tyers, R. and Yang, Y. (1997). 'Trade with Asia and Skill Upgrading: Effects on Labour Markets in the Older Industrial Countries', *Review of World Economics/Weltwirtschaftliches Archiv*, Vol. 133, 3, pp. 383–418.

Winchester, N. (2008). 'Searching For the Smoking Gun: Did Trade Hurt Unskilled Workers?' *Economic Record*, forthcoming.

Winchester, N. and Greenaway D. (2007). 'Rising Wage Inequality and Capital-Skill Complementarity', *Journal of Policy Modelling*, Elsevier, Vol. 29, 1, pp. 41–54.

Winchester, N., Greenaway, D. and Reed, G.V. (2006) 'Skill Classification and the Effects of Trade on Wage Inequality', *Review of World Economics*, Vol. 142, 2, pp. 287–306.

Wood, A. (1994). *North–South Trade, Employment and Inequality*. Oxford: Clarendon Press.

5
Unemployment in Models of International Trade

Udo Kreickemeier

5.1 Introduction

In recent years, there has been a growing interest among trade theorists in the links between international trade and labour market distortions. The contributions to this literature employ microeconomic models of labour market distortions and combine them with a multi-sector model of an open economy. Typically, the labour market models employed in this context use either search theory or efficiency wage theory. The chapter by Davidson and Matusz in this volume considers the search theoretic models in some detail, which is why the focus of this chapter is on the efficiency wage literature.

Much of the literature has used a modified Heckscher–Ohlin (HO) framework with two sectors and two factors of production that are mobile between sectors. Most of this chapter will focus on this framework as well. Rather then survey papers in the field in detail, I suggest a common framework – a 'prototype model' – that illustrates the channels through which international trade affects aggregate unemployment (and the labour market more generally) as well as welfare in these Heckscher–Ohlin models that allow for labour market distortions due to efficiency wages.

Compared to the standard HO model with perfectly competitive labour markets, (at least) three additional adjustment margins exist in the efficiency wage models surveyed here. First, the number of employed workers can vary. Second, the effort that these workers exert can vary. Third, there can be a wage differential between sectors, so the number of high wage (or low wage) workers can also vary. If an economy opens up to international trade, there are typically adjustments along all three margins. However, none of the extant models in the literature allows adjustment along all margins – the obvious reason being tractability issues. Rather, the existing models focus on, at most, two of those margins, which makes them difficult to compare.

The key contribution of this chapter is – hopefully – to increase the transparency by showing that, in principle, the three potential adjustment margins in the labour market can be consolidated into one. The principal idea is simple, and its essence is already contained in Albert and Meckl (2001). Basically, it consists of measuring units of labour in a way that these units are paid the same wage in all sectors. I suggest calling these 'normalised efficiency units' (NEUs) of labour. In this framework, moving a worker from the low wage sector to the high wage sector increases the economy-wide employment of labour in NEUs, *ceteris paribus*, while the standard way to think about this comparative static exercise would be that it improves the efficiency of the economy for a given level of aggregate employment. Changes in aggregate unemployment and aggregate effort influence the employment of labour in NEUs in the obvious way: higher unemployment reduces it, while higher effort increases it.

The prototype model presented in the main part of the chapter abstracts from variable effort and focuses on the remaining two adjustment margins (while making clear how the third could be included). These margins have been highlighted in an early contribution to the literature on efficiency wages in open economies by Matusz (1994). In Matusz's terminology, the change in the rate of unemployment caused by a reallocation of labour between sectors is the *level effect*. In addition, for a given level of employment, the reallocation of labour between high wage and low wage sectors has an impact on output via the *composition effect*. The prototype fair wage model presented in this chapter allows a very simple micro-foundation (different from that in Matusz, 1994) for a labour market with involuntary unemployment and inter-sectoral wage differentials. The framework makes it straightforward to discuss the two effects identified by Matusz (1994). Due to its simplicity it lends itself to a graphical representation that allows the analysis of a rich set of comparative statics, not all of which can be explored here. This representation is furthermore used to compare the model to two important reference frameworks in the literature, namely the Heckscher–Ohlin model with fully flexible wages and the Heckscher–Ohlin model with a binding minimum wage.

5.2 Trade and unemployment in a Heckscher–Ohlin world

5.2.1 The minimum wage model

The traditional way to introduce unemployment into a Heckscher–Ohlin trade model is to specify a binding wage floor for one of the factors, which can be fixed in units of either of the goods, or in terms of a price index (Brecher, 1974). This basic model is used to introduce the notation and the graphical tools employed throughout the chapter.

Consider a Heckscher–Ohlin economy with the two factors capital K and labour L, receiving returns r and w respectively, and two sectors, 1 and 2. Good 1 is relatively capital intensive, and there are no factor intensity reversals, i.e. the capital intensity in production of good 1 exceeds the capital intensity in production of good 2 at all common factor prices (formally: $k_1(w,r) > k_2(w,r)$). Good 2 serves as the numeraire, and p denotes the relative price of good 1. Consumers' preferences are homothetic. The return to capital is fully flexible, ensuring that capital is fully employed throughout. The return to labour is fixed in terms of the numeraire above the market clearing level. The determination of equilibrium is illustrated in Figure 5.1. It is taken, with slight modifications, from Davis (1998), and shows in a transparent way the effect of the minimum wage in the HO framework.

The GM locus in quadrant I gives combinations of p and the aggregate capital intensity k (defined as the capital stock K divided by aggregate employment L) that are compatible with goods market equilibrium. The GM locus is downward sloping because a higher aggregate capital intensity increases the relative output of the capital intensive good, and with homothetic preferences, a lower relative price is needed to clear the goods market. This is true independent of whether the economy is closed or a large open economy. The GM locus would be horizontal at the given world market price in the case of a *small* open economy. The ZP locus in quadrant II gives combinations of p and w that are compatible with zero profits under diversified production. The ZP locus is downward sloping due to the Stolper–Samuelson mechanism: a higher price of the capital intensive good leads to a lower return to labour. The KI locus is simply a graphical representation of the definitory relation $k \equiv K/L$ (for a given level of K).

All three loci are identical to what they would be in a standard Heckscher–Ohlin model with flexible factor prices. It is therefore possible to compare equilibria for both cases by using Figure 5.1. In the standard case with fully flexible wages, the determination of equilibrium in

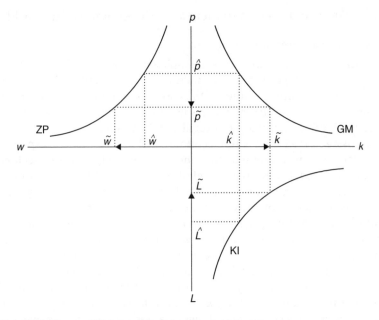

Figure 5.1: The equilibrium with and without minimum wages

Figure 5.1 is counter-clockwise, starting from quadrant IV: The employ-ment of labour $\hat{L}$ is equal to the exogenous endowment $\overline{L}$, which in turn – given the capital stock – determines aggregate capital intensity $\hat{k}$. The implied market clearing goods price is $\hat{p}$, and the resulting wage $\hat{w}$. In the minimum wage case, the determination of equilibrium is clockwise, starting from quadrant II: the wage is fixed at $\tilde{w} > \hat{w}$, which is compatible with zero profits in both sectors only at a lower relative price of the cap-ital intensive good $\tilde{p}$. Given this price, the goods market clears only if the relative supply of the capital intensive good increases (as consumers want to buy more of it), necessitating a higher aggregate capital inten-sity $\tilde{k}$. As capital is fully employed throughout, this can only be achieved if aggregate employment falls to $\tilde{L}$. The resulting unemployment rate is $U = (\overline{L} - \tilde{L})/\overline{L}$. The changes in the variables' equilibrium values relative to the flexible wage case are visualised by arrows in Figure 5.1.

There are two noteworthy features of the HO-Minimum-Wage framework. First, the minimum wage fixes the relative goods price in the economy, assuming – as in Davis (1998) – that the economy produces both goods.[1] In the case of a large open economy, which is (as shown above) covered by Figure 5.1 as well, the minimum wage therefore determines the relative world market price. Second, the equilibrium determines only the *number* of employed workers, with no particular role attached to the *rate* of employment (or unemployment). To be sure, the rate of unemployment can easily be inferred once the labour endowment of the economy is known. The latter, however, is essentially a non-binding constraint, and varying the labour endowment changes the number of unemployed one-for-one.

There are two ways to look at those features. On the one hand, they make the model readily tractable if the focus of the analysis is either a closed economy or a large open economy where the rest of the world (ROW) has fully flexible labour markets. This has been used to great effect by Davis (1998).[2] On the other hand, they are not fully satisfactory because they result from the arguably arbitrary combination of the minimum wage assumption with the Heckscher–Ohlin production structure.[3] And the fact that goods prices under diversified production are fully determined by the minimum wage makes the framework unattractive in two important economic environments: (i) the small open economy and (ii) the large open economy where home *and* the rest of the world have minimum wages. In both cases, the world market price is determined in ROW, by ROW supply and demand in case (i), and by the ROW minimum wage in case (ii). If the relative goods' price implied by the domestic minimum wage is different from the ROW price, a trade equilibrium with diversified production in both countries is not feasible.[4] In Figure 5.1, both cases would be represented by a horizontal GM locus in quadrant I (with its position determined solely by the ROW goods price), allowing a straightforward confirmation of the verbal argument made above.

5.2.2 An informal efficiency wage model

Combining an efficiency wage model of the labour market with the HO production structure eliminates both features of the minimum wage model mentioned above. While a detailed and more formal exploration is deferred to the next section, the main argument can be made informally with the help of Figure 5.2, a variant of which has been introduced in Kreickemeier and Nelson (2006). The key difference to Figure 5.1 lies in the addition of the upward sloping EW (efficiency wage) curve in quadrant III. Versions of this curve exist in most efficiency wage models.[5] In each case the EW curve derives from a set-up in which workers can alter the effort that they supply in the workplace. The better the workers' outside option, the higher is the wage that firms have to pay in order to make workers supply the effort level desired by the firms. *Ceteris paribus,* lower unemployment – and hence, for a given labour endowment, a

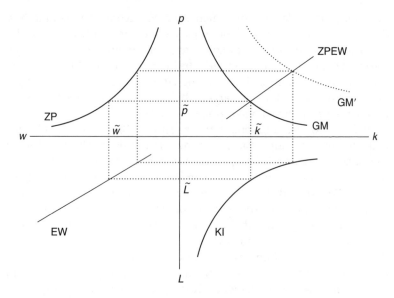

Figure 5.2: The equilibrium with efficiency wages

higher level of employment – improves workers' outside options, and hence firms choose to pay a higher wage. This results in an upward-sloping EW curve in wage-employment space, with the labour *endowment* a shift parameter of this curve.

The EW curve can now be used to derive a second relation between the capital intensity and the relative goods price in quadrant I. The upward sloping ZPEW curve gives combinations of k and p that are compatible with both the zero profit condition (quadrant II) and the efficiency wage curve (quadrant III). The equilibrium relative goods price and equilibrium capital intensity are determined by the intersection between ZPEW and GM (ignore GM' for the moment). Equilibrium values of the model variables are again denoted by a tilde. In contrast to the minimum wage model, the wage (and hence the relative goods price) is now endogenous. A change in the labour endowment would shift the EW curve, and hence can be seen to have an effect on equilibrium values of all variables – another important difference to the minimum wage model.

5.2.3 Comparing autarky and trade
Figures 5.1 and 5.2 can now be used to show how the transition from autarky to trade affects an economy ('Home') under different labour

market regimes. In all cases, the effect depends on whether the rest of the world is a net supplier of the capital intensive good or of the labour intensive good at the Home autarky goods' prices. For concreteness, the latter is assumed, which is compatible with the interpretation that Home is an industrialised country, starting to trade with a less developed rest of the world. In Figures 5.1 and 5.2, opening up to trade under this assumption shifts the GM locus outwards, leaving all other curves unaffected. In Figure 5.2 the new GM locus is denoted by GM'. For simplicity, GM' has been omitted from Figure 5.1.

Both the vertical distance between GM and GM' (measured at $k = \tilde{k}$) and the horizontal distance (measured at $p = \tilde{p}$) have a straightforward economic interpretation. The vertical distance measures the amount by which p, the relative price of the capital intensive good in Home, would have to go up without changing aggregate capital intensity, i.e. for a given level of employment. This price change has two effects: it shifts domestic demand towards the labour intensive good and domestic supply towards the capital intensive good, thereby eliminating the excess supply of the labour intensive good. The horizontal distance between the two curves at $\tilde{p}$ measures the amount by which the capital intensity of production in Home would have to increase in order to accommodate trade with the rest of the world at constant relative goods prices. The increase in the aggregate capital intensity (brought about by an increase in aggregate unemployment) is an alternative way of eliminating the excess supply of the labour intensive good because the decrease in aggregate employment has to be accompanied – via the standard Rybczynski effect – by a shrinking of the labour intensive sector and an expansion of the capital intensive sector.

In the minimum wage model, the relative goods price in Home is fixed at $\tilde{p}$, and opening to trade leads to a decrease in employment via the Rybczynski mechanism just described. In the efficiency wage economy, international trade leads to a decrease in both the wage rate and the level of employment, as can be seen in Figure 5.2, where adjustment to the new equilibrium occurs along the ZPEW locus. One can see that *ceteris paribus* the employment decrease is smaller in the efficiency wage model than in the minimum wage model, where the employment margin bears the full burden of adjustment. On the other hand, the wage decrease in the efficiency wage model is smaller than in an otherwise identical economy with fully flexible wages. This follows from the comparison of the wage decrease when there is constant capital intensity, with the wage decrease when there is adjustment of capital intensity along the ZPEW locus.[6]

The transition from autarky to trade in the case considered constitutes a negative shock to labour. Depending on the standard of reference there are two possible interpretations for the wage and employment effects of this transition:

(i) For a given level of employment, the negative demand shock to labour decreases the relative wage that is compatible with zero profits. Unemployment has to increase in order to make workers accept the lower wage. The relative supply of the labour intensive good decreases, and the negative shock is absorbed by a combination of lower wages and higher unemployment.

(ii) For a given relative wage, the negative demand shock increases unemployment, which gives firms the possibility to lower wages for labour without jeopardising full effort. They will do so, and the negative shock is absorbed by a combination of lower wages and higher unemployment.

Using the framework laid out in this section it is now straightforward to analyse the welfare effects of the transition from autarky to free trade. It is well known and does not need to be discussed here that in the standard trade model there are gains from trade (with constant economy-wide employment ensured by flexible factor prices) that can be decomposed into gains from exchange and gains from specialisation.

In the minimum wage model, if the economy continues to produce both goods and the minimum wage continues to be binding after trade liberalisation, both traditional effects that ensure gains from trade with flexible factor prices are absent because the relative goods price remains unchanged (Brecher, 1974). The welfare effect of the transition from autarky to free trade is therefore driven exclusively by the induced change in economy-wide employment. Hence, in the case considered here, where the rest of the world is a net supplier of the labour intensive good, welfare falls along with the level of employment. In the efficiency wage economy, it is clear from the previous analysis that the relative goods price adjusts qualitatively as in the standard model, and hence the traditional effects that increase welfare, *ceteris paribus*, are effective. The employment effect is added to these standard effects, and hence in case of a decrease in economy-wide employment the welfare effect of globalisation is determined by the relative size of the traditional and labour market effects. Put differently, a *negative* employment effect in the efficiency wage model is a necessary but not sufficient condition for *losses* from trade.[7]

5.3 A prototype Heckscher–Ohlin fair wage model

Having shown the basic mechanism of adjustment to globalisation in the Heckscher–Ohlin model under different labour market regimes, I now introduce a properly specified prototype model that allows the simultaneous consideration of unemployment and inter-sectoral wage differentials.

5.3.1 The model: basics

Consider a Heckscher–Ohlin economy that is identical to the one in the previous section but for the assumption that workers can choose their effort ε at work. I use the idea of Akerlof and Yellen (1990), that workers have an idea of what constitutes a 'fair' wage w^*, and that their effort depends on the wage they are paid relative to the fair wage, which forms their standard of reference.[8] Importantly, w^* is determined in general equilibrium and treated parametrically by all firms. In the present two-sector model, the effort supplied by a worker in sector j is assumed to be an increasing function of the wage in this sector, w_j, relative to w^*:

$$\varepsilon_j = f\left(\frac{w_j}{w^*}\right),\tag{5.1}$$

with $f' > 0$. Following Albert and Meckl (2001), I allow for the productivity of effort to be sector-specific. The efficiency e_j of a labour unit employed in sector j is formally given by

$$e_j = g_j\left(\frac{w_j}{w^*}\right) = G_j\left[f\left(\frac{w_j}{w^*}\right)\right]\tag{5.2}$$

where $g_j' > 0$, $g_j'' < 0$, and $g_j(a) = 0$ for some $a > 0$. As in the standard efficiency wage model by Solow (1979), the firm's hiring decision can be thought of as a two-stage process. In step one, firms in each sector set wages to minimise the cost of labour in efficiency units, w_j/e_j. In step two they hire workers up to the point where the value marginal product of labour is equal to the wage set in step one.

The properties assumed for the efficiency function g_j ensure that there is a unique minimum for w_j/e_j. This is illustrated in Figure 5.3, taking into account that w^* is treated parametrically by the firms. The cost minimising differential w_j/w^* is denoted by q_j, the associated efficiency by $\bar{e}_j$. Note that an inter-sectoral wage differential can only arise if the efficiency functions are different between sectors. While the efficiency functions fix the (potentially sector specific) q_js and $\bar{e}_j$s, wage rates are

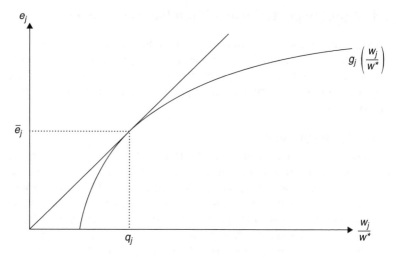

Figure 5.3: Equilibrium in sector j

determined in general equilibrium because the reference wage w^* is. Whenever wages are sector-specific, sector 2 is assumed to be the low wage sector, and without loss of generality we normalise $q_2 = 1$. Hence, the constant wage differential between sectors is $q = q_1 \geq 1$.

5.3.2 Determining the fair wage

While the set-up of the model so far is virtually identical to Albert and Meckl (2001), it is useful for the present purpose to use a specification for the fair wage that is different from theirs. In particular, let the reference wage be given by

$$w^* = A\overline{w}^k \qquad (5.3)$$

where $A > 0$ and $k < 1$ are two parameters and $\overline{w} = (w_1 L_1 + w_2 L_2)/\overline{L}$ is the average wage for all workers in the economy, including those who are unemployed. Note that $k < 1$ is a key behavioural assumption. It says that the reference wage of workers varies less than proportionally with the average wage in the economy, which can be interpreted as workers' expected outside option should they be separated from their current job. This assumption should be thought of as a shortcut that, in this prototype model, captures omitted variables in (5.3) that vary less than proportionally with $\overline{w}$.[9]

The average wage can obviously be re-written as $\overline{w} = (qw^* L_1 + w^* L_2)/\overline{L} = (w^*/\overline{L})L^e$, where $L^e \equiv qL_1 + L_2$. The new variable L^e is the economy-wide employment of labour, measured in *normalised efficiency units* (NEUs). These are labour units for which the value marginal product is equalised between sectors, and equal to w^*. Measuring labour units in this way simplifies the analysis dramatically, as the two adjustment margins present in the labour market are collapsed into one, namely the economy-wide employment of NEUs of labour. Using the definition of L^e, equation (5.3) can be rewritten as

$$L^e = (w^*)^{\frac{1-k}{k}} C \tag{5.4}$$

where $C \equiv A^{-1/k}\overline{L}$ is a positive parameter. Under the assumption $k < 1$ made above, $\partial L^e / \partial w^*$ is strictly positive. Whenever the reference wage in the economy increases, so does the economy-wide employment of labour, measured in NEUs. The reason is simple: firms adjust wages by less than would be compatible with constant employment, and hence employment adjusts in the same direction as the sectoral wage rates (w^* and qw^*, respectively).

Albert and Meckl (2001) consider the case $w^* = \overline{w}$, i.e. they set $A = k = 1$ in equation (5.3). Consequently, L^e is constant, which models the case where the level effect and the composition effect on aggregate output identified by Matusz (1994) exactly offset each other.[10] As stressed by Albert and Meckl, their model as a consequence behaves exactly as a flexible wage Heckscher–Ohlin model, with NEUs of labour replacing physical units of labour.

5.3.3 The closed economy equilibrium

The closed economy equilibrium can now be represented by Figure 5.4, which closely resembles Figure 5.2 above. For concreteness, it is assumed that good 1 (with relative price p) is capital intensive if labour is measured in NEUs: at all common factor prices w^* and r we have $k_1^e > k_2^e$. Under this assumption, the GM locus in quadrant I gives combinations of p and k^e that are compatible with goods market equilibrium. The ZP locus quadrant II gives combinations of p and w^* that are compatible with zero profits under diversified production. Both loci are directly analogous to the respective loci in a standard Heckscher–Ohlin model, where the two factors are capital and NEUs of labour, with the returns r and w^*.

The FW (fair wage) locus in quadrant III is the graphical representation of equation (5.4).[11] In analogy to Section 5.2, the KI locus in quadrant IV is the graphical representation of the definitory relation $k^e \equiv K/L^e$ between the economy-wide capital intensity, the exogenous capital stock, and the economy-wide employment of labour, measured in NEUs. The ZPFW locus in quadrant I is implied by the ZP, FW and KI loci, and

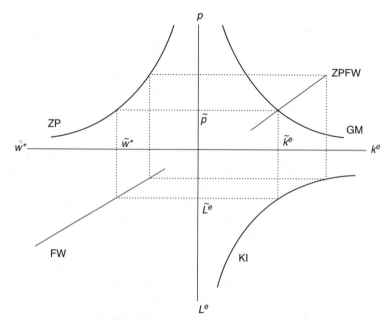

Figure 5.4: The one-country equilibrium

it gives combinations between the relative goods' price and the capital intensity that are compatible with both the fair wage constraint and the zero profit condition. There is a unique equilibrium for the closed economy, and the equilibrium values of p, w^*, L^e, and k^e are denoted by a tilde.

5.3.4   Comparing autarky and trade

The effect of a globalisation shock on the closed economy can now be deduced with the help of Figure 5.4. As in Section 5.2, the effect depends on whether at the Home autarky goods prices the rest of the world is a net supplier of the capital intensive good or of the labour intensive good, where the factor intensity this time is measured using NEUs of labour.[12] For concreteness, and in analogy to the previous discussion, the case where the rest of the world is a net supplier of the labour intensive good is considered. In Figure 5.4, opening up to trade under this assumption shifts the GM locus upwards, leaving all other curves unaffected. Employment of NEUs of labour falls along with the reference wage, and hence the wage in both sectors. The economic intuition for this adjustment is exactly as explained for the efficiency wage model in Section 5.2.3, and there is no need to repeat it here.

5.3.5 What about the unemployment effect?

It has been shown that, in a model with involuntary unemployment and an inter-sectoral wage differential, important comparative static properties can be derived by looking at NEUs rather than physical units of labour. The employment (or rather unemployment) of actual workers in many cases is of independent interest, however. From the definition of L^e it is immediate that aggregate employment $L \equiv L_1 + L_2$ can be written as

$$L = L^e - (q - 1)L_1. \tag{5.5}$$

This shows that, in principle, it is possible for L to decrease (and therefore the unemployment rate U to increase) despite an increase in L^e if the high-wage sector 1 expands. It follows immediately that in the model of Albert and Meckl (2001), where L^e is constant, unemployment increases if and only if globalisation leads to an expansion of the high-wage sector. On the other hand, in a model without an inter-sectoral wage differential (and therefore $q = 1$) we have $L = L^e$, and the composition effect on aggregate output identified by Matusz (1994) disappears.

5.3.6 Variants of the prototype model

The model of Matusz (1994) gives a micro-foundation of the wage differential between sectors that is different from the one in the prototype model presented here. Instead of the fair wage model by Akerlof and Yellen, Matusz uses the Shapiro–Stiglitz (1984) efficiency-wage model in which workers have to be supervised in order to prevent them from shirking. Matusz (1994) assumes that the rate at which shirking is detected is sector-specific, and in equilibrium the sector with the higher detection rate can pay a lower wage because the threat of being fired is more severe for these workers, who as a consequence moderate their wage demands. This difference to the prototype model is not important for the results derived, which are driven by the relative size of the level effect and the composition effect on the value of output.[13]

The first application of the fair wage approach in an open economy model is due to Agell and Lundborg (1995). Their approach features two major differences from the prototype model presented here. First, there is no inter-sectoral wage differential for labour. Second, the effort provided by workers is not constant in equilibrium. The second difference is triggered by the fact that Agell and Lundborg model the unemployment rate U and the relative returns to labour and capital r/w as separate arguments in the effort function.[14] Despite these differences, the Agell–Lundborg model could in principle be analysed using Figure 5.4. L^e is now the employment of labour in efficiency units (the need to normalise these efficiency units no longer arises, as there is no wage differential between sectors), and w^* the wage of an efficiency unit of labour. As in the prototype model, there are two sources for the change in L^e: the change in the employment of physical units of labour, and the change in the effort the workers supply. This latter *aggregate effort effect* replaces the composition effect that was triggered by the inter-sectoral wage differential in both the Matusz model and the prototype model.

All models discussed so far assume that the efficiency wage mechanism operates for only one of the factors, while the market for the other factor is perfectly competitive. This is appropriate if the two factors of production are thought of as being labour and capital, and the efficiency wage mechanism works only for labour. The assumption is less easy to justify if one thinks of the two factors as skilled and unskilled labour, respectively. Kreickemeier and Nelson (2006) follow the original modelling of Akerlof and Yellen (1990) in considering the two factors unskilled labour L and skilled labour K, whose returns are denoted with w and r, respectively. The fair wage mechanism operates for both factors symmetrically, and the respective fair wages are given by:

$$w^* = \theta r + (1 - \theta)\overline{w} \qquad (5.6)$$

$$r^* = \theta w + (1 - \theta)\overline{r} \qquad (5.7)$$

where, in analogy to the notation used earlier, $\overline{w} = (1 - U_L)w$, $\overline{r} = (1 - U_K)r$, and U_i is the rate of unemployment for factor i. Hence, for both factors, the fair wage is a weighted average of the wage the other factor is paid and the own-factor average wage. In contrast to the prototype model, it is assumed that there is a well-defined level of full effort (normalised to 1) which workers provide if they are paid the fair wage. Reducing the wage below the fair wage results in a proportional reduction of effort; paying more than the fair wage leaves effort constant. The effort function for unskilled labour is depicted in Figure 5.5 and there is an identical function for skilled labour.

With the additional assumptions that firms pay the fair wage if this does not reduce their profit and that in a (hypothetical) full employment equilibrium the wage for skilled workers would exceed the wage for unskilled workers, skilled labour is fully employed in equilibrium while there is unemployment of unskilled labour. Both types of labour provide

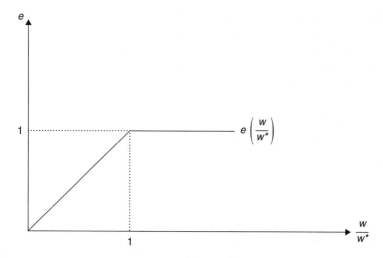

Figure 5.5: The effort function for unskilled labour

full effort, skilled labour receives a wage in excess of its fair wage, and unskilled labour is paid its fair wage.[15] The resulting framework is simpler than the prototype model because there is neither an inter-sectoral wage differential nor variable effort, and hence $L^e = L$. Solving equation (5.6) for L shows the level of employment in the economy as a function of the relative wage $\omega \equiv w/r$:

$$L = \frac{\omega - \theta}{\omega} D \tag{5.8}$$

where $D \equiv (1 - \theta)^{-1} \overline{L}$. It is easily checked that $\partial L/\partial \omega > 0$. Equation (5.8) is the analogue to equation (5.4) from the prototype model. Replacing w^* in Figure 5.4 by ω, the graphical representation of equation (5.8) gives the FW locus of this model.[16] The model then behaves qualitatively like the prototype model. Due to the simplifications stated above, the analogue to Figure 5.4 for the model from Kreickemeier and Nelson (2006) can furthermore be used to determine the employment effect for physical labour (rather than for efficiency units only, normalised or otherwise).

5.4 An asymmetric three-country world

The previous sections have featured analysis of a two-country world, consisting of Home and the rest of the world (ROW), and analysed what effects globalisation (i.e. opening up to trade with ROW) has on

Home. The analysis in Section 5.2.3 shows why and how this depends on the labour market regime in Home. One question that economists have been interested in, and that cannot be answered within this two-country framework, is the following. What is the effect of increased trade with newly industrialising countries on developed countries with different labour market institutions? The answer to this question has to take into account trade between the developed countries (as well as their trade with the newly industrialising countries), and hence the minimum number of countries needed in the model is three. The present section shows how the minimum wage framework and the prototype fair wage framework, respectively, can be modified to analyse this question.

For concreteness, in each case Home is labelled 'OECD', and it is assumed to consist of the two countries 'Europe' and 'America', which differ in their labour market characteristics. Consumer tastes and production technology are assumed identical between the countries, they both produce both goods and trade them freely with each other. Using standard Heckscher–Ohlin logic, this implies that factor prices between Europe and America are equalised. The third country is labelled 'China', and it is assumed to be a net exporter of the labour intensive good.

5.4.1   The minimum wage model

Davis (1998) looks at the case where Europe has a binding minimum wage, while the wage in America is fully flexible.[17] He then considers the effect on European and American labour markets if the OECD opens up to trade with China, assuming that both OECD countries continue to produce both goods. The comparative static effects can be shown with the help of Figure 5.6, which is a modified version of Figure 5.1 adapted to allow the analysis of the three-country case.

Quadrant I of Figure 5.6 is the result of a 'merger' of quadrants I and II from Figure 5.1, which is needed to make room for a new quadrant III in Figure 5.6 (see below). The GMZP locus consequently combines the old GM and ZP loci. It gives combinations of $1/w$ (common to Europe and America) and the aggregate capital intensity k_o of the OECD that are compatible with goods market equilibrium *and* the zero profit conditions in both sectors. It follows immediately from the arguments used in the explanation of Figure 5.1 that the GMZP locus is downward sloping and that p (no longer visible in the figure) decreases as k_o increases. In analogy to the above, the *KI* locus is the graphical representation of the definitory relation $k_o \equiv K_o/L_o$, where K_o and L_o are the aggregate capital stock and the aggregate employment of the OECD, respectively. Fixing the minimum wage in Europe at $\tilde{w}$ implies an aggregate capital intensity

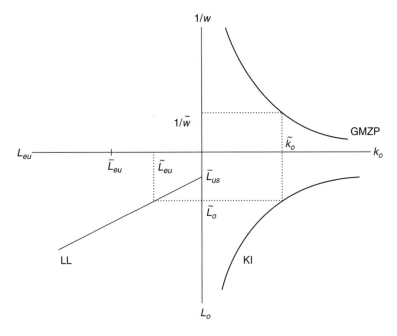

Figure 5.6: The two-country equilibrium with minimum wages

$\tilde{k}_o$, and an aggregate employment level in the OECD of $\tilde{L}_o$. LL in quadrant IV shows how OECD employment is distributed across Europe and America. Because labour markets in America are fully flexible, American employment equals the endowment $\bar{L}_{us}$. European employment $\tilde{L}_{eu}$ is then simply the difference between OECD employment and American employment. Formally, LL is simply given by $L_o = \bar{L}_{us} + L_{eu}$.

Opening up to trade with China shifts the GMZP locus to the right and leaves all other loci in Figure 5.6 unchanged, where the reasoning is exactly as in the case of the two-country model. Given the European minimum wage $\tilde{w}$, the capital intensity in the OECD $\tilde{k}_o$ increases and employment $\tilde{L}_o$ falls. This translates one-for-one in a decrease in European employment $\tilde{L}_{eu}$, while labour in America remains fully employed. This is one facet of the 'insulation result' emphasised by Davis (1998). The minimum wage in Europe insulates America from the consequences of the globalisation shock.[18] Davis thereby highlights the effect that labour market institutions in third countries (Europe) can have on the effects of economic integration between two countries (America and China).

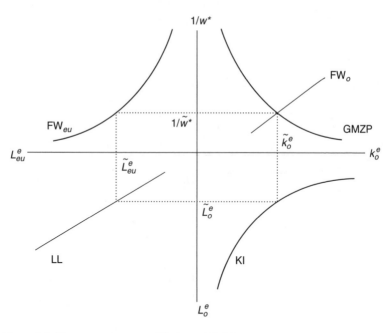

Figure 5.7: The two-country equilibrium with fair wages

5.4.2   The prototype fair wage model

Kreickemeier and Nelson (2006) revisit the set-up used by Davis, but assume a less stark asymmetry between Europe and America. In their model, there is unemployment in both countries due to the fair wage mechanism described earlier, but the fair wage constraints – and there-fore the unemployment rates – differ between countries. In this section, I show how the prototype fair wage model from Section 5.3 can be used in a set-up of asymmetric fair wage constraints to derive the country-specific effects of globalisation.

Figure 5.7 is a modified version of Figure 5.4, and the analogue in the fair wage model to Figure 5.6 from the minimum wage model. The GMZP and KI loci are identical to those in Figure 5.6, while FW_{eu} is the European fair wage constraint, relating European employment to the European ref-erence wage, in analogy to the FW locus in Figure 5.4. In order to close the model one needs – as in the minimum wage model – a function relating European employment and OECD employment, which in this framework is measured in normalised efficiency units. As shown, this is trivial in the asymmetric minimum wage model because employment in

America does not change, and a change in European employment goes hand in hand with a change in OECD employment of the same magnitude. Things are more complicated here because employment is endogenous in both countries: $L_o^e = L_{eu}^e + L_{us}^e$ as before, but L_{us}^e is now variable.

The employment levels in both countries are linked, however, by the condition that factor prices for capital and NEUs of labour are equalised between them. We therefore have fair wage constraints like equation (5.4) for both countries, where k and C are country-specific, but w^* is not.[19] Using this information, one can express L_{us}^e as a function of the model parameters as well as the European employment level. OECD employment is then given by

$$L_o^e = L_{eu}^e + (L_{eu}^e)^\kappa C_{eu}^{-\kappa} C_{us} \qquad (5.9)$$

where $\kappa \equiv [k_{eu}(1 - k_{us})]/[k_{us}(1 - k_{eu})] > 0$ and $C_i \equiv A^{-1/k_i}\overline{L}_i$. One can immediately see that L_o^e increases with L_{eu}^e. The graphical representation of equation (5.9) in Figure 5.7 is the LL locus. Equation (5.9) shows that the position of LL is determined by the fair wage parameters and labour endowments of both countries. Together, FW_{eu}, LL and KI imply the upward sloping FW_o locus in quadrant I, and its intersection with GMZP determines wages and employment levels in the OECD countries.

Opening up to trade with China shifts GMZP to the right, and the OECD adjusts to a new equilibrium along FW_o. It is easily checked that this reduces the wage rate in the OECD, and it furthermore reduces employment measured in NEUs of labour in Europe and America. The insulation result of Davis (1998) therefore turns out to be specific to the minimum wage model he considers. At a more general level, however, the basic insight stressed by Davis that labour market institutions in one country do have effects on the results of globalisation in another country if goods markets between those two countries are integrated, survives the transition to an alternative model of the labour market. For the simple fair wage model without inter-sectoral wage differentials, this is shown in Kreickemeier and Nelson (2006).

5.5 Unemployment and intra-industry trade

While the majority of contributions to the trade and unemployment literature uses the Heckscher–Ohlin framework, there are some exceptions. In this section I briefly describe two models that introduce labour market imperfections into standard models of intra-industry trade and analyse the effect of trade on welfare and unemployment.

Matusz (1996) combines the standard model of intra-industry trade in intermediate products by Ethier (1982) with an efficiency wage model of the labour market. International trade in this framework increases the number of intermediate products that are available in each market. Producers in both countries specialise in non-overlapping sets of intermediates, and it is profitable for all firms to export part of their output. Final good producers benefit from the increase in the number of intermediates due to the 'love of variety' effect standard in this literature. Aggregate output of the final good increases in both countries. For a given level of employment, this would lead to an increase in the wage rate, because all income in the economy is wage income. With a higher wage, the outside option of being unemployed (and thereby getting nothing) becomes relatively less attractive. This situation is not an equilibrium because firms (who have wage setting power) now pay more than is necessary to elicit the profit maximising effort. Rather than increase wages by an amount compatible with constant employment, firms will therefore increase wages by less, triggering additional entry into the intermediates sector and increasing aggregate employment. This improves the outside option of the workers, and in the new equilibrium firms again just pay the wage that is necessary to make workers supply the profit maximising effort. The trading equilibrium therefore features both a higher wage rate and lower unemployment than the autarky equilibrium.

Egger and Kreickemeier (2006) develop an alternative model of intra-industry trade in intermediate products in the presence of efficiency wages that builds on the heterogeneous firm model by Melitz (2003). As in the model by Matusz (1996), international trade raises aggregate output, but at least in part for a reason that is absent in the Matusz model. As in all models of the Melitz-type, intermediate good producers are assumed to have different productivities and there are fixed costs to exporting that only the most productive firms find worthwhile bearing. High productivity firms therefore expand and produce a larger share of aggregate output. In addition, the least productive firms are forced to exit the market due to increased import competition. As a consequence, the average labour productivity of active firms goes up, and so does aggregate output. There are now two opposing effects on aggregate employment: Higher aggregate output increases employment, *ceteris paribus*, while higher average labour productivity reduces employment. In contrast to the model by Matusz (1996), where the productivity of all firms is identical and therefore the second effect is absent, in the model by Egger and Kreickemeier (2006) unemployment may rise or fall as a consequence of globalisation. In the benchmark specification of their model, welfare, average firm profits, average wages and unemployment all increase, thereby pointing to distributional conflicts of globalisation that have not been accounted for in the previous literature.

5.6 Conclusions

This chapter has focused on the presentation of an easily tractable framework for the analysis of involuntary unemployment in international trade models. The prototype Heckscher–Ohlin fair wage model allows a rich set of comparative statics in either the two-country or three-country setting, using the respective four-quadrant diagrams presented here.[20] The same graphical tool also allows the straightforward comparison between models of the fair wage (or more generally efficiency wage) type and the traditional minimum wage model of Brecher (1974) that is still popular among trade theorists modelling unemployment in open economies, as well as with the standard Heckscher–Ohlin model with flexible wages.

The main aim of this chapter was to show that the comparative static properties of a broad range of Heckscher–Ohlin type trade models with efficiency wage unemployment can be inferred if one analyses changes in the employment level of a single key variable, normalized efficiency units (NEUs) of labour. I have derived a simple condition under which a negative shock to (unskilled) labour, defined as a shock that would decrease the wage in a standard Heckscher–Ohlin model, decreases employment of NEUs of labour. This happens if and only if, as a consequence of a negative shock, the reference wage of workers decreases by less than the average wage in the economy (taking into account those who are unemployed). This condition is relevant because the average wage itself, as an indicator of workers' outside options, can be expected to play a role in the determination of the reference wage. In fact, in Albert and Meckl (2001) the average wage is the *only* determinant of the reference wage. A less than proportionate adjustment in the reference wage (the case which I focus on in this chapter) occurs for example if the remuneration of the second factor (capital or skilled labour) plays a role in the determination of the reference wage, implying that there is an inter-group fairness motive present in workers' fair wage preferences (Akerlof and Yellen, 1990).

International trade in the Heckscher–Ohlin framework with efficiency wages influences aggregate unemployment because it influences the sectoral structure of production. Wage setting firms that consider the incentive effect of wages on worker effort do not find it profit maximising to adjust wages to the full extent necessary to keep aggregate employment constant, and part of the adjustment occurs on the employment margin. Losses from trade are possible if employment falls by too much. In models of intra-industry trade there are typically gains from trade, and the value of output increases. With identical firms this translates into an increase in employment, while in the presence of heterogeneous firms employment may fall as a consequence of trade because aggregate productivity in the industry increases, and hence – at least *ceteris paribus* – the labour requirement falls.

Notes

1. If the economy specialises in the production of one good, the ZP locus as drawn in Figure 5.1 is no longer relevant. Oslington (2002) analyses the case where an open economy that imposes a minimum wage is forced to shut down its labour intensive sector.
2. See the discussion in Section 5.4 below.
3. Adding a third factor to the model, for example, would eliminate the first of the two features. See Oslington (2005) for a discussion.
4. There is a noticeable resemblance of the HO minimum wage model with diversified production to the Ricardian model (one fully employed flex-price factor and two sectors, implying a linear transformation curve).
5. This is true for one-sector efficiency wage models as well as multi-sector efficiency wage models without inter-sectoral wage differentials. The modifications needed to apply the concept in a model with inter-sectoral wage differentials are introduced in the next section.
6. Krugman (1995) compares the effect of globalisation on a flexible wage country ('America') and a country with a binding minimum wage ('Europe'), using the Heckscher–Ohlin framework presented here.
7. For a graphical analysis in the context of specific efficiency wage frameworks, see Agell and Lundborg (1995) and Kreickemeier and Nelson (2006).
8. There is considerable microeconomic evidence across virtually all sectors, as well as experimental evidence, for the fair wage model. Recent reviews of the evidence can be found in Howitt (2002) and Bewley (2005).
9. Most importantly, in the present Heckscher–Ohlin framework, one could think of the return to capital as an omitted variable. Akerlof and Yellen (1990) argue that in determining their reference (fair) wage, workers take into account the wage of other factors of production, with their own wage demands increasing *ceteris paribus* if the remuneration of the other factor increases. In the Heckscher–Ohlin framework w and r move in opposite directions, and the movement of r can therefore be expected to have a dampening effect on w. We will return to this below.
10. Albert and Meckl (2001) use the label 'labour absorption' for what I call 'normalised efficiency units of labour'.
11. The FW locus is linear, as drawn in Figure 5.4, if $k = 0.5$.
12. In principle, with a wage differential between sectors, it is possible for the factor intensity ranking in terms of physical labour units and NEUs of labour to

diverge. Specifically, if the capital intensive sector, measured in terms of physical labour, is also the high wage sector, it may be labour intensive in terms of NEUs if the wage differential is sufficiently large. See Jones (1971) for a discussion of this issue in the case of a full employment model with an exogenous inter-sectoral wage differential. In that framework, Jones distinguishes capital intensity in the physical sense and in the value sense.

13. In contrast to the prototype model of Section 5.2, the inter-sectoral wage differential is not constant in the Matusz model. Eliminating this additional adjustment margin is what allows the simple graphical representation in Figure 5.4.

14. In the prototype model, the relative wage is omitted as an explicit argument, but taken into account by the assumption that the reference wage adjusts by less than the expected average wage $(1 - U)\overline{w}$. Given the efficiency function shown in Figure 5.3, the effort that minimises w_j/e_j is then constant in each sector. In Agell and Lundborg (1995), the efficiency function of Figure 5.3 is replaced by a three-dimensional effort surface in $w/r - U - e$ space, and the effort no longer needs to be constant.

15. Hence, while in principle the fair wage mechanism is operating for both types of labour, it is effective only for unskilled workers. Formally, equation (5.7) is a non-binding constraint while equation (5.6) is binding. See the discussion in Akerlof and Yellen (1990) and Kreickemeier and Nelson (2006).

16. Invoking standard Heckscher–Ohlin reasoning, it is easily checked that the zero profit locus in quadrant II is downward sloping in $\omega - p$ space, just as it is in $w^* - p$ space.

17. Davis considers the two factors to be skilled and unskilled labour. In analogy with the previous sections, we stick with capital and labour.

18. Meckl (2006) shows that the insulation result breaks down if workers differ in their ability, and the minimum wage fixes the hourly wage, rather than the wage for an effective unit of labour.

19. Wages for physical labour units (i.e. workers) can vary across countries if q is country-specific.

20. This includes the analysis of global technological change (which affects the ZP locus) as well as the analysis of changes in country-specific fair wage constraints (which affects the FW locus and, in the three-country model, the LL locus).

References

Agell, J. and Lundborg, P. (1995). 'Fair Wages in the Open Economy', *Economica*, Vol. 62, pp. 335–51.

Akerlof, G. and Yellen, J. (1990). 'The Fair Wage-Effort Hypothesis and Unemployment', *Quarterly Journal of Economics*, Vol. 105, pp. 255–83.

Albert, M. and Meckl, J. (2001). 'Efficiency-Wage Unemployment and Intersectoral Wage Differentials in a Heckscher–Ohlin Model', *German Economic Review*, Vol. 2, pp. 287–301.

Bewley, T. (2005). 'Fairness, Reciprocity, and Wage Rigidity', in H. Gintis, S. Bowles, R. Boyd and E. Fehr (eds), *Moral Sentiments and Material Interests: the Foundations of Cooperation in Economic Life*. Cambridge, MA: MIT Press, pp. 303–38.

Brecher, R. (1974). 'Minimum Wage Rates and the Pure Theory of International Trade', *Quarterly Journal of Economics*, Vol. 88, pp. 98–116.

Davis, D. (1998). 'Does European Unemployment Prop Up American Wages?' *American Economic Review*, Vol. 88, pp. 478–94.

Egger, H. and Kreickemeier, U. (2006). 'Firm Heterogeneity and the Labour Market Effects of Trade Liberalisation', GEP Research Paper 2006/26.

Ethier, W. (1982). 'National and International Returns to Scale in the Modern Theory of International Trade', *American Economic Review*, Vol. 72, pp. 389–405.

Howitt, P. (2002). 'Looking Inside the Labor Market: a Review Article', *Journal of Economic Literature*, Vol. 40, pp. 125–38.

Jones, R. W. (1971). 'Distortions in Factor Markets and the General Equilibrium Model of Production', *Journal of Political Economy*, Vol. 74, pp. 437–59.

Kreickemeier, U. and Nelson, D. (2006). 'Fair Wages, Unemployment and Technological Change in a Global Economy', *Journal of International Economics*, Vol. 70, pp. 451–69.

Krugman, P. R. (1995). 'Growing World Trade: Causes and Consequences', *Brookings Papers on Economic Activity*, pp. 327–62.

Matusz, S. J. (1994). 'International Trade Policy in a Model of Unemployment and Wage Differentials', *Canadian Journal of Economics*, Vol. 27, pp. 939–49.

Matusz, S. J. (1996). 'International Trade, the Division of Labor, and Unemployment', *International Economic Review*, Vol. 37, pp. 71–84.

Meckl, J. (2006). 'Are US Wages Really Determined by European Labor-Market Institutions?' *American Economic Review*, Vol. 96, 5, pp. 1924–30.

Melitz, M. J. (2003). 'The Impact of Trade on Intra-Industry Reallocations and Aggregate Industry Productivity', *Econometrica*, Vol. 71, pp. 1695–1725.

Oslington, P. (2002). 'Factor Market Linkages in a Global Economy', *Economics Letters*, Vol. 76, pp. 85–93.

Oslington, P. (2005). 'Unemployment and Trade Liberalisation', *World Economy*, Vol. 28, pp. 1139–55.

Shapiro, C., and Stiglitz, J. (1984). 'Equilibrium Unemployment as a Worker Discipline Device', *American Economic Review*, Vol. 74, pp. 433–44.

Solow, R. (1979). 'Another Possible Source of Wage Stickiness', *Journal of Macroeconomics*, Vol. 1, pp. 79–82.

6
Human Capital and Adjustment to Trade

Rod Falvey, David Greenaway and Joana Silva

6.1 Introduction

The labour market consequences of globalisation are controversial. Fears that the process of increased integration into world markets implies increasing job losses and downward pressure on wages are widespread, often resulting in demands for import protection. Growing concerns about the importance of such adjustment costs are evident in the policy community. This debate also has a direct consequence for policy: there have been recent reforms of the USA's compensation scheme for trade-displaced workers and a new EU Globalisation Adjustment Fund has been created.

Academic economists typically respond to public and policy-maker concerns by explaining that, while there are adjustment costs in the short run, in the long run there are aggregate gains from freer trade. Until recent years, the long-run consequences of increased globalisation have been the central focus in the theoretical literature, while the transitional dynamics have received less focused treatment. But to realise these potential long-run gains, trade-displaced workers must become re-employed and the historical record seems to suggest that this can take some time and may entail earnings losses, especially for workers with characteristics associated with greater adjustment difficulties. A widely held perception is that both adjustment costs and benefits depend on a worker's age, experience, skills and ability in some way.

Adjustment to trade liberalisation involves more than the involuntary relocation of workers among jobs of the same or similar skill levels. The product price changes that follow from trade liberalisation induce changes in skill premia. If trade liberalisation in developed countries leads to an increase in the relative return to skilled labour, skill upgrading by the existing workforce will be an important part of the adjustment process, and whether a worker chooses to upgrade or not will depend on that worker's age and ability. Like all human capital accumulation, skill upgrading can be time consuming, thus extending the adjustment process beyond the short term.

In this chapter we discuss the main theoretical and empirical developments that provide insights into the link between trade liberalisation and human capital formation. In each of the trade models reviewed in this chapter, the labour force is divided into skill categories and individuals must decide on which category to join on entry to the workforce. Some choices involve investment in human capital, and they may or may not be reversible. The models reviewed in Section 6.2 involve a 'training' element. In Section 6.2.1 this is a process of general skill acquisition through formal education and the focus tends to be on the steady state. In Section 6.2.2 industry-specific training is involved, and the focus is on the costs of adjustment. The work reviewed in Section 6.2 either considers the steady state, or infinitely lived workers. In contrast, Section 6.3 explicitly considers adjustment by the existing workforce, where a worker's age becomes important in determining their choices. Section 6.4 then looks at some recent developments and Section 6.5 concludes.

6.2   The role of training in labour market adjustment

The role that human capital formation may play in the economy's response to a trade shock is a relatively unexplored topic in the trade literature. Changes in trade policy, through its effects on relative factor returns, also change the incentives for workers to acquire skills. This observation applies not only to new entrants to the labour force, but also to those currently employed. Two different approaches have been considered for the role of human capital, and therefore formal education and training in trade adjustment, depending on whether the skills acquired apply economy-wide or are industry-specific.

6.2.1   Trade models with investment in formal education

The analysis of the effects of trade (or trade liberalisation) on the acquisition of general skills requires a model in which skilled labour can be employed in more than one sector. The familiar two factor, two sector Heckscher–Ohlin–Samuelson (HOS) model is an obvious candidate, once the factors are interpreted as skilled and unskilled labour. Besides its familiarity, this model has the advantage that factor returns are determined by product prices and are independent of factor endowments, provided production is non-specialised. From a modelling perspective this considerably simplifies the analysis of investment in human capital, since an individual contemplating the choice between remaining unskilled or becoming skilled can be assumed to know the wage rates applicable in each case and that these will not be altered by the outcome of her choice and those of others in a like position. Although this is unrealistic, the broad outcomes would remain unaffected by more realistic but complicated alternatives. Factor supplies are exogenous in the standard formulation of the HOS model. The innovation in Findlay and Kierzkowski (1983) is to allow workers entering the labour force a choice of whether to remain unskilled or to become skilled, thereby endogenising factor supplies. Skilled workers are an output of the educational sector, whose other input is educational-specific capital which is assumed to be in fixed exogenous supply. This sector transforms, after a fixed amount of time, unskilled workers into skilled workers, each embodied with a number of efficiency units of skill which is positively related to the educational-capital to student ratio. Each individual has a potential working life of T periods, E periods of which are lost if the worker decides to become skilled. The working population is stationary, with the number of workers who retire being replaced by an equal number of new entrants. The income of a skilled worker (for the remaining $T-E$ periods of her working life) is the skilled wage per efficiency unit multiplied by the number of efficiency units of skill that they acquired in school. An unskilled worker earns the unskilled wage for the full T periods of her working life.

The benefit from education is the present value of the higher earnings which skilled workers receive. The cost of education has two components: the direct educational cost (fees to the education specific input[1]); and the opportunity cost of the forgone income as an unskilled worker whilst a student. If the net benefits from education are positive, individuals decide to invest. With a fixed amount of educational capital, the higher the number of students in the educational system, the lower the number of efficiency units acquired by each student and therefore the lower the net benefit of education. The number of skilled workers then depends on the size of the working population, relative wages (and therefore, as the production side is purely HOS, on the relative prices of the final goods), the stock of educational capital and the interest rate. Since workers are homogeneous to begin with, the lifetime incomes of skilled and unskilled workers are identical in the steady state equilibrium.[2]

If two countries have identical technologies and preferences (specifically rates of time preference) then, starting from a steady state autarky equilibrium, trade will be motivated by differences in the relative supplies of skilled and unskilled labour which will in turn reflect differences in the endowment ratios of educational capital to population. Trade will induce an increase in the relative price of the skill-intensive good in the educational-capital abundant country. Consequently, by the Stolper–Samuelson Theorem the relative wage of skilled labour increases. This change will increase the number of students, reduce the supply of unskilled labour and, eventually, increase the supply of skilled labour. Applying the Rybczynski Theorem, we see that these factor supply changes will shift specialisation towards the skill-intensive good beyond that implied by the change in product prices at fixed factor supplies. The converse happens in the other (unskilled labour abundant) country. Findlay and Kierzkowski (1983) put it as follows: 'The incentive to acquire skills is reduced if the goods requiring skills more intensively can be imported more cheaply from abroad, while for the exporter there is the additional stimulus to acquire skills from the additional world demand' (p. 970). Since trade leads to an income reduction for low-skilled workers in the educational capital abundant country, and all workers are identical ex-ante, the income of high-skilled workers must also fall. The winners of the trade expansion in the educational-capital abundant country will be the owners of the specific educational input. Again the opposite occurs in the other country.

The focus of Findlay and Kierzkowski (1983) is on steady state outcomes and the income distribution in their model consists of just two points, since skilled and unskilled workers are two homogeneous groups. The task of broadening the model to generate a wider income distribution was taken up by Borsook (1986), whose analysis can be considered as an extension of Findlay and Kierzkowski (1983). The new feature is that differences in abilities among individuals determine the skill levels acquired in school. Borsook assumes an exogenous distribution of individual ability. While the length of the time spent in school is fixed, more able students receive a more intensive education, because the optimal capital/student ratio is increasing in ability. Earnings differentials then reflect the interaction of ability and schooling and not just schooling alone. Again, the relative stock of educational capital is an important determinant of the pattern of trade.[3] In equilibrium, all workers above an endogenously determined ability threshold will become skilled. In contrast to Findlay and Kierzkowski (1983), the lifetime incomes of skilled and unskilled workers are not equal, as the lifetime earnings of skilled workers are increasing in their ability.

Trade will lead to skill upgrading and will raise the return to educational capital in the skilled labour abundant country, which again is the country with the higher ratio of educational capital to population. In that country, trade adjustment proceeds as follows: trade leads to an increase in the relative price of the skill-intensive good, increasing the skill premium and therefore the demand for education. The new long-run equilibrium is characterised by a lower threshold level of ability and a higher return on educational capital. Trade opening has two major effects: first, the number of unskilled (skilled) workers decreases (increases); second, the return to educational capital increases. The opposite occurs in the other country. Again, by affecting relative wages, trade will have long-run effects on the skill composition of the workforce. While the net effect on the earnings of skilled labour in each country is ambiguous, the effect on the earnings of unskilled labour is not: they fall in the educational-capital abundant country and increase in the other country. In this context, trade can widen the earnings differential between unskilled and skilled workers.

The Borsook model of human capital accumulation has several notable features. The distribution of income primarily reflects the distribution of ability in the workforce. In turn, this distribution may be the outcome of the interaction of the inherent abilities of individuals and the compulsory stages of education (which are not modelled). These differences in ability are only relevant to some tasks. The marginal productivity of an unskilled worker is independent of her ability, reflecting the relatively standardised and routine tasks undertaken by these workers. In contrast, the marginal productivity of a skilled worker depends on the efficiency units of skill embodied in that worker, which in turn is primarily a function of the worker's ability. Finally, a costly education process must be undergone before the production potential in that ability is realised. In Findlay and Kierzkowski (1983) and Borsook, this education process involves both time and educational capital inputs. In a recent contribution, Weigert (2007) provides an interesting reinterpretation and extension of these education structures as public and private university systems. His public system provides tuition-free education, but with a uniform student/teacher ratio for all students. The private system, on the other hand, involves tuition fees but allows a continuum of student/teacher ratios to the student's taste. He also considers cases where both systems coexist, and examines comparative advantage based on differences in educational institutions.

For many purposes an educational process that takes time is sufficient. Thus, Deardorff (2000) assumes that schooling is necessary to become skilled, but that the only resource needed for schooling is time. His interest arises from the trade and wages debate, which sought to determine whether the relative decline in unskilled wages in advanced countries was caused by increased trade with developing countries, or by technological change. Specifically, he asks whether the appropriate choice of redistribution policy depends on the source of the rise in income inequality. He shows that it does not. He also notes that the increase in the skill premium will alter relative factor supplies as described above, and that this supply shift will further increase income inequality. The policies available to reduce income inequality – taxes and subsidies on factors, production and trade – all introduce familiar by-product distortions. Deardorff shows that we can add the skill choice of individuals to the list of distortions.

Other work has exploited the simplicity of a model where workers differ in their abilities and skill upgrading requires time only. Dinopoulos and Segerstrom (1999) insert such a structure into a two-sector model, where the two sectors involve research and development (R&D) or the manufacturing of final products. They focus on R&D based trade driven by differences in knowledge between countries. A distinctive feature is that firms in the manufacturing sector are assumed to be heterogeneous, differing in their rates of product quality enhancing innovation. Trade liberalisation increases firms' incentive to innovate, which implies that more firms will decide to invest in R&D, increasing the rate of technological change. Assuming that R&D is the skill-intensive activity, the relative wage of skilled labour increases and, therefore, a higher fraction of the labour force chooses to become skilled. A similar mechanism is applied by Neary (2002) in an oligopoly context. He argues that a reduction in trade barriers induces home firms to increase investment in response to the increased threat from foreign competition, thereby blocking entry by reducing the equilibrium output of every other firm. Assuming that investment uses only skilled labour and production uses only unskilled labour, this increases the relative demand for skilled labour which feeds back into the skill premium, encouraging greater skill acquisition.

Finally, Blanchard and Willman (2006) develop a two period overlapping generations model, where individuals differ in ability, and skill acquisition and trade policy are both endogenous. In each period the current population (both young and old) vote on trade policy, which determines the skill premia for that period. Young agents therefore take into account both the current and expected future trade policies in deciding whether to acquire skills. The outcome is an interesting feedback mechanism, where trade policy determines the skill composition of the population, which determines the identity of the median voter, which in turn determines trade policy. They show that both a protectionist and a liberal trade policy steady state may exist in this framework, and consider policies to induce transition from the former to the latter.

6.2.2 Trade models with investment in industry-specific human capital

The models discussed so far have involved worker investment in skills which can be used in more than one sector of the economy. Trade liberalisation changed relative product prices, which changed relative factor prices and caused skill upgrading and a reallocation of workers between sectors. The skills of a worker moving out of the import competing sector were equally applicable in the expanding export sector, and therefore retraining of skilled workers was unnecessary. While this seems a sensible way to model the acquisition of skills through a formal education process that is not tied to any particular producing sector, in practice some of the skills that workers acquire may be industry-, firm- or even job-specific and cannot be fully transferred to alternative jobs.

Modelling the consequences of industry-specific human capital for the adjustment process is the focus in Davidson and Matusz (2000, 2001, 2002). They consider industry-specific training costs (which involve both time and resources) in a model with one factor (labour) and labour market search frictions. Workers differ in ability and jobs differ in terms of training requirements. Jobs in the low-tech industry require little search and little training, but these jobs have high turnover rates and are poorly paid. In contrast, jobs in the high-tech sector require longer search and more training (involving the acquisition of job-specific and general skills) but last longer and pay well. The key parameters of the model are therefore the worker turnover rates (namely, the rate at which workers exit the training process, the rate at which workers lose their jobs and the rate at which unemployed workers searching for a job find one), the resource cost of training and the probability of having to retrain after losing a job. On entering the workforce, each worker decides to train in a particular sector based on discounted lifetime income which depends on her ability level. After training is completed, the worker becomes a searcher until she finds a job. Workers cycle between periods of employment, searching and training whose lengths depend on the turnover rates in the relevant sector.

Higher ability workers are more productive than their lower ability counterparts in both sectors, but have a comparative advantage in the high-tech sector. Thus, in the steady state equilibrium, higher ability workers sort into the high-tech sector and lower ability workers sort into the low-tech sector. Then, in the high-tech exporting country, trade liberalisation will shift specialisation further towards the high-tech good, with more workers in each of the three categories (training, searching and employed) in the high-tech sector and fewer in the low-tech sector. However, the transition between long-run equilibria will be progressive: the number of workers training in the low-tech sector shrinks immediately, while the number of workers in employment in this sector shrinks gradually as they lose their jobs through an exogenous process of job destruction. New entrants to the high-tech sector begin as trainees and gradually become searchers as they complete training. In the short run, trade liberalisation will lead to a higher level of unemployment and a lower national income net of training costs evaluated at world prices. These two effects are adjustment costs. Davidson and Matusz show that even with modest assumptions on the key parameters, adjustment costs are a significant fraction of the gross benefits of trade reform.

6.3   The role of workers' age in the trade adjustment literature

While the distributional effects of trade liberalisation have been at the core of trade analysis, the role of workers' age in determining these effects for the existing workforce has been largely neglected to date. This might seem puzzling, since the adjustment difficulties facing older workers are prominent in the popular perception of adjustment costs.

There is also evidence that worker age is an important aspect of the adjustment process. Kletzer's (2001, 2004) findings on the post-displacement employment prospects and earnings losses of trade displaced workers indicate that the probability of re-employment is higher for younger than older workers and age is an important determinant of earnings losses due to displacement.[4] However, explicitly accommodating workers of different ages requires a dynamic model, with a corresponding increase in modelling complexity.

Until recently, Davidson and Matusz (2004) has been the only theoretical work explicitly considering the age dimension to worker adjustment. The model that they employ is an interesting extension of those discussed above. Workers differ in ability but, in this case, ability is only relevant to an individual's marginal product (and hence wage) in one of the two sectors (specifically the high-tech export sector), rather than one of two occupations. All workers have the same marginal product in the low-tech sector. This fits in with the models discussed above, if we consider the low-tech sector as using only unskilled labour, and the high-tech sector as using only skilled labour. Davidson and Matusz then add a simple, overlapping generations structure, with each individual in the workforce for two periods, and the possibility that those searching for employment in the high-tech sector will be unsuccessful. Their specific interest is in exploring the efficiency consequences of using temporary protection to smooth out the adjustment process following an unexpected, permanent improvement in the terms of trade.

All new entrants to the workforce must decide in which sector to seek employment. The high-tech sector offers higher wages (proportional to ability), but at the risk of being unemployed. This risk is increasing in the number of workers searching for employment – a congestion externality. A worker can always obtain a job in the low-tech sector, and a job obtained in either sector as an entrant can be retained as a mature worker in the second period. In the steady state equilibrium, those entrants with ability above an endogenous threshold seek employment in the high-tech sector. If an entrant finds a job in the high-tech sector, they stay in that sector in the second period. However, if they are unsuccessful and are unemployed or working in the low-tech sector, they can try the high-tech sector again in the second period. But only those that have a level of ability higher than the relative wage of the low-tech sector weighted by (the inverse of) the probability of finding a job in the high-tech sector will choose to do so. Their decision therefore depends on both relative wages and the size of the pool of searchers.

In this context, an unexpected permanent improvement in the country's terms of trade increases the incentive to search for a job in the high-tech sector, by reducing the relative wage in the low-tech sector. This increases the fraction of the population searching for a job in the high-tech sector, which decreases the probability of finding a job. Young workers make their decisions after the terms of trade improvement occurs, taking account of the new relative wages and lower probability of finding a job in the high-tech sector. Old workers, however, made their decisions based on the old relative wages and probability of finding a job. If the change in the terms of trade is sufficiently large and if the probability of finding a job in the high-tech sector does not become too low, there will be a 'surge of old workers entering the export sector labour market for the first time that can cause the congestion that the government may want to ease ... The existence of the congestion externality leaves open the possibility that government intervention could successfully increase economic welfare' (Davidson and Matusz, 2004: 756–9).

Temporary protection of the import competing activity reduces the number of searchers in the export sector and reduces congestion thereby ensuring a smoother transition to the steady state.[5]

The theoretical insights from human capital theory on earnings functions and the empirical insights from labour economics on wage determinants, both show that age is crucial in determining, for example, workers' skill upgrading decisions. However, by treating workers within each skill group as homogeneous, most trade models implicitly assume all skilled and unskilled workers are affected equally and, therefore, have similar incentives to upgrade. This assumption prevents trade economists from analysing the potential role of trade in explaining important labour market trends regarding within-group dimensions of wage inequality and the different evolution of relative factor supplies for younger and older workers. The paucity of trade models incorporating worker heterogeneity along this dimension and including the possibility of retraining by the existing workforce seems to be an important gap in the literature. Such models could provide a better understanding of workers' reactions to trade liberalisation and the channels influencing skill upgrading in this context. These could inform policies better targeted to expedite this process.

6.4   Recent developments

In this section we review two recent papers. The first is work of our own that extends the models of Section 6.2 to examine adjustment by the existing workforce. The second is a paper by Long, Riezman and Soubeyran (2007), which focuses on the effects of trade on the incentives for firm-specific skill acquisition.

6.4.1   Adjustment by the existing workforce

In Falvey, Greenaway and Silva (2007) we modify and extend the earlier work by Findlay and Kierzkowski (1983) and Borsook, in order to highlight the way in which workers of different age and ability are affected by anticipated or unanticipated trade expansion.[6] We consider a small economy which consists of a manufacturing and an educational sector. The manufacturing sector is HOS in structure and produces two traded goods using the services of skilled and unskilled labour. Unskilled workers enter the labour force without training. Education transforms unskilled individuals into skilled workers but takes time and resources. Workers who choose to become skilled spend a fraction of their working life in an educational system which also uses the services of skilled labour,[7] with a fixed staff–student ratio. Education thus involves a direct cost (compensating the 'teachers') and an opportunity cost in terms of forgone earnings as an unskilled worker. Since this educational process has the same length and skilled labour input for all students, regardless of ability, this model assumes that their productivity as skilled workers depends only on their ability. The income of unskilled workers is independent of ability. In the steady state equilibrium all workers above an ability threshold become skilled.

The major difference between our work and the previous literature in this area is that we focus on the medium-term adjustment by the existing workforce. To do this we allow individuals to change labour status at any time in their working lives. The decision to enter the labour market as unskilled can be reversed later through schooling. We also follow Becker (1964), Becker and Chiswick (1966) and Mincer (1974, 1993), in modelling the educational investment decision accounting for the relationship between earnings profiles, ability and age. The return to education is an increasing function of ability and youth. The long-run effects of a trade liberalisation on the steady state ability threshold, relative factor supplies and hence outputs are as discussed in Section 6.2.1. It is the medium-run effects on the skill composition of the workforce existing at the time the liberalisation occurs where new insights are available. From the perspective of a relatively skill abundant country, these arise in five main areas.

First, what is the role of age in the process of skill acquisition by the existing workforce? The change in relative factor returns will induce the more able unskilled workers to upgrade. Current unskilled workers balance the costs of human capital acquisition with the future benefits, and more able workers receive a higher return to skill upgrading. But here the age dimension becomes important, since older workers have a shorter remaining working life over which the higher skilled wage can be earned. The outcome is a trade-off between age and ability – the older the age cohort the more able the marginal worker who upgrades.

Second, adding a time dimension to the model also permits a comparison of adjustment under anticipated and unanticipated liberalisations. If a trade liberalisation is anticipated, when does most of the skill upgrading by the existing workforce occur? We find that the announcement of a future liberalisation will induce current workers close to the old ability threshold to upgrade immediately following the announcement. Others further away from the threshold will upgrade immediately before the liberalisation and, if the liberalisation is sufficiently large, a third group will upgrade immediately after the liberalisation. The important feature is that much of the upgrading by the current workforce will take place after the announcement but *before* the liberalisation actually occurs. Measures of adjustment that fail to take this into account may result in significant underestimates of the actual adjustment.

Third, how does the transition to the long run occur? The long-run effects on the composition of traded goods production follows from the Rybczynski Theorem – output of the relatively skilled labour intensive good increases and output of the other good falls. This is consistent with Findlay and Kierzkowski (1983) and Borsook, and also models of variable factor supplies in a HOS setting (e.g. Martin, 1976; Neary, 1978; Woodland, 1982). However, this process need not be monotonic. Some unskilled workers switch from manufacturing to education immediately following the liberalisation (or its announcement). This expansion in the number of students draws in more skilled labour to act as teachers. Thus, the supply of both unskilled and skilled labour allocated to manufacturing fall, which will tend to reduce both traded outputs, and may lead to biased outcomes through a negative Rybczynski effect, depending on the changes in relative factor supplies. However, once the existing upgraders have made their way through the education system, there will be a progressive shift in outputs towards their long-run levels. Until the new long-run equilibrium is achieved, a skilled (unskilled) labour abundant country will have a skill endowment below (above) its steady state. In the latter periods the retiring cohort includes increasing numbers of workers who upgraded immediately after liberalisation. By exposing the time dimension this model also shows that adjustment can take a long time.

Fourth, how does trade liberalisation affect wage dispersion? In skilled labour abundant countries, trade liberalisation will be associated with increased wage dispersion among skilled workers and income inequality in the long run. Moreover, this increase is progressive. Interestingly, in the context of this model, trade liberalisation could play a role in explaining differences in the evolution of the relative supply of skilled labour between younger and older workers and therefore help in explaining differences in the evolution of the college to high-school wage gap for different age cohorts.[8] For the existing workforce, the strength of the incentive to become skilled following a trade liberalisation depends on a worker's age. A smaller fraction of older age cohorts become skilled. The post-liberalisation unskilled wage is the same for all age cohorts, but the average skilled wage will be higher for older cohorts. The latter is a result of skill upgrading involving workers of lower ability than the existing skilled workforce. The larger the fraction upgrading, the lower the average income of the upgraders. The outcome is that the ratio of average skilled to average unskilled earnings is higher in older cohorts during the adjustment process.

Finally, what are the implications of these results for the design of programmes of adjustment assistance? Not all workers who upgrade 'gain' from the liberalisation. Given that the liberalisation has taken place, they are better off upgrading than remaining unskilled, but for some their discounted lifetime earnings may still be less than before the liberalisation. In each ability group, the younger upgraders gain and the older upgraders lose from trade liberalisation, and the age cut-off between winners and losers is increasing in ability. However, any compensation scheme based on age alone (as ability is neither observable nor revealed in this model by a worker's unskilled income) is likely to fail to capture some losers with low ability while rewarding some gainers of high ability. An additional issue arises if the liberalisation is anticipated, because assistance is typically only provided to members of the existing workforce adjusting *after* the liberalisation has occurred. But, as noted above, if the liberalisation is anticipated much of the upgrading takes place before it occurs. If adjustment assistance is only made available post-liberalisation, this will distort and delay the timing of adjustment for an anticipated liberalisation.

6.4.2 Trade and investment in firm-specific human capital

The effects of trade liberalisation on firm-specific human capital formation have recently been analysed by Long et al. (2007). They note that firm-specific human capital introduces a non-competitive element to wage determination, since a worker is more productive employed in a specific job, than by any other firm. They therefore assume that the wage of a skilled worker arises as the Nash bargaining solution between the worker and the firm. Firms do not take the wages of skilled workers as given therefore, which provides them with an incentive to negotiate the wage after the skills have been accumulated. Recognising this, workers tend to underinvest in skills, since they know they will not receive the full benefit of their investment. How is this decision affected by trade liberalisation?

Long et al. build a two-sector model where the low-tech sector employs only unskilled labour and the high-tech sector employs skilled labour and capital. There are two periods. Workers, who are homogeneous on entering the workforce, have to decide whether to work in the low-tech sector and remain unskilled in the next period, or to work in the high-tech sector and acquire skills, part of which are firm-specific, which will raise their productivity in the next period. Workers can only acquire skills by working, and skill acquisition is costly. They equate the marginal cost of skill acquisition with the marginal private benefit, which, as noted above, is less than the marginal social benefit because some of the productivity increase is captured by the firm. Investment in skills is thus suboptimal from a social perspective.

A higher price for the high-tech good will raise the return to skill accumulation, and move it towards the social optimum, albeit at the expense of the accompanying by-product distortions. Thus trade liberalisation, which reduces the relative price of the import competing good, will convey an extra gain to the high-tech exporter and a loss to the high-tech importer. Long et al. note the implication that a developing country (a high-tech importer) may be harmed by trade, because of this distortion in its labour market.

6.5   Conclusions

The historical record seems to suggest that adjustment to trade shocks can be lengthy and that the longer-run benefits can be preceded by significant short and medium-run disturbances. Until recently, the long-run effects of trade received the bulk of the attention in the theoretical literature. The dynamic adjustment of the economy towards this long run received less attention. Moreover, trade models tend to treat workers within each skill group as homogeneous, thereby leaving important dimensions of the adjustment process unexplored. The perception that trade adjustment is a dynamic phenomenon, whose costs and benefits depend on workers' individual characteristics is widely held, as is the view that education and training may play a role in facilitating transition. The omission of these features from trade models is understandable, since the dynamics involved are especially difficult in the type of general equilibrium setting required to analyse trade-related issues. But until they are included, it will be difficult to relate the theory to the concerns of the policy-making community. Progress is being made, however, as discussed above. The labour market search process is beginning to be included in trade models, and the implications of worker age and experience have also begun to be included in the analysis of the adjustment process.

As noted in the Introduction, academic analysis tends to focus on the sources of the aggregate gains from trade and the impact of trade on the domestic income distribution. It is straightforward to demonstrate that, were an appropriate redistribution mechanism available, the gainers could compensate the losers and still be better off. How such compensation might proceed in practice is far from straightforward however. Ichida (2005) provides a careful and detailed analysis of the difficulties of constructing compensation schemes based on factor and commodity taxes when individuals are heterogeneous and can move freely between different sectors. The primary difficulty is identifying gainers and losers among those who switch industries. In practice there is no specific attempt to use policy to redistribute the general gains from trade. What compensation there is is typically targeted at easing adjustment, by covering (part of) the costs incurred by those who adjust. The problems in designing such policies can be illustrated in the context of adjustment through skill upgrading in our model discussed in Section 6.4. Workers of the same age who upgrade their skills may gain or lose as a result of the liberalisation, depending on their ability levels. If age is observable and ability is not, then compensation to adjusters (upgraders) based on age alone will lead to 'compensation' of some workers who are in fact gaining from the liberalisation, while no compensation is provided to other workers who are losing. These problems are amplified for an anticipated liberalisation, where a policy of post-liberalisation adjustment assistance will bias the adjustment strategies of the more able workers away from their efficient strategy of upgrading earlier.

Trade liberalisation, or globalisation more generally, will affect the incentives of individual workers to acquire skills. These induced changes in human capital formation, whether of general, industry-specific, firm-specific or even job-specific skills, will be an important aspect of the adjustment process. Of course, they are also important for other aspects of the economy's performance, such as determining its comparative advantage and its ability to undertake the technological innovation (or even imitation) now recognised as a crucial element of sustained growth. To date, there has been limited modelling in this area, but this is beginning to change.

Empirically, it has proved difficult to provide comprehensive evidence on the adjustment experience of workers and whether international trade caused their job loss, because of the absence of direct data on the characteristics of displaced workers. Fortunately this is changing with the recent provision of access to large longitudinal matched employer–employee datasets, containing complete work histories as well as individual and firm characteristics, for Portugal, Sweden, Germany and France for example. These may make it possible to analyse workers' decisions induced by trade liberalisation, such as the decisions to skill upgrade or move industry, and the impact of these choices on earnings and unemployment duration. Furthermore, they allow for the analysis of how firms' characteristics interplay with workers' characteristics in trade adjustment and the investigation of the sources of earnings losses among workers and industries. Finally, they permit the examination of the mechanisms through which openness affects the earnings of specific groups of workers.

Research on adjustment in developing countries should not be neglected. These countries exhibit a wider variety of labour market institutions, and are the location of many of the larger and more recent trade reforms. They are also countries where the problems of poverty and inequality are likely to be more severe, since many lack income support mechanisms that can sustain a period of job search. Importantly, countries like Mexico, Colombia, Argentina, Brazil, Chile, India and Hong Kong, now have good household survey data that would allow for detailed examination of the proposed issues.

Notes

1. Education is assumed to be a perfectly competitive sector with the returns of each unit of capital equal to its marginal value product.
2. Besides skilled and unskilled workers, students and owners of the educational capital, Findlay and Kierzkowski (1983) also consider another type of agent in the economy: providers of finance to education. Their role is to make loans to students. The underlying assumptions are that both types of workers have identical preferences and all agents have a common, constant rate of time preference (reflected in a horizontal supply of loans) equal to the market rate interest. In this context, both skilled and unskilled workers will want to consume the unskilled wage rate per unit of time. Loan repayment will occur over their working life. Importantly, with a horizontal supply curve for loans no producer surplus will exist in the provision of finance to education.
3. Note that there is perfect mobility of capital among individuals with different abilities resulting in returns to the educational capital equalised in the educational sector.
4. For details see Chapter 7.
5. Davidson and Matusz also demonstrate conditions under which congestion externalities can lead to multiple steady-state equilibria that can be Pareto ranked. Temporary protection can then also be used to divert the economy to a preferred steady state.
6. While we specifically analyse the case where the cause of the change in relative output prices is trade, any other policy change or shock that changes relative wages, and is exogenous to the wage setting conditions within the country, will yield the same results. This framework could also be used to analyse the effects of changes in the length of schooling, birth rates and the efficiency of the educational sector on workers' educational decisions.

7. While this might appear to create a 'chicken and egg' problem, in that skilled labour is required to produce skilled labour, it is straightforward to suppose that there is an alternative education technology under which high ability individuals can acquire skills themselves if they devote sufficient time to studying. This technology would then become dominated by that in the text once the skilled wage is sufficiently low.
8. For discussion of the evolution of relative wages and factor supplies by different age groups and cohorts see, for example, Card and Lemieux (2001) and Autor, Katz and Kearney (2005).

References

Autor, D., Katz, L. and Kearney, M. (2005). 'Trends in US Wage Inequality: Re-Assessing the Revisionists', NBER Working Paper No. 11627.

Becker, G. (1964). *Human Capital*. Columbia University Press, New York: NBER.

Becker, G. and Chiswick, B. (1966). 'Education and the Distribution of Earnings', *American Economic Review*, Proceedings, Vol. 56, pp. 358–69.

Blanchard, E. and Willman, G. (2006). 'Political Stasis or Protectionist Rut? Policy Mechanisms for Trade Reform in a Democracy', University of Virginia.

Borsook, I. (1986). 'Earnings, Ability and International Trade', *Journal of International Economics*, Vol. 22, pp. 281–95.

Card, D. and Lemieux, T. (2001). 'Can Falling Supply Explain the Rising Return to College for Younger Men? A Cohort-Base Analysis', *Quarterly Journal of Economics*, Vol. 116, pp. 705–46.

Davidson, C. and Matusz, S. (2000). 'Globalisation and Labour-Market Adjustment: How Fast and at What Cost?', *Oxford Review of Economic Policy*, Vol. 16, 3, pp. 42–56.

Davidson, C. and Matusz, S. (2001). 'On Adjustment Costs', GEP Research Paper 2001/24, Leverhulme Centre for Research on Globalisation and Economic Policy, University of Nottingham.

Davidson, C. and Matusz, S. (2002). 'Globalisation, Employment, and Income: Analysing the Adjustment Process', in D. Greenaway, R. Upward and K. Wakelin (eds), *Trade, Investment, Migration and Labour Market Adjustment*, IEA Conference, Vol. 35. New York: Palgrave Macmillan.

Davidson, C. and Matusz, S. (2004). 'An Overlapping-Generation Model of Escape Clause Protection', *Review of International Economics*, Vol. 12, pp. 749–68.

Deardorff, A. V. (2000). 'Policy Implications of the Trade and Wages Debate', *Review of International Economics*, Vol. 8, pp. 478–96.

Dinopoulos, E. and Segerstrom, P. (1999). 'A Schumpeterian Model of Protection and Relative Wages', *American Economic Review*, Vol. 89, 3, pp. 450–72.

Falvey, R., Greenaway, D. and Silva, J. (2007). 'Trade Liberalisation and Human Capital Adjustment', GEP Research Paper 07/34, Leverhulme Centre for Research on Globalisation and Economic Policy, University of Nottingham.

Findlay, R. and Kierzkowski, H. (1983). 'International Trade and Human Capital: a Simple General Equilibrium Model', *Journal of Political Economy*, Vol. 91, pp. 957–78.

Ichida, T. (2005). 'Occupational Choice and Compensation for Losers from International Trade', Waseda University.

Kletzer, Lori (2001). *Job Loss from Imports: Measuring the Costs.* Institute for International Economics, Washington, D.C.

Kletzer, Lori (2004). 'Trade-related Job Loss and Wage Insurance: a Synthetic Review', *Review of International Economics*, Vol. 12, pp. 724–48.

Long, N., Riezman, R. and Soubeyran, A. (2007). 'Trade, Wage Gaps, and Specific Human Capital Accumulation', *Review of International Economics*, Vol. 15, pp. 75–92.

Martin, J. (1976). 'Variable Factor Supplies and the Heckscher–Ohlin–Samuelson Model', *Economic Journal*, Vol. 86, pp. 820–31.

Mincer, J. (1974). *Schooling, Experience, and Earnings.* New York: NBER Press.

Mincer, J. (1993). *Collected Essays of Jacob Mincer.* Aldershot: Edward Elgar.

Neary, P. (1978). 'Short-run Capital Specificity and the Pure Theory of International Trade', *Economic Journal*, Vol. 88, pp. 488–510.

Neary, Peter (2002). 'Foreign Competition and Wage Inequality', *Review of International Economics*, Vol. 10, pp. 680–93.

Weigert, B. (2007). 'Educational Systems and Globalisation', Justus-Liebig-University Giessen.

Woodland, A. (1982). *International Trade and Resource Allocation.* Amsterdam: North-Holland.

7
Trade Adjustment and Occupational Mobility

Richard Upward and Peter Wright

7.1 Introduction

It is widely agreed that there has been a dramatic shift in demand away from unskilled towards skilled workers in many OECD countries.[1] This has manifested itself both in deteriorating employment prospects and worsening wage outcomes for low-skilled workers.

However, workers are not immutably either low- or high-skilled. One way of modelling this is to consider the decision of workers to invest in human capital, as discussed in Falvey, Greenaway and Silva (Chapter 6) of this volume. In this chapter we take a different approach, and consider explicitly the role of *firms* in the shift towards a more skill-intensive workforce. When firms change their desired skill mix of workers, they can do so either by hiring new workers, or by retraining their existing workforce. Thus, a 'shock' which changes the relative demand for skilled and unskilled workers may change the pattern of mobility between occupations.

To illustrate the potential importance of firms in the process of skill upgrading, consider Table 7.1. We use a representative panel of workers in the UK from the British Household Panel Survey (BHPS).[2] The first row shows that 76 per cent of those in private sector employment were working for the same firm in the previous year; the remaining 24 per cent entered from another firm, another sector, or from non-employment. Of those in a private sector firm at time t, 28 per cent exit the firm before $t+1$.

The second panel shows that, even amongst those who remain with the same employer, there is considerable promotion from non-managerial to managerial or supervisory roles.[3] There is relatively little demotion amongst those who remain with the same employer. Amongst

Table 7.1: Worker reallocation in the UK, 1991–2004 (proportion)

	Remains in firm	Enters new firm	Exits firm
Total	0.76	0.24	0.28
Promoted	0.09	0.11	0.08
Same-level	0.86	0.79	0.79
Demoted	0.05	0.10	0.13
From non-employment	—	0.45	—
To non-employment	—	—	0.46
Voluntary	—	0.83	0.73
Involuntary	—	0.17	0.27

those who enter or exit a new firm at *t* to or from another job, rates of promotion and especially demotion are higher.

The bottom panel shows the proportion of individuals who move voluntarily or involuntarily.[4] Of those who enter a new firm at *t* about 17 per cent report that they left their last job involuntarily. Of those who leave their firm between *t* and *t* + 1 far more (27 per cent) report leaving involuntarily.

Thus, we observe considerable movement of workers between broadly defined skill-groups both within and between firms. Workers might be characterised as attempting to climb an occupational 'ladder', while facing a risk that they may also be moved to a lower occupational rung. The existence of occupational ladders implies that the consequences of shocks may be more complex than in a world where workers have a fixed skill-type. Workers may suffer career dislocation as a result of changes to the structure of the economy. The cost of losing a job is therefore not simply the immediate pecuniary one, but also the fact that the intended career path, on which the individual has embarked, may be disrupted. But shocks may also bring opportunities. Job openings which were previously unavailable may now be obtainable by an individual, and their long-term career prospects may be improved.

Globalisation may provide exactly the kind of shocks which cause firms to change their relative demand for skilled and unskilled labour. Dluhosch (Chapter 8) and Geishecker, Görg and Maoli (Chapter 9) in this volume consider how the increased fragmentation of production ('offshoring') leads to a within-firm and within-industry shift towards more skill-intensive production.[5]

In Section 7.2 we review the theoretical literature on occupational mobility. It turns out that there is surprisingly little explicit discussion of the relationship between structural change and occupational mobility. In Section 7.3, therefore, we outline a model which explicitly links the decisions of firms (who offer both high-skill and low-skill jobs) with the decisions of workers, some of whom are trying to reach a higher rung on the occupational ladder. We then turn to the empirical evidence on skill upgrading and occupational mobility in Section 7.4. Once again, there is little direct evidence on the relationship between structural change and mobility, and so Section 7.5 presents recent empirical evidence which examines how the changing patterns of demand have affected the employment prospects and occupational mobility patterns of individual workers.

7.2 Theoretical literature

Much of the modern literature on career mobility stems from the work of Sicherman and Galor (1990). They consider how fully informed, forward-looking agents choose their optimal human capital investment, and subsequently their optimal career path, in order to maximise their lifetime income. This serves as a useful extension to the basic model of human capital investment. However, although the individual's career may involve movements up and across occupational ladders, the demand side in this model is taken as given. Hence workers progress smoothly, and with perfect foresight, along their chosen career paths with no prospect of being knocked off or back down their chosen career ladder.

Jovanovic and Nyarko (1997) provide an alternative characterisation of the human capital model, and argue that jobs lower in the occupational ladder provide 'stepping-stones' to more senior positions. Their basic model has just two occupations A and B. Each occupation requires a technique which has some randomness associated with it. This randomness has a bivariate distribution across the two occupations with a squared correlation coefficient ρ. The greater the variance of this randomness, the more 'skilled' is an occupation, because the greater the risk of an unskilled person performing that task. The first period reveals the value of randomness in that occupation, and this is the way in which learning is modelled. If the randomness is highly correlated across occupations, learning in one occupation helps the worker to learn about the other occupation, and in this way the generality of skills is modelled. Because there are only two occupations and two time periods, there are just four possible careers (AA, BB, AB, BA). The expected value of a career (e.g. V_{AB} and V_{BA}) is increasing with ρ. A key result is that individuals should engage in the less-skilled activity first (because it has a lower variance), and then move onto the high-skilled occupation if ρ is sufficiently high, or if the relative wage in the other occupation is sufficiently high. In this model, 'those at the top of the occupational ladder earn more partly because they have spent time on lower rungs, where they have learned something' (Jovanovic and Nyarko, 1997: 289).

Jovanovic and Nyarko contrast the human capital approach with that of 'bandit' models of career progression, in which a worker's innate suitability to perform jobs higher up the occupational ladder is revealed by experience, and it is this revelation that leads to an occupational switch.

Jovanovic and Nyarko also consider separately a 'sectoral shock' model of career progression, in which changes in the relative profitability of a sector affect the labour demand and hence the number of individuals choosing each occupation in each sector. However, they argue that such a model explains 'time effects' rather than why individuals change occupation at particular ages – the 'age effect' – and hence dismiss it as uninteresting.

Siow (1994) develops a model in which both the demand and supply side considerations are important. All workers are initially unskilled, but firms can train workers to make them skilled, at a cost of lost output. This skill is assumed to be generic across all firms in the same industry, so a market in skilled labour develops. Firms can, subject to a screening cost, attempt to hire a high-skill worker. Siow goes on to informally outline a model of upgrading within firms. The supply side is driven by standard human capital and job-matching considerations, the demand side by standard labour demand considerations with hiring costs.

Mortensen and Pissarides (1998) is not explicitly a model of career progression, but is nevertheless informative of the relationship between technological progress and the decision of a firm to upgrade an existing worker, or to end an existing employment relationship. In their model they consider a stylised firm that employs a single worker. The arrival of a new technology causes a shock to the product market, and means that some current matches between workers and firms become unprofitable. Firms can then choose whether to dissolve the match and exit production, or to invest in a renovation cost in order to continue production with the same worker. One obvious aspect of this renovation cost is the cost of retraining the worker to be able to use the new technology. Clearly, the impact on the individual worker will be very different in these two cases. In the first, an increase in the rate of technological change (and hence in the rate of skill upgrading) will cause job loss and the interruption of individual careers. In the second case, however, workers move to a higher skill level to accommodate the increased demand for higher skill workers.

7.3   A model of shocks, job turnover and worker turnover

In this section we outline a model which captures the intense job reallocation patterns identified by Davis, Haltiwanger and Schuh (1996), and the complex patterns of worker reallocation which have been recognised and studied for rather longer; see for example Farber (1999). A more detailed exposition of the model can be found in Bougheas, Davidson, Upward and Wright (2007). Crucially, we allow workers to move not only between jobs and sectors, but also between non-managerial and managerial positions. Thus workers have 'careers' which are affected not only by their own decisions, but also by the decisions of firms. This contrasts with the extant literature on career mobility, which typically considers only the decisions of one side of the market, as discussed in Section 7.2. The model will allow us to assess the impact of structural shocks on worker turnover, job turnover, relative wages and workers' promotion patterns.

The economy consists of a single low-tech sector and two high-tech sectors. This is illustrated in Figure 7.1. The low-tech sector (denoted *B*) uses a simple production process and requires only unskilled operatives. The two high-tech sectors (denoted 1 and 2) have a more sophisticated production process, and firms in this sector need to employ both a blue-collar worker and a manager.

Within the economy there is a clear hierarchy of jobs. At the bottom are *operative* jobs, then *blue-collar*, then *managerial* jobs. It is assumed that

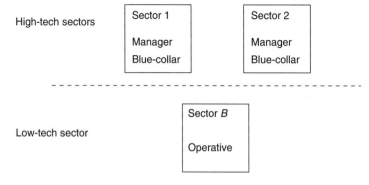

Figure 7.1: The sectoral structure of the economy

the tasks performed in the low-tech sector *B* are simple, and all workers are capable of these. Thus, all workers are equally productive in this sector. Further, this market clears, so a worker will always be able to find a job in this sector. In the high-tech sectors, however, the production processes are more sophisticated, and workers differ both in their ability to perform the blue-collar tasks and in their ability to be managers in this sector. Workers therefore differ in their productivity in each role.

The ability of a worker to perform blue-collar tasks in the high-tech sector is assumed to depend on two factors. Firstly, a worker's particular aptitudes may be more suited to one sector than another. Secondly, even within the same sector, firms differ in their ethos and organisation, and workers are better suited to work in some firms than others. The productivity of the worker therefore also depends on the quality of the match between the worker and the firm.

As well as offering the possibility of blue-collar jobs, the high-tech sector also offers the prospect of a managerial job. We assume that managerial skills are more generic than blue-collar skills and hence sectoral match quality is not important. However, aptitude is important, and what determines a worker's success as a manager is their innate ability to perform managerial tasks.

Within even such a relatively simple framework, the possible career movements of individuals can be complicated and affected by the decision of the firm, the decision of the worker, and changes in the external environment. The various possibilities for movement are illustrated in Figure 7.2.

A crucial factor in determining the initial position at which a worker enters will be their innate ability to perform managerial tasks. Those with an aptitude for management will seek to enter into one of these positions immediately. However, the number of managerial jobs is constrained, so not all those seeking managerial posts will obtain one. Such individuals will seek blue-collar jobs, since here they have an opportunity for promotion into a managerial job in the next period. It is this feature which means that blue-collar jobs are viewed as superior to operative jobs in the career hierarchy.

The ability of the worker is also an important factor in determining the subsequent career path of the individual. Those individuals with a high ability that were previously unable to find a managerial job will again attempt to obtain one in the next period. Note that some managerial posts will be filled by internal promotions. Here, those in blue-collar jobs already in the firm will face an advantage because their firm may promote them if there is a vacancy and they are well matched.

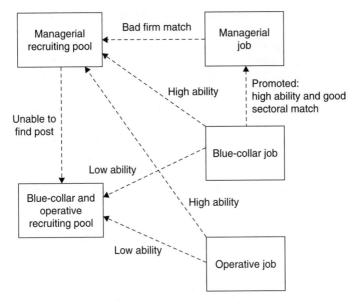

Figure 7.2: Worker movement between jobs and recruiting pools

The quality of the match between the worker and their firm and the general match of the worker to the sector in which their firm is located will also be crucial in determining mobility. If a worker is badly matched then, in the next period, they will re-enter the job market. This is either because they seek to find a job to which they are better suited, or because the firm in which they work fires them in the hope of finding a better replacement.

The model therefore allows for a rich variety of worker movements between firms and jobs. Separations may be both voluntary and involuntary. Workers may be promoted within firms if they are well matched with a firm and have managerial ability. Workers who separate may find new jobs at the same level or may be forced to move to a lower occupation.

Using this model, we examine the impact of 'skill biased technological change' and 'sector biased technological change' on worker movement.[6] A shock of the former type, which increases the productivity of managers relative to blue-collar workers, will increase the number of viable high-tech firms and both more managers and more blue-collar workers will be employed. Hence, the demand constraint on managerial and blue-collar jobs will be relaxed. Such a change will be particularly beneficial to high ability workers, since the number finding themselves stuck in blue-collar (or operative) positions will decline. Workers in the high-tech sector will also benefit in terms of greater job security because their firms will now be less vulnerable to temporary shocks. Interestingly, this serves to slow down the number of promotions because worker 'churning' (which includes promotions) falls.

How do these results contrast with those induced by sector-biased technological change? Such a shock will increase the expected profitability, and the size of the sector concerned, and hence the demand for managers and blue-collar workers in that sector. This will mean that the other high-tech sector will diminish in size and will suffer relatively higher rates of job churning as the firms in it become relatively more vulnerable to temporary shocks. As this sector shrinks, wages will fall, and it will release workers of both high and low ability. These workers will seek employment in the other sector, whose relative wages are increasing in line with sector profits.

Note that in this model there are, in the terminology of Jovanovic and Nyarko (1997), both 'age' and 'time' effects. Individuals whose match qualities are revealed are promoted *ceteris paribus*. However, sectoral shocks may thwart movements that would otherwise have occurred and prompt movements to other sectors.

7.4 Empirical literature

The changing skill structure, and in particular the dramatic shift in demand away from unskilled and towards skilled workers in many OECD countries, has been well documented. Industry level studies for the US, such as Berman, Bound and Griliches (1994) find that skill upgrading is primarily a within-industry phenomenon which is correlated with indicators of technological change. Berman, Bound and Machin (1998) find similar patterns in most other developed countries.

These findings have also been corroborated by plant-level studies of skill-upgrading. In the US, Dunne, Haltiwanger and Troske (1997) find that changes in the share of skilled labour is driven first by continuing plants 'retooling and reorganising', and second, by new, more skill-intensive plants entering to displace less skill-intensive plants which exit. In the UK, Haskel and Heden (1999) reach similar findings. Skill-upgrading is accounted for almost entirely by within-plant changes and by net entry of new, more skill-intensive plants.

Although it seems to be a stylised fact that skill-upgrading is, to a large extent, a within-plant phenomenon, plant level data cannot tell us *how* firms upgrade their workforce, which is the focus of this chapter. Mortensen and Pissarides' (1998) model makes clear that within-plant skill upgrading can be achieved either by replacing existing workers with new, more skilled workers, or by upgrading the existing workforce. Of course, entry and exit of plants is one mechanism by which the former occurs, but to examine what happens within existing plants one requires data on plants linked to workers so that one can observe job flows and worker flows. A growing literature uses such linked data to investigate the relationship between job flows and worker flows,[7] but these papers do not separate worker or job flows by skill level. Bauer and Bender (2004) is an exception, using data from Germany. They find some evidence that plants upgrade the skills of their incumbent workforce. However, these effects are very small compared to the effect of external worker flows. In other words, plants upgrade the skills of their workforce by laying off unskilled workers and hiring skilled workers.

Bartel and Sicherman (1998) measure the relationship between industry level measures of technological change and rates of training provision. They find that higher rates of technological change are associated with *greater* training provision for production workers and for less skilled non-production workers. This accords with our earlier intuition that technological change may not necessarily harm less skilled workers. If, as seems likely, those in receipt of training have a higher probability of movement to higher skill levels, then technological change and career progression will be positively correlated.

7.5   Skill upgrading and occupational mobility

In Upward and Wright (2007), we address the issue of structural change and career progression directly, by examining how the changing patterns of aggregate employment have impacted both on the employment prospects and on the occupational mobility patterns of individual workers. We do this using individual-level panel data from both the US (the Panel Study of Income Dynamics, PSID) and the UK (the British Household Panel Study, BHPS).[8]

We seek to address two major questions. First, does the speed of skill upgrading in an industry lead to greater upward mobility of workers, or does it lead to a greater rate of job loss and downward movement? Second, is the speed of skill upgrading in an industry a quantitatively important component of occupational mobility, or is it relatively unimportant compared to other influences such as the worker's level of human capital?

This analysis serves to fill a number of gaps in our knowledge of the skill-upgrading process. It allows us to address the question 'what is the impact of skill-upgrading on individual workers?' We examine the characteristics of those workers who have improved employment prospects and the characteristics of those whose job prospects worsen. By focusing on individual workers, we are also able to assess the extent of individual wage gains and losses for those who move job as a result of changes in the skill structure. The 2007 paper also sheds light on the mechanism by which firms upgrade the skill composition of their workforce. For example, do they retrain and promote individuals already working within the firm or do they lay off low-skill workers and recruit external high-skill workers?

7.5.1   A simple framework

Consider an economy with two types of job, low skill (1), and high skill (2). Given the current state of technology, firms decide on their optimal mix of jobs. In aggregate, there are initially N_1 workers employed in low-skilled jobs and N_2 workers employed in high-skilled jobs.

We suppose that firms are then potentially subject to two types of shock. First, technology shocks, which occur with probability λ per period per job, cause firms to change their optimal mix of jobs. More precisely, a technology shock causes an unskilled job to become unprofitable, but at the same time opens up a new profitable opportunity for a skilled job. A technology shock therefore causes firms to destroy low-skill jobs and create high-skill jobs. In aggregate, this causes the destruction of λN_1 low-skill jobs and the creation of λN_1 high-skill jobs.

Second, in the absence of a technology shock any particular job may be subject to an idiosyncratic shock, which occurs with probability τ per period per job. These occur when either a firm or a worker decides to end a particular worker–firm match. These shocks leave the profitability of high- and low-skill jobs unchanged, and so the firm replaces the worker who leaves with another worker of the same skill level.

When faced with a technology shock, a firm can either replace their existing worker with a new worker, or they can retrain an existing worker. In the first case the firm must pay a search and recruitment cost. In the second case, the firm must pay the cost of retraining the worker. The relative cost of each strategy differs across firms, so not all firms adopt the same response to a technological shock.[9] A firm chooses to 'renovate' the match (and retrain its worker) with probability π, and to destroy the match and search for a new worker with probability $1 - \pi$.

Given this setup, four different outcomes are possible for workers in the low-skill group. Firstly, an individual who is subject neither to a technology shock nor an idiosyncratic shock will stay at the same skill level within the same firm:

$$s' = (1 - \lambda)(1 - \tau). \tag{7.1}$$

Secondly, if they are subject to a technology shock but their job is renovated then they will move up the job ladder but stay in the same firm:

$$v' = \pi\lambda. \tag{7.2}$$

If, on the other hand, the worker is laid off, with probability $(1 - \pi)\lambda$, or they are subject to an idiosyncratic shock, with probability $(1 - \lambda)\tau$, then the individual will seek employment in another firm. Define θ_1 as the probability of finding a new low-skilled job, and θ_2 as the probability of finding a new high-skilled job. Then the probability of moving to another job at the same skill-level in a new firm is

$$s'' = (1 - \pi)\lambda\theta_1 + \tau(1 - \lambda)\theta_1, \tag{7.3}$$

and the probability of moving to a high-skilled job in a new firm is

$$v'' = (1 - \pi)\lambda\theta_2 + \tau(1 - \lambda)\theta_2. \tag{7.4}$$

If individuals fail to find either a low-skilled or a high-skilled job then they become unemployed.

$$u = (1 - \pi)\lambda(1 - \theta_1 - \theta_2) + \tau(1 - \lambda)(1 - \theta_1 - \theta_2). \tag{7.5}$$

Our estimates may be viewed as an attempt to recover the underlying parameters which determine probabilities (7.1) to (7.5) above. This procedure would directly answer the question that we initially posed: if there is a technology shock, what are the relative chances of being upgraded and of being made unemployed?[10]

In this framework, the only reason for a change in the skill structure of the labour market is a technology shock. Thus, the percentage change in low-skill employment is a perfect proxy for the probability that a job is affected by a technology shock. That is, since

$$\Delta N_1 = N_{1,t+1} - N_{1,t} = -\lambda N_{1,t}, \tag{7.6}$$

then the probability of a technology shock is given by:

$$\lambda = -\frac{\Delta N_1}{N_{1,t}} \tag{7.7}$$

This suggests that once we have estimated the probability of a shock by observing the percentage change in unskilled employment, equation (7.2) would allow us to obtain an estimate of π. We could similarly extract the value for the remaining parameters. This is largely the strategy that we adopt in this paper. We relate the probability of movement up the 'occupational ladder' to the percentage change of employment in the skill group in the industry i in which the individual works at time $t - 1$. For example:

$$v'_{it} = \Phi \left(\beta \frac{-\Delta N_{it}}{N_{it}} + \gamma x_{i,t-1} + \delta_j \right). \tag{7.8}$$

Each movement probability (7.1) to (7.5) has an empirical counterpart of the form given by (7.8), estimated using a Probit model. We include in these regressions a vector of individual characteristics x to control for other factors which might influence the probability of movement. These include age, gender, marital status, years of education, union status, health, tenure and current hourly wage. The δ_j are a set of industry dummies to allow for the possibility that turnover rates differ across industries for other reasons.

There are two important extensions to this basic framework which must also be considered before estimation. First, it is straightforward to allow for more than two skill groups. Second, we have so far assumed that technology shocks are purely 'skill-upgrading' in the sense that they destroy low-skill jobs but create high-skill jobs. However, Davis, Haltiwanger and Schuh (1996) show that, in reality, we observe simultaneous job creation and destruction within skill groups. A simple way to accommodate this feature is to extend the framework to allow for the possibility of shocks arriving at both low-skill and high-skill jobs. This modification allows for the possibility that technological change can cause movements both up and down the job ladder.

Allowing for movements down as well as up the ladder implies that, in addition to the movement probabilities (7.1)–(7.5) we must also estimate the probability of moving down the ladder within and between firms, giving a total of seven probabilities to estimate.

7.5.2 Results

The first row in Table 7.2 verifies that increased skill upgrading (i.e. a reduction in the size of each skill group) reduces the probability of staying in the same skill group in the same firm. It is noticeable that this effect is larger in the US than in the UK. The estimated effect is negative in all

Table 7.2: Impact of $\Delta N_{it}/N_{it}$ on movement probabilities

	All skill groups	Level 1	Level 2	Level 3	Level 4
(a) United States					
Same level, same firm	−0.1016	−0.0981	−0.1305	−0.0614	−0.0527
	(0.000)	(0.024)	(0.001)	(0.143)	(0.163)
Same level, new firm	0.0026	0.0111	0.028	0.0137	−0.0205
	(0.763)	(0.456)	(0.158)	(0.398)	(0.291)
Higher level, same firm	0.0173	0.0296	0.0187	0.0015	
	(0.001)	(0.021)	(0.051)	(0.847)	
Higher level, new firm	0.0126	−0.001	−0.0008	0.016	
	(0.008)	(0.953)	(0.977)	(0.076)	
Lower level, same firm	−0.0009		0.0026	0.004	0.0029
	(0.776)		(0.603)	(0.280)	(0.692)
Lower level, new firm	−0.0064		0.0061	0.0107	0.0027
	(0.170)		(0.987)	(0.349)	(0.796)
Out of employment	0.0517	0.0479	0.0446	−0.0027	0.0650
	(0.000)	(0.120)	(0.139)	(0.919)	(0.011)
(b) United Kingdom					
Same level, same firm	−0.0646	−0.0629	−0.0646	−0.0066	−0.0639
	(0.0001)	(0.1037)	(0.0001)	(0.8291)	(0.0415)
Same level, new firm	−0.0138	−0.0202	−0.0099	−0.0168	0.0011
	(0.1109)	(0.0633)	(0.6120)	(0.2497)	(0.9447)
Higher level, same firm	0.0038	0.0219	0.0015	−0.0082	
	(0.3511)	(0.0152)	(0.8104)	(0.1135)	
Higher level, new firm	0.0094	0.0201	0.0017	−0.0018	
	(0.0503)	(0.1994)	(0.8382)	(0.7354)	
Lower level, same firm	0.0082		0.0045	0.009	0.008
	(0.0017)		(0.0719)	(0.0225)	(0.2522)
Lower level, new firm	0.0028		0.0148	−0.0011	0.0069
	(0.4943)		(0.0109)	(0.8181)	(0.4849)
Out of employment	0.0455	0.0433	0.0862	0.0132	0.0387
	(0.0000)	(0.1100)	(0.0001)	(0.4978)	(0.0464)

skill groups, and tends to be larger in lower skill groups. This effect is, of course, essentially tautological: a reduction in the size of a worker's skill group in their industry *must* reduce the probability that a worker can stay in that skill group in that industry.

What is of more interest is where these workers go. In a framework where workers' skills are fixed, then a reduction in the number of jobs of a certain skill will always harm workers of that type. But in our framework, even low-skill workers may benefit from skill-upgrading because they may be promoted.

The final row of Table 7.2 shows that, in almost every case, a reduction in the size of a skill group does increase the probability of entering unemployment, and that this effect is slightly larger in the US. In the UK there is also evidence that the probability of demotion within the firm is increased, although the size of the marginal effect is smaller. This effect is not significant in the US; nor is it significant for between-firm moves.

Workers can also benefit from this process of skill-upgrading. For both countries we see evidence of an increased probability of upward movement. For workers in the US, the probability of moving up the skill ladder is increased both within and between firms. This effect is also evident in the UK, though only the between-firm component is statistically significant.

What is the overall balance of these effects on individual workers? Table 7.2 shows that, in both countries, whilst the probability of movement up the job ladder goes some way to offset the increased probability of unemployment, the average overall impact is negative because the increased probability of unemployment is greater.

Our results also show how the impact of structural change affects the movement probabilities of workers in different skill groups. If we think of the process of upgrading as a relative decline in lower skill groups and an expansion of the higher groups, then this table allows us to make some judgement about how this change comes about. Interestingly, those on the lower rungs are *not* necessarily more likely to exit to unemployment as a result of greater skill upgrading. Expansion of the upper skill groups is therefore achieved via a number of sources. First, job stability in the higher skill groups is increased, with the probability of remaining in this group rising and the probability of moving into unemployment from this group falling. Second, there is significant movement from the lower skill groups with promotion playing a role.

7.5.3 The wage effects of occupational mobility

We are also able to provide an insight into the wage effects of this occupational mobility. In the previous discussion it has implicitly been assumed that movements up are preferable to movements down or off the skill ladder. Table 7.3 shows the results of these investigations, and reports the result of wage regressions which examine that impact of worker movement. These control for those individual characteristics which might impact on wage changes independently of movement (such as age, sex and educational level).

The results indicate the deleterious impact to an individual of downward movement to a new employer. The measured impact in the US

Table 7.3: Conditional wage effects of occupational movement

	Same employer		New employer	
	Coeff.[a]	p-value	Coeff.	p-value
(a) United States				
level 2	0.0031	[0.457]	0.0306	[0.318]
level 3	0.0057	[0.265]	0.0560	[0.114]
level 4	0.0200	[0.000]	0.1158	[0.001]
level 2 (down)	−0.0137	[0.411]	−0.1079	[0.000]
level 3 (down)	0.0548	[0.019]	−0.1563	[0.000]
level 4 (down)	−0.0090	[0.628]	−0.1719	[0.000]
level 1 (up)	0.0296	[0.115]	0.0478	[0.201]
level 2 (up)	0.1019	[0.000]	0.0908	[0.000]
level 3 (up)	0.0862	[0.002]	0.0308	[0.417]
(b) United Kingdom				
level 2	0.0046	[0.451]	−0.0258	[0.620]
level 3	0.0099	[0.164]	−0.0065	[0.909]
level 4	0.0149	[0.029]	−0.0263	[0.632]
level 2 (down)	0.0427	[0.406]	−0.0431	[0.363]
level 3 (down)	−0.0346	[0.156]	−0.1225	[0.035]
level 4 (down)	−0.0155	[0.407]	−0.1362	[0.000]
level 1 (up)	0.1074	[0.000]	0.0390	[0.543]
level 2 (up)	0.0554	[0.001]	0.0714	[0.028]
level 3 (up)	−0.0321	[0.127]	0.0683	[0.245]

Source: Upward and Wright (2007).
[a] Shows percentage change in wages as a result of the movement indicated. Estimates control for age, sex and educational level.

ranges from 11 per cent for those moving down from level 2 to 17 per cent for those moving from level 3. In the UK the equivalent impacts range from 4 per cent to 14 per cent. There is no evidence of a wage penalty for downward movement within firms.

Table 7.3 also emphasises the benefit of upward movement within a current employer, both for the US and the UK. By contrast, only when moving from skill group 2 to skill group 3 is there a mean pecuniary advantage to an individual of changing firm. This latter result is rationalised by noting that those that move employer consist of two groups: those who move voluntarily to better jobs who get wage increases; and those whose movement is enforced. The latter group often end up in lower paying jobs. Similar patterns are observed for the United Kingdom and the United States.

7.6   Conclusions

In this chapter we have examined the impact of 'skill-upgrading' when workers are not immutably either high or low skill. This seems to be an important extension to traditional models, because we observe large numbers of workers moving between skill levels both within and between firms. The consequences of a shock which changes the relative demand for different skill types are therefore more complex. Shocks may serve to interrupt career paths, but they may also provide new opportunities for workers to climb up the skill ladder.

We outlined a model where workers can move not only between jobs and sectors, but also between non-managerial and managerial positions. Thus, workers have 'careers' which are affected not only by their own decisions, but also by the decisions of firms.

Our empirical approach has been to use individual level data linked to industry level measures of skill upgrading. A fruitful avenue for further research will be the use of linked employer–employee data which can examine precisely how a change in the skill composition of the workforce is achieved. Such data would allow us to measure the flow of jobs of different skill levels and the flows of workers between and within firms.

Our results, and those of Bauer and Bender (2004), suggest that skill-upgrading is primarily achieved by replacing existing workers with new workers, rather than by promoting existing workers. In the context of Mortensen and Pissarides' (1998) model, this implies that the shocks firms face are such that retraining the existing workforce is more costly than hiring and firing. Of course, such a result is dependent on the nature of the shock and the institutional arrangements which govern the hiring and firing of workers.

The impact of globalisation (or technological change) on workers' patterns of occupational mobility appears to be an under-researched area, but it seems likely to be an increasingly important component of the adjustment process emphasised by Davidson and Matusz in Chapter 2 of this volume. Concerns about the impact of globalisation have shifted away from worries about traditional international trade, and towards the more recent phenomenon of fragmentation, by which firms can divide segments of the production process across countries. Fragmentation is fundamentally a 'within firm' process which affects particular occupations rather than industries. Thus, adjustment in which workers retrain and change occupations may become even more crucial.

Notes

1. See, for example, Murphy and Welch (1993) and Berman, Bound and Griliches (1994) for US evidence; Berman, Bound and Machin (1998) for international evidence.
2. Detailed information on the BHPS is available from http://www.iser.essex.ac.uk/ulsc/bhps/. See also Taylor, Brice, Buck and Prentice-Lane (2006).
3. The BHPS asks individuals if they have any managerial duties or if they supervise other employees. We use this information to determine whether individuals are promoted or demoted.
4. The BHPS asks individuals who changed jobs between interview dates why they left their previous jobs. We code someone as having left involuntarily if they respond 'Made redundant', 'Dismissed/sacked' or 'Temporary job ended'.
5. Of course, various forms of skill-biased technological change can have the same effect.
6. Although we refer to the source of structural change as 'technology', one could equally well consider some aspect of globalisation which changes the relative profitability of firms in different sectors, or workers of different skill groups.
7. For example, Anderson and Meyer (1994); Abowd, Corbel and Kramarz (2000); and Burgess, Lane and Stevens (2000).
8. To ensure maximum comparability of the results for the two countries, we use a common data period from 1991 to 2001.
9. Mortensen and Pissarides (1998) suggest that 'For example, if implementing the latest technology requires that the job move to a new location, then the implementation [renovation] cost would include the cost of moving as well as retraining the worker. These could well exceed the cost of recruiting and training a new worker already located in the appropriate place. Alternatively, a different type or level of education may be needed by the new technology. In this case it may be cheaper to destroy the current job rather than retrain a current employee' (p. 745).
10. An equivalent set of movement probabilities can be derived for someone in the high-skill group.

References

Abowd, J., Corbel, P. and Kramarz, F. (2000). 'The Entry and Exit of Workers and the Growth of Employment: an Analysis of French Establishments', *Review of Economics and Statistics*, Vol. 81, 2, pp. 170–87.

Anderson, P. and Meyer, B. (1994). 'The Extent and Consequences of Job Turnover', *Brookings Papers on Economic Activity: Microeconomics*, pp. 177–248.

Bartel, A. and Sicherman, N. (1998). 'Technological Change and the Skill Acquisition of Young Workers', *Journal of Labor Economics*, Vol. 16, 4, pp. 718–55.

Bauer, T. and Bender, S. (2004). 'Technological Change, Organizational Change, and Job Turnover', *Labour Economics*, Vol. 11, pp. 265–91.

Berman, E., Bound, J. and Griliches, Z. (1994). 'Changes in the Demand for Skilled Labour within US Manufacturing: Evidence from the Annual Survey of Manufactures', *Quarterly Journal of Economics*, Vol. 109, 2, pp. 367–97.

Berman, E., Bound, J. and Machin, S. (1998). 'Implications of Skill-biased Technological Change: International Evidence', *Quarterly Journal of Economics*, Vol. 113, 4, pp. 1245–80.

Bougheas, S., Davidson, C., Upward, R. and Wright, P. (2007). 'The Impact of Shocks on Worker Mobility and Job Turnover', GEP Working Paper. Leverhulme Centre for Research on Globalisation and Economic Policy, University of Nottingham.

Burgess, S., Lane, J. and Stevens, D. (2000). 'Job Flows, Worker Flows and Churning', *Journal of Labor Economics*, Vol. 18, 3, pp. 473–502.

Davis, S., Haltiwanger, J. and Schuh, S. (1996). *Job Creation and Destruction*. Cambridge, MA: MIT Press.

Dunne, T., Haltiwanger, J. and Troske, K. (1997). 'Technology and Jobs: Secular Changes and Cyclical Dynamics', *Carnegie-Rochester Conference Series on Public Policy*, Vol. 46, pp. 107–78.

Falvey, R., Greenaway, D. and Silva, J. (2007). 'Trade, Human Capital and Labour Market Adjustment', in D. Greenaway, R. Upward and P. Wright (eds), *Globalisation and Labour Market Adjustment*. Basingstoke: Palgrave Macmillan.

Farber, H. (1999). 'Mobility and Stability: the Dynamics of Job Change in Labor Markets', in O. Ashenfelter and D. Card (eds), *Handbook of Labor Economics*, Vol. 3B, Amsterdam: North-Holland, chapter 37, pp. 2439–83.

Haskel, J. and Heden, Y. (1999). 'Computers and the Demand for Skilled Labour: Industry- and Establishment-level Panel Evidence for the UK', *Economic Journal*, Vol. 109, 454, pp. C68–C79.

Jovanovic, B. and Nyarko, Y. (1997). 'Stepping-stone Mobility', *Carnegie-Rochester Conference Series on Public Policy*, Vol. 46, pp. 289–325.

Mortensen, D. and Pissarides, C. (1998). 'Technological Progress, Job Creation and Job Destruction', *Review of Economic Dynamics*, Vol. 1, pp. 733–53.

Murphy, K. and Welch, F. (1993). 'Occupational Change and the Demand for Skill 1940–1990', *American Economic Review*, Vol. 83, 2, pp. 122–6.

Sicherman, N. and Galor, O. (1990). 'A Theory of Career Mobility', *Journal of Political Economy*, Vol. 98, pp. 169–92.

Siow, A. (1994). 'Hierarchical Careers', *Industrial Relations*, Vol. 33, pp. 83–105.

Taylor, M., Brice, J., Buck, N. and Prentice-Lane, E. (2006). 'The British Household Panel Survey User Manual', University of Essex.

Upward, R. and Wright, P. (2007). 'Snakes or Ladders? Skill Upgrading and Occupational Mobility in the US and UK during the 1990s', GEP Working Paper. Leverhulme Centre for Research on Globalisation and Economic Policy, University of Nottingham.

8
The Labour Market Implications of Fragmentation and Trade Under Imperfect Competition

Barbara Dluhosch

8.1 Introduction

Trade statistics suggest that, while international commerce has risen by more than value added, the growth in trade has been concentrated within rather than between industries.[1] Furthermore, there is also evidence that global sourcing of parts and components outpaced even trade in final goods (for data on cross-border production fragmentation see, for instance, Yeats, 2001; Yi, 2003; and Jones, Kierzkowski and Lurong, 2005). In other words, increased trade is at least partly associated with the 'fragmentation' of the production process rather than simply trade in finished products.

At the same time, labour markets in many countries underwent substantial shifts in labour demand, both with respect to skills and occupations. The labour market prospects of the low skilled deteriorated in particular, but other changes affected all skill groups. For example, employment in services gained in importance, both at the lower and upper end of the wage scale. Empirical work also suggests that composition of the labour force within industries and firms has changed along both skill and occupation dimensions (e.g. Bauer and Bender, 2004).

The simultaneous increase in intermediates trade and these changes in the labour market has given rise to a new wave of research on the phenomena of fragmentation, outsourcing, vertical specialisation and their implications for factors of production, income distribution and welfare, with a particular focus on possible links between the dislocation of production and labour market developments.

Most work on vertical specialisation has concentrated on 'north–south' dislocation of components production which is driven by

Heckscher–Ohlin differences in factor endowments across countries. In this literature, firms outsource labour-intensive parts of production from high to low wage countries in order to save on labour costs. Because of this, cross-border production fragmentation is considered to be a possible source of deteriorating labour market prospects, especially with regard to low-skilled workers (e.g. Feenstra and Hanson, 1996; Görg, Hijzen and Hine, 2005; and the overview by Feenstra and Hanson, 2003).[2] However, although Heckscher–Ohlin related vertical specialisation is surely one avenue through which trade may have affected labour markets, it is more closely associated with inter- rather than intra-industry trade, even if some of the components fall into the same industry as the final good. Hence, vertical trade along Heckscher–Ohlin lines is to some extent at variance with the relative growth of intra-industry trade.

Work by François and Nelson (2000), Burda and Dluhosch (2002), Ekholm and Midelfart Knarvik (2005) and others suggests that the process of fragmentation itself may be associated with intra-industry trade and labour market effects in addition to those that arise because of traditional factor-proportions trade. This is for two reasons. First, trade-induced fragmentation may alter the structure of labour demand because it requires more management and services to co-ordinate a production process which is split into a number of production stages, especially if some of those stages are geographically separated. Fragmentation thus affects labour demand with respect to skills and occupations.

Second, and probably more importantly, the process of fragmentation is associated with economies of scale and thus involves imperfect competition and a link towards intra-industry trade. The economies of scale arise from the fixed-cost character of the service links, which primarily depend on the number of production steps but much less on the scale of production within each production block. The role of service links in this process has been pointed out by Jones and Kierzkowski (1990) and, more recently, by Deardorff (2001) and Riezman (2005).[3] François (1990) and Markusen (1989) have examined the economies of scale and increasing returns properties of fragmentation, while increasing returns of intermediates trade has been emphasised by Ethier (1982). If fragmentation is associated with increasing returns it might give rise both to intra-industry trade and to additional labour market and welfare effects.

In fact, as shown in Dluhosch (2006b), even exposure to north–north trade may induce production fragmentation, without any factor-proportion effects driving the process. This will be the case if those services which are required to manage a fragmented production (often called 'business services') are themselves associated with increasing returns. An increase in market size will then increase the productivity of business services, which will encourage firms to switch towards a finer vertical division of labour in order to exploit economies of scale more intensively. In contrast with Heckscher–Ohlin driven fragmentation, the economies of scale aspect seems to have the potential to alleviate Stolper–Samuelson effects of vertical specialisation, even allowing for a trade-off between scale and variety.

This chapter discusses the labour market consequences and implications for individual welfare under imperfect competition, with a particular focus on the cost effectiveness of fragmentation. Section 8.2 presents a model based on the micro-foundations of fragmentation as developed by Burda and Dluhosch (2002) for the integrated economy and by Dluhosch (2006c) for fragmentation and trade with imperfect competition.[4] Section 8.3 links the model to empirical evidence which finds that a considerable (and growing) fraction of trade between industrialised countries is intra-industry in character. Section 8.4 shows that the labour market implications of fragmentation may nevertheless be similar, whether or not fragmentation is associated with inter- or intra-industry trade. Finally, Section 8.5 demonstrates that the welfare effects of fragmentation differ from simple Stolper–Samuelson effects when there is an imperfect competition element, with fragmentation actually extending the range of parameters for which trade proves to be mutually beneficial.

8.2 Fragmentation under imperfect competition

Consider two countries (Home and Foreign) engaged in horizontal trade of (two) sorts of final goods: one homogeneous good x_0 (which also serves as the numeraire); and a number of differentiated goods $x_i(i = 1, \ldots, n)$. Individuals in Home and in Foreign have the following Dixit–Stiglitz (1977) utility function across both groups of goods:

$$U = x_0^{1-\mu} \left(\sum_{i=1}^{n} x_i^{\rho} \right)^{\frac{\mu}{\rho}} \tag{8.1}$$

with μ and $(1 - \mu)$ denoting the expenditure shares of the numeraire and differentiated goods respectively. The elasticity of substitution between the differentiated goods is approximately $1/(1 - \rho) \equiv \eta$ if the number of goods, n, is large. Each of the countries is considered to be populated by a number of high- and low-skilled individuals, $\overline{H}$ and $\overline{L}$, each inelastically supplying one unit of labour to the market and receiving income w_H and w_L respectively. With factor proportions $\kappa \equiv \overline{L}/\overline{H}$, the macroeconomic budget constraint with both of the factors of production fully employed is thus $Y = (w_H + w_L \kappa) \overline{H}$. For a given national income Y and relative price $p_{i,j}$ of the differentiated goods i,j, optimisation gives rise to the following aggregate demand functions $x_0 = (1 - \mu) Y$ (numeraire) and $x_i = \left(\sum_{j=1}^{n} p_j^{\rho/(\rho-1)} \right)^{-1} \mu Y p_i^{-1/(1-\rho)}$ (differentiated good i).

If countries are incompletely specialised, the supply side in each country consists of the two sectors, the numeraire and the differentiated goods sector. In order to simplify the analysis, the numeraire sector is assumed to be a constant returns industry whose production requires low-skilled labour with output $x_0 = L_0$.[5] Production in the differentiated goods sector, in contrast, is characterised by increasing returns and may be subject to fragmentation into a number of production blocks, with final goods supplied under monopolistic competition.

The differentiated goods sector can be further decomposed into three sub-sectors. First, a *manpower industry* combines high- and low-skilled labour (H_P, L_P) into an intermediate service input with $(1-\theta)H_P/(\theta L_P)$ being the marginal rate of substitution between both skill groups.[6] This intermediate service is sold in perfect competition to the second sub-sector, *direct production*, where it is used to produce differentiated goods. The production process in each firm can be fragmented into a number of production blocks, with the extent of fragmentation measured by index z_i. Due to the benefits of specialisation within each production block, marginal costs are lower the more fragmented the production. However, the more fragmented the production, the more it requires the third sub-sector of *management services* (or business services) to co-ordinate the various production stages. Although management depends on the extent of fragmentation, and not on the scale of production x_i, switching towards a more management intensive production may nevertheless pay off because a larger market sustains a higher scale of production and thus allows economies of scale to be exploited. Since management is on average more skill-intensive than many other parts of the economy, we assume that it is produced with high-skilled labour according to the linear production function $Z = H_S$.

If each of the n firms producing differentiated goods has a fragmentation index z_i, total demand for business services is nz_i and price p_Z equilibrates supply and demand. The production costs of firms producing the different varieties can then be decomposed according to whether costs are fixed or variable with respect to output. Some of the costs of the labour service are variable with respect to output and depend on the extent of fragmentation. These costs are assumed to be lower the more extensive the fragmentation. In particular, we will assume that these costs follow the iso-elastic function $\bar{v}z_i^{-\gamma}x_i$, with the parameter γ denoting the effectiveness of fragmentation in cost reduction.[7] However, with multistage production, firms also incur fixed costs in the form of the business services required for co-ordinating the production blocks. With fragmentation index z_i and business services marketed at price p_Z, these fixed costs amount to $p_Z z_i$ for each firm. Rather than treating these costs as exogenous, as in Jones and Kierzkowski (1990), we consider these costs to be determined endogenously by supply and demand. Finally, and in line with conventional approaches to increasing returns, some of the labour service composite is required in the direct production of each firm, independent of the scale of operation, thus giving rise to fixed costs $\bar{F}$. Hence, the profit function of the i-th firm in the differentiated-goods sector is

$$\pi_i = p_i x_i - (\bar{F} + \bar{v}z_i^{-\gamma}x_i + p_Z z_i) \tag{8.2}$$

If firms supply the varieties in monopolistic competition à la Chamberlin to the market, as is traditionally assumed in trade models with increasing returns, optimal behaviour yields output, price, the extent of fragmentation and (via the zero-profit condition) the number of firms in the differentiated goods sector as a function of the relative price of business services. If firms are symmetrical, each will operate on the same scale $x_i = x$, and index of fragmentation $z_i = z$, and each firm will charge the same price $p_i = p$. Hence, we obtain supply and demand for final goods as a function of the relative price of business services (supply) and income (demand).

Both of these variables are in turn determined by labour market conditions. If mobility between sectors in each country is costless, labour will be allocated according to the value marginal product in each sector. With labour markets segmented by skill level, equilibrium in the high-skill labour market thus requires wages to equal value marginal products in the production of differentiated goods and in business services, whereas the low-skill labour market is in equilibrium if wages equal value marginal products in direct production and in the production of the numeraire. With labour markets for both types clearing, sectoral employment of high- (low-) skilled labour adds up to high- (low-) skilled labour supply $H_P + H_S = \bar{H}$ ($L_P + L_S = \bar{L}$). Thus, sectoral output and employment, national income, and the firm level extent of fragmentation are a function of endowments, especially factor proportions.

If the world consists of two identical countries except for differences in endowments (with variables of Foreign distinguished from those of Home by an asterisk), and if both countries are integrated by trade, the relevant endowment is the world supply of high- and low-skilled labour, $\overline{H} + \overline{H}^* = \overline{H}^{ie}$ and $\overline{L} + \overline{L}^* = \kappa\overline{H} + \kappa^*\overline{H}^* = \overline{L}^{ie}$ respectively. Factor proportions in the (integrated) world economy are given by $\kappa^{ie} \equiv (\overline{L} + \overline{L}^*)/(\overline{H} + \overline{H}^*)$. In order to illustrate results in two dimensions, we will assume that both countries hold equal amounts of high-skilled labour so that relative factor supply in the world economy is $\kappa^{ie} = (1 + \omega)\kappa/2$ with $\omega \equiv \kappa^*/\kappa$ a measure of the factor proportions differential. Assuming that the theorem of factor price equalisation holds (that is, countries do not differ too much in terms of factor proportions so that they are incompletely specialised in trading equilibrium), relative wages in terms of the numeraire are a function of factor proportions in the world economy as well as of parameter values of expenditure shares for differentiated goods (μ), the marginal rate of substitution between skill levels in the differentiated-goods production (as measured by θ), the elasticity of substitution between those goods (as described by ρ), and, in particular, the cost effectiveness of fragmentation with respect to variable costs (γ).

8.3   Fragmentation and intra-industry trade

Standard intra-industry trade measures such as the Grubel–Lloyd (1975) index suggest that intra-industry trade (IIT) has increased faster than inter-industry or Heckscher–Ohlin trade. Trade amongst OECD countries is largely IIT (OECD, 2002): in the US, the share of IIT in total manufacturing trade climbed from 64 per cent (1988–91) to 69 per cent (1996–2000). In Germany, the share of IIT rose from 67 per cent to 72 per cent over the same period; in the UK from 70 per cent to 74 per cent. In some Eastern European countries IIT outpaced Heckscher–Ohlin trade by even more: in Poland, it increased from 56 per cent (1992–5) to 63 per cent (1996–2000); in Hungary from 55 to 72 per cent; and in the Czech Republic from 66 to 77 per cent.

If fragmentation is related to economies of scale, the increase in IIT may be linked to fragmentation.[8] We can show this by decomposing world trade with fragmentation into inter-industry and intra-industry trade. Consider first the value of intra-industry trade (in terms of the numeraire) by subtracting the inter-sectoral part of trade from world trade. If Home is the skill-abundant country ($\omega > 1$), world trade is the sum of both countries' gross exports in differentiated goods, plus Home's imports of the numeraire, that is:

$$xpn^T(Y^*/Y^{ie}) + xpn^{T^*}(Y/Y^{ie}) + (x_0^c - x_0^p)$$

where n^T and n^{T^*} denote the number of firms in Home and in Foreign in trading equilibrium, Y, Y^*, Y^{ie} are aggregate income in Home, Foreign and the world economy, and x_0^c, x_0^p the consumption and production of the numeraire. This expression for world trade can be rewritten by noting that, under balanced trade, Home's imports in the numeraire $(x_0^c - x_0^p)$ match its net exports in differentiated goods $(xpn^T(Y^*/Y^{ie}) - xpn^{T^*}(Y/Y^{ie}))$. Taking trade-balance equilibrium into account, world trade is thus twice Home's gross exports in differentiated goods $(2xpn^T(Y^*/Y^{ie}))$. Furthermore, with Foreign being a net exporter of the relatively low skill intensive numeraire, inter-sectoral trade equals Foreign's exports of the numeraire $(x_0^p - x_0^c)$ plus Home's net exports in differentiated goods $xp(n^T(Y^*/Y^{ie}) - n^{T^*}(Y/Y^{ie}))$. Hence, the difference (that is, IIT) is twice Foreign's gross exports in differentiated goods (8.3).

$$\text{IIT} = 2n^{T^*}(Y/Y^{ie})xp = \left(1 + \frac{(\theta + (1-\theta)\gamma\rho)\mu(1+\omega)}{2((1-\mu\theta) - (1-\theta)\mu\gamma\rho)}\right)\mu\kappa\overline{H} \qquad (8.3)$$

If, on the other hand, Home is relatively low skill abundant ($\omega < 1$), IIT is $2n^T(Y^*/Y^{ie})xp$. However, the first derivative of IIT with respect to the cost effectiveness of fragmentation γ is still positive, so IIT unambiguously increases the more effective is fragmentation in curbing marginal production costs. That is, the larger γ and the more extensive the fragmentation, the more intra-industry trade takes place.[9] The economic intuition behind this result is that, as productivity increases with γ, so does (world) market size (measured in terms of world income Y^{ie}), and IIT is known to be increasing in market size.

As well as the volume of IIT increasing, it also accounts for a growing share in world trade (SIIT). With Foreign being the low skill abundant country, that is $\omega > 1$, SIIT is

$$\text{SIIT} = \frac{IIT}{2xpn^T(Y^*/Y^{ie})} = \frac{2 + (\theta + (1-\theta)\gamma\rho)\mu(\omega - 1)}{2\omega - (\theta + (1-\theta)\gamma\rho)\mu(\omega - 1)} \qquad (8.4)$$

which shows that within the relevant parameter range of factor-price equalisation, and for given relative factor proportions ω, SIIT increases with γ. The same holds true for Home being relatively low skill abundant,

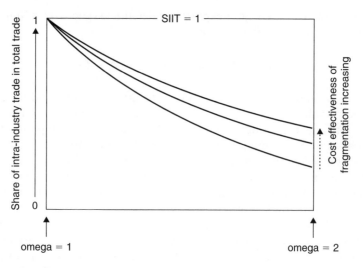

Figure 8.1: Share of intra-industry trade as a function of the differential in factor proportions (ω) and cost effectiveness of fragmentation (γ)

and with SIIT then the reciprocal of (8.4). Hence, the share of intra-industry trade in total trade unambiguously increases in γ, as does fragmentation.

Figure 8.1 displays the share of intra-industry trade as a function of the differential in factor proportions for $1 < \omega < 2$. If countries are the same in every respect, all trade is of the intra-industry type. The more dissimilar the countries are in terms of factor proportions (the larger is ω), the lower is the share of intra-industry trade. However, given $\omega > 1$, the share of intra-industry trade increases in the cost effectiveness of fragmentation (γ), so that the SIIT-function rotates counter-clockwise around the point ($\omega = 1$, SIIT $= 1$). A similar result holds for $\omega < 1$ (not shown), again with the share larger the more similar the countries are in terms of factor proportions, and with SIIT larger the more cost effective the fragmentation, so that in any case, SIIT is larger the larger γ, given the differential in factor proportions.

Because more fragmented production pays in terms of lower marginal costs, differentiated goods whose production is subject to economies of scale also account for a growing share in Home's imports (as can be seen from (8.4)). By the same reasoning, Foreign's exports in differentiated goods represent a larger share in gross exports the more extensive the fragmentation.

IIT, however, is generally regarded as much less disruptive with respect to labour markets, because it is considered to affect the regional compos-ition of product demand, but not necessarily labour demand (Balassa, 1966). Although the general validity of this presumption has been doubted in the literature (see for instance Finger, 1975; Lovely and Nelson, 2002; Greenaway, Haynes and Milner, 2002; Brülhart, Murphy and Strobl, 2004), their findings have not been explicitly linked to the process of fragmentation.

8.4 Fragmentation and labour market adjustment

Though a number of studies have shown that IIT may require more labour adjustment than previously thought, there is still a widespread presumption that IIT has less strong distributional consequences than the Stolper–Samuelson effects of inter-industry trade. We have shown that fragmentation primarily boosts IIT. However, fragmentation may also be accompanied by intra- and inter-sectoral changes in employment similar to those of conventional factor-proportions trade. This is because the demand for skills and occupations changes as firms switch towards a more fragmented production process. Hence, the distinction between inter- and intra-industry trade in terms of labour market effects may in fact be less pronounced than is often thought. In order to focus on the associated labour adjustment induced by fragmentation and trade, in this section we concentrate on the implied shifts in the demand for skills and occupations, while holding labour supply constant.

Consider first inter-sectoral shifts in employment. If business services that are needed for managing a fragmented production process are com-pletely produced in-house, inter-sectoral skill shifts are primarily related to low-skilled labour. That is, provided that Home is the skill abun-dant country, it specialises in high skill intensive differentiated goods, while Foreign expands its production of the numeraire good. For $\omega < 1$, the reverse holds. This fragmentation-augmented specialisation follows traditional comparative advantage along Heckscher–Ohlin lines, where each country specialises in the production of the good in which it enjoys a comparative advantage due to factor abundance.[10]

The magnitude of this inter-sectoral shift largely depends on the cost effectiveness of fragmentation. If Home is relatively skill abundant ($\omega > 1$), employment decreases by less the larger is γ. With constant expenditure shares on both groups of goods, the productivity gains from fragmentation are responsible for the fact that the contraction of Home's numeraire sector is smaller than otherwise. In Foreign, the number of differentiated goods declines by less. Hence, the larger γ, the milder is the effect. The corollary of the inter-sectoral specialisation is a change in the skill intensity of the differentiated goods sector.

However, if, rather than produced in-house, business services are partially outsourced and supplied by a separate business-service sector to firms producing differentiated goods, the impacts of fragmentation and trade on the allocation of labour between direct production and business services depend on parameter values such as the extent of outsourcing, differential factor abundance, the elasticity of substitution between varieties, and the cost effectiveness of fragmentation.

If business services are completely outsourced, the joint impact of fragmentation and trade may be ambiguous, because it may induce either a rise or fall of the skill ratio in the direct production of each firm. For instance, given $\omega > 1$, and with the elasticity being low, the skill ratio increases in Home (Foreign) at high (low) values of γ. The lower the elasticity of substitution between the differentiated goods, the more likely it is that firms employ relatively more high skilled labour as γ becomes larger. In contrast, if the elasticity of substitution is high, domestic firms tend to lower the skill intensity of direct production since operating at larger scale allows them to spread the fixed costs of fragmentation over more units and to gain more from fragmentation. Moreover, the results also depend on factor proportions: the more similar countries are in terms of factor proportions, the smaller is the set of parameter values for which firms in either Home or Foreign employ more high-skilled labour.

However if, at the same time, more business services are produced in-house, the skill ratio may remain unchanged or even increase. Let α be the fraction of business services outsourced. There is a curve of combinations α and γ for which the skill ratio remains unaffected – despite opening up. Figure 8.2 shows the iso-skill-ratio curves of each country assuming that $\omega > 1$. The shaded area above Home's curve represents the set of parameter values for which firms in Home increase their skill ratio while the area below Foreign's curve shows the corresponding set for Foreign.[11] The more low skill abundant Foreign is relative to Home, the further the iso-skill-ratio curves drift apart for any γ and the smaller is thus the range of α, α^* for which all industries employ relatively more high-skilled labour than before opening up to trade. In any case, there is a trade-off in the sense that a larger γ may require a lower α in order for the labour force in direct production to remain unaffected. Yet, if the fraction of business services $(1-\alpha)$ produced in-house differs across countries (that is $\alpha \neq \alpha^*$), skill ratios may increase across all of the industries in all of

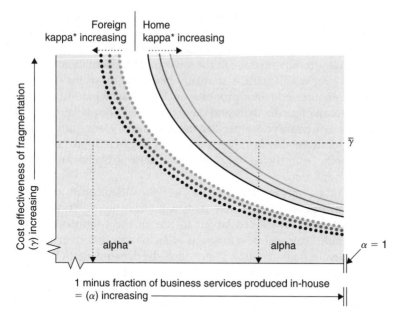

Figure 8.2: Iso-skill-ratio curves with fragmentation augmented trade as a function of α and γ

the countries when opening up, even for a given cost effectiveness of fragmentation.

In contrast to inter-sectoral skill shifts in labour demand, intra-sectoral skill shifts mainly concern high-skilled labour. Due to the factor proportions effect of opening up, firms lower their high-skilled labour force in the skill-abundant country, given the cost effectiveness of fragmentation. The labour thus released, however, finds employment in new firms as the high skill abundant country specialises in differentiated goods. In the low skill abundant country, firms enlarge their high-skilled labour force by absorbing labour from firms closing down, and with the expansion, there is a corresponding increasing in γ.

8.5   Welfare effects of trade with fragmentation

While the labour market effects discussed above resemble those induced by inter-industry trade in a number of aspects, the effects on welfare may differ considerably because there is also an intra-industry trade component involved. Since variety and productivity affect welfare and, since both are subject to change when opening up, factor proportion effects, as described in the previous section, are just one aspect by which trade affects welfare. The intra-industry trade aspects may give rise to additional Pareto-improving trade in the sense that fragmentation increases the range over which trade is mutually beneficial, even for larger differences in countries' factor proportions. With fragmentation, positive effects in terms of productivity and variety are an additional source which may outweigh negative Stolper–Samuelson effects. Hence, unlike pure factor proportions driven trade, trade with fragmentation may result in everybody being better off, thus even passing Buchanan's (1959) unanimity criterion.

If utility functions are described by (8.1), the difference in individual welfare between autarky and free trade will yield the conditions under which high- and low-skilled labour in any of the countries is better off with trade. This will be a function of factor proportions ω and cost effectiveness of fragmentation γ. Provided the demand elasticity is sufficiently elastic so that low-skilled labour is absorbed by the numeraire sector, high-skilled labour in the low skill abundant country may be impaired by Stolper–Samuelson effects as the country specialises away from differentiated goods. Yet, fragmentation relaxes the condition on ω for high-skilled labour to enjoy gains from trade. The difference is due to the productivity effect of trade which the low skill abundant country is able to enjoy when opening up to trade: the price of business services for fragmenting production declines and the fragmentation of production increases. The latter effect makes for a gain which outweighs the loss of income for the scarce factor for a number of parameter values ω. In fact, the critical ω is smaller with fragmentation than without for all parameter values μ, θ, ρ.[12] The first derivative of the condition for an increase in welfare with respect to γ is positive for low- and high-skilled labour in the skill poor country for all values of $\omega < 1$. In contrast to the low skill abundant country, high-skilled labour in the skill abundant country not only enjoys welfare gains from a larger variety of goods but also from an increase in compensation which ensures that it gains from trade. Hence, we can concentrate on tracking down welfare effects for both factors of production in the low skill country. Accordingly, (8.5) and (8.6) show conditions for welfare to improve in this country for low and high skilled labour respectively.

$$\frac{\partial \left(A^{\frac{\mu}{\rho}-\mu} \left(\frac{2}{A}\right)^{\gamma\mu} - 1 \right)}{\partial \gamma} = 2^{\mu\gamma} \mu A^{\frac{\mu(1-\rho(1+\gamma))}{\rho}} \left(\ln 2 - \ln A \right) > 0 \qquad (8.5)$$

$$\frac{\partial (A^{\frac{\mu}{\rho} + (1-\mu) - \gamma\mu} 2^{\gamma\mu - 1} - 1)}{\partial \gamma} = 2^{\mu\gamma} \mu \left(\frac{A}{2} \right) A^{\frac{\mu(1-\rho(1+\gamma))}{\rho}} (\ln 2 - \ln A) > 0 \qquad (8.6)$$

with $A \equiv (1 + \omega)$ for $\omega < 1$ and $A \equiv (1 + \omega)/\omega$ for $\omega > 1$.

Hence, the condition for welfare to increase due to trade is less restrictive on the lower and the upper bound on ω which ensures that all factors enjoy a welfare gain. Therefore, fragmentation also widens the range of parameter values ω for which both economies do better with trade than without. That is, given everything else, Home's (or Foreign's, depending on factor abundance) endowment with low-skilled labour may be larger than otherwise.

As is generally the case with intra- cum inter-industry trade, the critical value of ω depends on the substitutability of products (for the case without fragmentation see Krugman, 1981). Taking the logarithm of the conditions for gains from trade for high- and low-skilled labour in the low skill country and differentiating these expressions with respect to $\rho \equiv (\eta - 1)/\eta$, shows that the impact of trade on individual welfare is a decreasing function of ρ as $-(\mu/\rho^2) \ln(1 + \omega) < 0$ for all $0 < \omega < 1$.[13] The larger ρ, the less likely it is that the country's high-skilled labour gains from trade. Fragmentation again makes a difference, because it lowers the critical ρ for high skilled labour if it is the relatively scarce factor.[14] Solving for ρ, we obtain the critical ρ below which trade is mutually beneficial

$$\rho < \frac{\mu \ln(1 + \omega)}{\ln 2 - (1 - \mu)\ln(1 + \omega) - \mu\gamma(\ln 2 - \ln(1 + \omega))} \qquad (8.7)$$

The last term in the denominator on the RHS is related to the cost effectiveness of fragmentation. Since the RHS of inequality (8.7) increases in γ, fragmentation increases the range of parameter values ρ for which all factors gain from trade, given $\omega < 1$.[15] The condition for ρ can also be restated in terms of a critical γ (given the elasticity of substitution) for which even the scarce factor gains from trade (despite loss of income):

$$\gamma > \frac{\ln 2 - \left(1 + \frac{(1-\rho)}{\rho}\mu\right)\ln(1 + \omega)}{\mu(\ln 2 - \ln(1 + \omega))} \qquad (8.8)$$

Consequently, there exists a curve in $\omega - \gamma$ space that separates those combinations of (ω, γ) for which trade is mutually beneficial from those in which there are conflicts of interest. This curve, which is similar to Figure 8.3 in Krugman (1981) for the case of trade without fragmentation, is displayed in Figure 8.3 for various parameter values ρ.

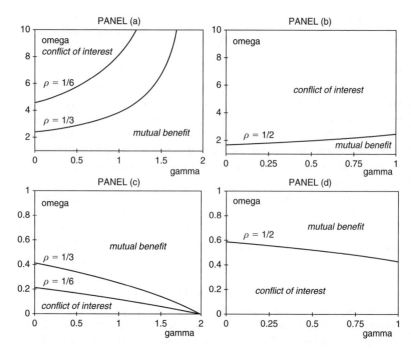

Figure 8.3: Gains from trade as a function of the elasticity of substitution ρ, cost effectiveness of fragmentation γ and factor proportions ω

Assuming that $\omega < 1$, the upper panels show how the elasticity of substitution and the cost effectiveness of fragmentation affect the condition for trade to be mutually beneficial. The lower panels refer to the case of $\omega > 1$. In the upper part of panels (a) and (b), the effects of inter-industry trade dominate: either economies of scale are not all that important or countries are too different in terms of factor proportions. Previously scarce high-skilled labour suffers from a decline in income which is not compensated for by gross benefits from trade. In this case, there is a conflict of interest between high- and low-skilled labour as regards opening up to trade.

The set of parameter values below each curve, by contrast, comprises combinations of ω and γ for which both factors gain from trade – despite its distributional effects. Given ρ, the range of parameter values ω increases in γ, or, to put it differently, a larger γ outweighs the negative effects of a larger ρ (that is less variety). However, for given γ, the region of mutually beneficial trade is smaller the larger ρ.[16] In panels (c) and (d), all combinations of ω and γ above the iso-impact curves are Pareto-superior. Again, the range of mutually beneficial trade increases in γ (for given ρ) and decreases in ρ (for given γ).

As ω approaches zero, the critical γ goes to $\gamma > 1/\mu$; if ω approaches unity, the RHS of (8.8) goes to negative infinity, so that the condition holds for all $0 < \rho < 1$. That is, the less similar countries are, the larger must be the effectiveness of fragmentation in cost reduction if both factors are to gain from trade.

If $\omega < 1$, and if high-skilled labour in the skill-poor country does better with trade than without, both factors in the skill abundant country fare better too. The logged conditions for low- and high-skilled labour are symmetrical to those of the skill-poor country, except for an additional, positive, term.[17] Hence, within the range of parameter values for which trade is mutually beneficial from the perspective of factors in the skill-poor country, both of the other country's factors also benefit. Due to the symmetry of the model, the same applies for $\omega > 1$, with both countries changing roles.

8.6   Summary and directions for future research

This chapter provided a model of the process of production fragmentation and has shown what effect this fragmentation has on the pattern of trade, on consequent labour market adjustment and on welfare. In contrast with much of the early literature, which primarily viewed fragmentation as the result of Heckscher–Ohlin trade in fragments according to comparative advantage, this chapter emphasises the potential of a north–north perspective in that it links the process of production fragmentation to intra-industry trade.

In the spirit of work on increasing returns of intermediates trade under imperfect competition, Section 8.2 presented a model in which the fragmentation of production is related to economies of scale. If fragmentation becomes more effective in reducing variable costs, firms tend to adopt a production process which is more fragmented, with the share of intra-industry trade in total trade increasing. The increase in productivity not only tends to enlarge the range of parameter values for which trade is Pareto-improving, but the larger market also sustains a higher range of fixed costs associated with the business services necessary in the management of a fragmented production process. However, insofar as fragmentation is also tied to factor proportions trade, the labour market implications do in some respects depend on parameter values.

Three areas suggest themselves as promising areas for further research. First, a closer theoretical and empirical examination of economies of scale within the business services sector itself is required. Second, the fact that business services are key to managing a fragmented production process also suggests that occupations should be considered more closely, rather than simply focusing on a single skill-premium. Finally, frictions and rigidities in the labour market are a straightforward extension as they may lead to over-specialisation. However, while rigidities may foster outsourcing, they also may prompt firms to implement less fragmented production, thus actually reducing intra-industry trade. Hence, labour market rigidities may prove more costly than under Heckscher–Ohlin trade with constant returns.

Notes

1. In 2002, the OECD devoted a whole chapter of its *Economic Outlook* to the surge in intra-industry trade.
2. However, recent (empirical) research suggests that the notion of the low skilled being hurt need not generally hold true (see Geishecker and Görg, 2005; Grier, François and Nelson, 2005). On theoretical reasons for off-shore production not necessarily being harmful for labour-intensive industries see Arndt (1998) and Jones and Kierzkowski (2001). On winners and losers see also Deardorff (2005).
3. Although Jones and Kierzkowski highlighted the requirement for service links, they concentrated more on the allocation of fragments with differing factor intensities according to comparative advantage while continuing to assume that production is subject to constant returns.
4. Dluhosch (2006a), in contrast, analyses welfare by comparing trading equilibria with and without fragmentation (rather than investigating what happens when economies open up, as is the perspective adopted in this chapter). Naturally, effects on labour markets and welfare differ in some respects.
5. This assumption reflects the empirical fact that a considerable amount of low-skilled labour is employed, for instance, in the retail sector.
6. The notion of a separate manpower industry serves as a sort of 'can opener' as regards the general equilibrium effects of fragmentation with increasing returns.
7. In order to ensure economically meaningful results in general equilibrium, the cost effectiveness is assumed to be bounded by $\gamma < (1 - \rho)/\rho$.
8. This applies even more if business services are themselves characterised by increasing returns (see Dluhosch, 2006b).
9. Note that with $\omega < 1$, intra-industry trade is

$$IIT = \left(\frac{((2 - \mu\theta) - (1 - \theta)\mu\gamma\rho)(\omega + 1)}{2((1 - \mu\theta) - (1 - \theta)\gamma\mu\rho)} - 1 \right) \mu\kappa\overline{H}$$

which increases in γ as well.

10. Hence, as low-skilled employment in the differentiated goods sector changes in tandem with the number of firms, the skill ratio is driven by countries specialising in the number of firms on the one hand and the allocation of high-skilled labour between occupations (direct production or business services) on the other hand.

11. For parameter values of α between both iso-skill-ratio curves, industries in Home and in Foreign employ relatively more low-skilled labour. Hence, in these cases, the decline in high-skilled employment due to business services expanding is stronger than the firm-level decline in low-skilled employment.

12. See Dluhosch (2006c) for a detailed sensitivity analysis with respect to various parameter values.

13. Therefore, Krugman observes that there exists a critical ρ for which gross benefits from trade outweigh its distributional effects. However, his findings are restricted to trade without fragmentation.

14. The logged condition for welfare to improve for high-skilled labour can be described by the following characteristics: (*i*) as $\omega \rightarrow 1$, it converges to $(\mu(1-\rho)/\rho)\ln 2 > 0$, independent of fragmentation; (*ii*) as $\omega \rightarrow 0$, it approaches $\gamma\mu\ln 2 - \ln 2$, which may be smaller or larger than zero, depending on parameter values μ and γ; (*iii*) it is strictly increasing in ω since the derivative with respect to ω is positive $((\rho + \mu(1 - \rho(1 + \gamma)))/\rho(1 + \omega) > 0)$.

15. Note that, without fragmentation, as ω approaches unity, so does the critical ρ, as in the case of Krugman (1981), so that for all ρ below unity both factors gain from trade.

16. Note that not all values of γ correspond to economically meaningful equilibria. Since fragmentation must not be too effective, the critical γ is bounded by $\gamma < (1 - \rho)/\rho$.

17. For low-skilled labour in the skill-abundant country this is the term $-(\mu(1 - \rho(1 + \gamma))/\rho)\ln \omega$, for high-skilled labour it is $-(\mu(1 - \gamma\rho)/\rho)\ln \omega$. If $\omega < 1$ and $(1 - \rho(1 + \gamma))/(1 - \rho) > 0$ (as assumed), both are positive.

References

Arndt, S. W. (1998). 'Super-Specialization and the Gains from Trade', *Contemporary Economic Policy*, Vol. 16, pp. 480–5.

Balassa, B. (1966). 'Tariff Reductions and Trade in Manufacturing Among the Industrial Countries', *American Economic Review*, Vol. 56, pp. 466–73.

Bauer, T. K. and Bender, S. (2004). 'Technological Change, Organizational Change, and Job Turnover', *Labour Economics*, Vol. 11, pp. 265–91.

Brülhart, M., Murphy, A. and Strobl, E. (2004). 'Intra-industry Trade and Job Turnover', mimeo, University of Lausanne, UCD and University of Louvain.

Buchanan, J. M. (1959). 'Positive Economics, Welfare Economics, and Political Economy', *Journal of Law and Economics*, Vol. 2, pp. 124–38.

Burda, M. and Dluhosch, B. (2002). 'Cost Competition, Fragmentation and Globalization', *Review of International Economics*, Vol. 10, pp. 424–41.

Deardorff, A. V. (2001). 'International Provision of Trade Services, Trade and Fragmentation', *Review of International Economics*, Vol. 9, pp. 233–48.

Deardorff, A. V. (2005). 'Gains from Trade and Fragmentation', University of Michigan Discussion Paper No. 543.

Dixit, A. and Stiglitz, J. E. (1977). 'Monopolistic Competition and Optimum Product Diversity', *American Economic Review*, Vol. 67, pp. 297–308.

Dluhosch, B. (2006a). 'Intra-industry Trade and the Gains from Fragmentation', *North American Journal of Economics and Finance*, Vol. 17, pp. 49–64.

Dluhosch, B. (2006b). 'Intra-industry Trade Exposure, Fragmentation and Labour Adjustment', *Journal of Economic Integration*, Vol. 21, pp. 318–39.

Dluhosch, B. (2006c). 'Integration, Fragmentation, and the Geography of Welfare', *Scandinavian Journal of Economics*, Vol. 108, pp. 459–79.

Ekholm, K. and Midelfart Knarvik, K. H. (2005). 'Relative Wages and Trade-induced Changes in Technology', *European Economic Review*, Vol. 49, pp. 1637–63.

Ethier, W. F. (1982). 'National and International Returns to Scale in the Modern Theory of International Trade', *American Economic Review*, Vol. 72, pp. 389–405.

Feenstra, R. C. and Hanson, G. H. (1996). 'Globalization, Outsourcing, and Wage Inequality', *American Economic Review*, Vol. 86, pp. 240–5.

Feenstra, R. C. and Hanson, G. H. (2003). 'Global Production Sharing and Rising Inequality: a Survey in Trade and Wages', in E. K. Choi and J. Harrigan (eds), *Handbook of International Trade*. Oxford: Basil Blackwell.

Finger, J. M. (1975). 'Trade Overlap and Intra-Industry Trade', *Economic Inquiry*, Vol. 13, pp. 581–9.

François, J. (1990). 'Producer Services, Scale, and the Division of Labour', *Oxford Economic Papers*, Vol. 42, pp. 715–29.

François, J. and Nelson, D. R. (2000). 'Victims of Progress: Economic Integration, Specialization and Wages for Unskilled Labour', CEPR Discussion Paper No. 2527.

Geishecker, I. and Görg, H. (2005). 'Do Unskilled Workers Always Lose from Fragmentation?', *North American Journal of Economics and Finance*, Vol. 16, pp. 81–92.

Görg, H., Hijzen, A. and Hine, R. (2005). 'International Outsourcing and the Skill Structure of Labour Demand in the United Kingdom', *Economic Journal*, Vol. 115, pp. 860–78.

Greenaway, D., Haynes, M. and Milner, C. (2002). 'Adjustment, Employment Characteristics and Intra-Industry Trade', *Weltwirtschaftliches Archiv*, Vol. 138, pp. 254–76.

Grier, K., François, J. and Nelson, D. R. (2005). 'Globalization, Roundaboutness and Relative Wages', mimeo, University of Oklahoma, Tinbergen Institute, Tulane University and Leverhulme Centre.

Grubel, H. and Lloyd, P. (1975). *Intra-industry Trade*. London: Macmillan.

Jones, R. W. and Kierzkowski, H. (1990). 'The Role of Services in Production and International Trade: a Theoretical Framework', in R.W. Jones and A. O. Krueger (eds), *The Political Economy of International Trade*. Oxford: Basil Blackwell, pp. 31–48.

Jones, R. W. and Kierzkowski, H. (2001). 'Globalization and the Consequences of International Fragmentation', in R. Dornbusch, G. Calvo, and M. Obstfeld, (eds), *Money, Capital Mobility and Trade*. Cambridge, MA: MIT Press, pp. 365–84.

Jones, R. W., Kierzkowski, H. and Lurong, C. (2005). 'What Does Evidence Tell Us About Fragmentation and Outsourcing?', *International Review of Economics and Finance*, Vol. 16, pp. 305–16.

Krugman, P. R. (1981). 'Intraindustry Specialization and the Gains from Trade', *Journal of Political Economy*, Vol. 89, pp. 959–74.

Lovely, M. and Nelson, D. R. (2002). 'Intra-industry Trade as an Indicator of Labour Market Adjustment', *Weltwirtschaftliches Archiv,* Vol. 138, pp. 179–206.

Markusen, J. R. (1989). 'Trade in Producer Services and in Other Specialized Inputs', *American Economic Review,* Vol. 79, pp. 85–95.

OECD (2002). *Economic Outlook.* Paris: OECD.

Riezman, R. G. (ed.) (2005). 'Fragmentation and Services in the Modern Economy'. *Special Issue North American Journal of Economics and Finance,* Vol. 16, No. 1.

Yeats, A. J. (2001). 'Just How Big is Global Production Sharing?', in S. W. Arndt and H. Kierzkowski (eds), *Fragmentation: New Production Patterns in the World Economy.* Oxford: Oxford University Press, pp. 108–43.

Yi, K.-M. (2003). 'Can Vertical Specialization Explain the Growth of World Trade?', *Journal of Political Economy,* Vol. 111, pp. 52–102.

9
The Labour Market Impact of International Outsourcing

Ingo Geishecker, Holger Görg and Sara Maioli

9.1 Introduction

Over recent years the phenomenon of international outsourcing has provoked a considerable amount of public concern and anxiety. Despite the advocated benefits in terms of efficiency gains, the prevalent view appears to be that international outsourcing severely threatens domestic jobs and wages, in particular for low-skilled workers. However, this view is mainly fuelled by anecdotal evidence since, despite the strong public interest, academic research which analyses the phenomenon of outsourcing empirically is only in its infancy. Also, from a theoretical point of view, the effects of international outsourcing on the labour market outcomes for low-skilled workers seem to be ambiguous.

If one looks at labour markets across industrialised countries it is a common stylised fact that over the past decades the share of low-skilled workers in total employment has been steadily declining and, importantly, this process has been taking place within most manufacturing industries (see, for example, Berman, Bound and Machin, 1998; Machin and Van Reenen, 1998 for a number of OECD countries). At the same time, the relative wages of low-skilled workers have been falling substantially in many countries (Feenstra and Hanson, 2001) while in some countries, such as Germany, relative wages appear to have remained constant (Fitzenberger, 1999), accompanied by sharp increases in relative unemployment rates of low-skilled workers (Reinberg and Hummel, 2005). While it is widely accepted in the literature that skill biased technological change is at least partly responsible for this development, the role of international trade, and more specifically international outsourcing, is still surrounded by much controversy.

This chapter gives an overview of a number of recent studies on the labour market impact of international outsourcing. It surveys evidence on the extent to which outsourcing affects the demand for low-skilled workers and, thus, poses a threat to low-skilled jobs and wages. In Section 9.2, we first discuss ways of quantifying international outsourcing and provide an overview of its development over recent years in Germany and the UK. We focus on these two countries for a number of reasons: firstly, they are two of the main economies in the European Union but, as noted above, have shown different developments in terms of labour market outcomes for low-skilled workers, and have different labour market institutions; secondly, as we discuss below, much of the empirical evidence for European countries looks at these two economies.

Section 9.3 briefly discusses the theoretical literature on international outsourcing and summarises the predicted labour market impact. Section 9.4 gives an overview of the large body of literature that empirically assesses the impact of international outsourcing within an industry panel framework. However, industry level studies suffer from a number of shortcomings such as aggregation bias, potential endogeneity bias or poor skill classifications. A number of more recent papers take these shortcomings into account and analyse the effects of outsourcing using individual worker data. This literature is introduced in Section 9.5. Section 9.6 summarises and draws some conclusions.

9.2 Stylised facts on outsourcing

As a working definition, we understand outsourcing to be the process of splitting production processes into several stages that are carried out at different locations. In principle this process can be entirely domestic, leaving all production stages within a single country. However, in open economies, firms may economise on lower production costs abroad. Outsourcing therefore becomes international; it reorganises production within a potentially global network of domestic firms, foreign subsidiaries and subcontractors and is characterised by an intensive trade in intermediate goods. Anecdotal evidence on firms shifting production stages abroad by subcontracting to legally independent suppliers or establishing foreign production sites is manifold. However, systematically measuring the process of international outsourcing presents a challenge.

Most authors rely on trade statistics, exploiting the close relation between international outsourcing and trade in intermediate goods.

Authors such as Yeats (2001) seek to measure international outsourcing or, as he calls it, production sharing, by directly quantifying trade in intermediate goods, assessing the intermediate character of the traded goods on the basis of disaggregated goods classifications. His calculations indicate that trade in machinery and transport equipment parts and components accounts for about 30 per cent of total trade in that sector and is growing rapidly. Within the machinery and transport equipment sector, imported parts and components in 1995 accounted for 14.1 per cent of the production value in the European Union, 6.7 per cent in Japan and 11.6 per cent in North America. Clearly, this indicates the large role of international outsourcing within this industry. However, these calculations most likely are upward biased, as imported parts and components (of machinery and transport equipment) are assumed to be intermediate goods imports of the respective broader industry that produces such parts and components itself (machinery and transport equipment industry). This abstracts from the possibility that parts and components from one industry can also be used by other manufacturing and service industries or by final consumers.

Authors such as Feenstra and Hanson (1999) or Campa and Goldberg (1997) quantify international outsourcing by combining input coefficients from input-output tables and trade data. The estimated value of imported intermediate inputs of an industry thereby largely depends on whether one applies a 'narrow' or a 'wide' definition of international outsourcing.

Campa and Goldberg (1997) assume that the total sum of imported intermediate goods in each industry as a share of the respective industry's production value represents a reasonable indicator for international outsourcing. They present industry level calculations for four OECD countries. In US manufacturing, the calculated average outsourcing intensity doubled from 4.1 per cent in 1975 to 8.2 per cent in 1995. In the UK, the outsourcing intensity in manufacturing increased from 13.4 per cent in 1974 to 21.6 per cent in 1993, while over the same period it rose from 15.8 to 20.2 per cent in Canadian manufacturing. Only in Japan did the average manufacturing outsourcing intensity fall, from 8.2 per cent in 1974 to 4.1 per cent in 1993.

However, according to Feenstra and Hanson (1999), the above definition might be too broad if one understands international outsourcing to be the result of a make-or-buy decision. Following this approach, it is not the total sum of imported intermediate inputs, but only the part that could be produced within the respective domestic industry that actually constitutes outsourcing. However, depending on the aggregation level, the range of products that an industry can produce varies. Accordingly, the more highly aggregated the industries are, the broader the definition of international outsourcing becomes. Specifically, Feenstra and Hanson (1999) show that, in US manufacturing, narrowly defined outsourcing intensity, calculated as the sum of intermediate imports of an industry from the same two digit industry in relation to total industry expenditure for non-energy inputs, increased from 2.2 per cent in 1972 to 5.7 per cent in 1990.

In a related article, Hummels et al. (2001) combine input-output tables and trade data to measure what they call vertical specialisation by quantifying inputs that are both imported and subsequently processed and used in exported goods. Although the concept of vertical specialisation is different from international outsourcing, it is at least loosely related in that it is concerned with the specialisation of a country in a specific segment of the international value chain of production. The authors' calculations for thirteen countries indicate that between the early 1970s and the early 1990s, vertical specialisation significantly increased in all countries except Japan.

An alternative approach to quantifying international outsourcing draws heavily on data on 'outward processing trade'. Regularly, tariff regulations of industrialised countries provide specific exemptions for goods that are exported, further processed or assembled abroad and subsequently reimported. As a result, customs authorities collect specific data on these transactions. Yeats (2001) reports that in 1989, imports to the US under the outward processing trade regulation accounted for about 16 per cent of all US imports. Görg (2000), using Eurostat data for EU countries, shows that this type of trade accounted for roughly 20 per cent of imports from the US into the EU in 1994, while Egger and Egger (2001) find that outward processing exports by EU manufacturing increased by 6 per cent per year between 1995 and 1997.

However, it is important to stress that the available data most likely underestimate the true importance of outward processing trade, because many imports are already exempt from tariffs due to bilateral and multilateral trade agreements, and are therefore not separately measured, even though they constitute outward processing trade (Yeats, 2001). Also, more importantly, outward processing trade, even if accurately measured, by definition only constitutes a fraction of international outsourcing. Inputs from foreign affiliates or subcontractors that are not outward processing trade are completely neglected. Hence, arguably, the aforementioned strategies that combine trade data and input-output tables are better suited to measure international outsourcing.

To quantify and compare outsourcing intensity in the United Kingdom and Germany we construct two measures of international outsourcing that follow the concepts proposed in Feenstra and Hanson (1996, 1999) and Campa and Goldberg (1997). Narrow international outsourcing is measured as the shift of a two digit industry's *core activities* abroad, represented by the value of the industry's imported intermediate inputs from the *same* industry abroad, as a share of the domestic industry's production value. The challenge is to measure the respective industry's imports of intermediate goods. A simple procedure would be to assume that all imports from a certain industry i^* abroad are directed towards the respective domestic industry i and nowhere else. Essentially, this would amount to the construction of industry level import penetration ratios, which are however rather poor measures of industries' outsourcing activities. Instead, input-output data are utilised in order to allocate imports according to their usage as input factors across industries.

The use of input-output tables renders obsolete the differentiation of intermediate goods on the basis of disaggregated goods classifications. Imports are always counted as intermediate goods imports if they are used in the production of manufacturing industries.

Formally, narrow outsourcing is constructed as:

$$OUTS_{it}^{narrow} = \frac{IMP_{i^*t} \times \Omega_{i^*it}}{Y_{it}} \tag{9.1}$$

with IMP_{i^*t} denoting imported inputs from industry i^* abroad and Y_{it} the production value of industry i at time t. Ω_{i^*it} denotes the share of imports from the foreign industry i^* consumed by the domestic industry i in t with $\sum_{i=1}^{I} IMP_{i^*t} \times \Omega_{i^*it} = total$ *imports* from industry i^* used in manufacturing in t. Adding imports used in agriculture, mining, services, private and public consumption, investment, supply inventory and exports yields the total amount of imports from the foreign industry i^*.

Loosening the concept of an industry's *core activities* and following Campa and Goldberg (1997), wide outsourcing is defined somewhat less conservatively as a two digit industry's purchase of intermediate goods from abroad represented by the respective industry's sum of imported intermediate goods from *all* manufacturing industries j relative to the

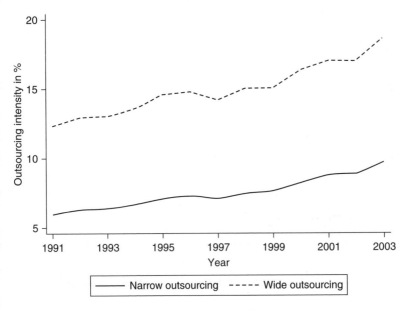

Figure 9.1: International outsourcing in UK manufacturing

domestic industry's production value:

$$OUTS_{it}^{wide} = \frac{\sum\limits_{j^*=1}^{J} IMP_{j^*t} \times \Omega_{j^*it}}{Y_{it}} \quad (9.2)$$

Figures 9.1 and 9.2 show the development of international outsourcing in the manufacturing sector in the UK and Germany between 1991 and 2003.[1] In the UK in 2003 the outsourcing intensity was 9.5 per cent following the narrow definition (as in Equation (9.1)) and 18.5 per cent applying the wide definition (as in Equation (9.2)). In Germany narrow outsourcing is, with 7.2 per cent, somewhat less pronounced while wide outsourcing, with 19.6 per cent, slightly exceeds the UK value.

As is apparent in Figures 9.1 and 9.2, in both countries international outsourcing has grown substantially over recent years, and the development of narrowly and broadly defined outsourcing appears to be fairly parallel. For the UK, narrowly defined international outsourcing increased significantly by around 59 per cent while broadly defined outsourcing increased by around 50 per cent between 1991 and 2003.

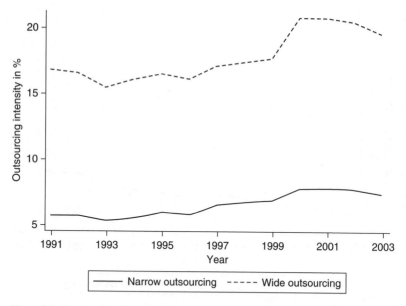

Figure 9.2: International outsourcing in German manufacturing

Over the same period, increases in the outsourcing intensity were significantly less pronounced in German manufacturing, with 27 per cent for narrow and 16 per cent for wide outsourcing.

As demonstrated by Geishecker (2006), by differentiating imports by source countries, one can construct outsourcing proxies for different geographic regions, at least if one is willing to assume that Ω_{i*it} is constant across regions. Equations (9.3) and (9.4) show the decomposition of the outsourcing measure by geographic region, which is simply additive since the denominator is always the same and the weight Ω_{i*it} is assumed to be constant across regions:

$$OUTS_{it}^{narrow} = \frac{IMP_{i*t} \times \Omega_{i*it}}{Y_{it}} = \frac{\sum\limits_{c=1}^{C} IMP_{i*ct} \times \Omega_{i*it}}{Y_{it}} \tag{9.3}$$

$$OUTS_{it}^{wide} = \frac{\sum\limits_{j*=1}^{J} IMP_{j*t} \times \Omega_{j*it}}{Y_{it}} = \frac{\sum\limits_{c=1}^{C} \sum\limits_{j*=1}^{J} IMP_{j*ct} \times \Omega_{j*it}}{Y_{it}} \tag{9.4}$$

where c indicates the geographic region.

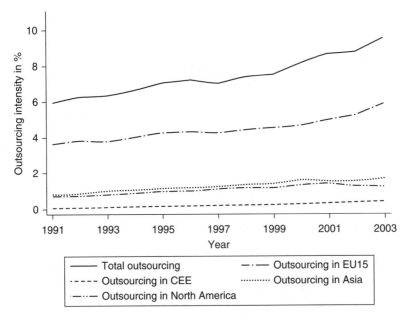

Figure 9.3: Narrow outsourcing in UK manufacturing by region

Figures 9.3 and 9.4 show the development of narrowly defined international outsourcing to the European Union (EU15), Central and Eastern Europe (CEE), Asia, North America and the whole world for the entire manufacturing sector for the UK and Germany, respectively.[2] From the figures it is evident that for the UK as well as Germany the large majority of outsourcing takes place within the European Union (EU15). In comparison, outsourcing to North America, Asia or Central and Eastern Europe is of much lower magnitude, although for Germany outsourcing towards Central and Eastern Europe is growing rapidly. Evidently most outsourcing does not occur in the direction of low wage countries, but takes place among countries with reasonably similar productivity and wages. This indicates the importance of other factors, such as economies of scale, as determinants of international outsourcing.

Summarising, international outsourcing has grown substantially, particularly in the UK, but also in German manufacturing. Nevertheless, the intensity of international outsourcing is somewhat more pronounced in German than in UK manufacturing. However, regarding the geographic distribution of international outsourcing, both countries have similar patterns with outsourcing towards the EU15 taking the largest share.

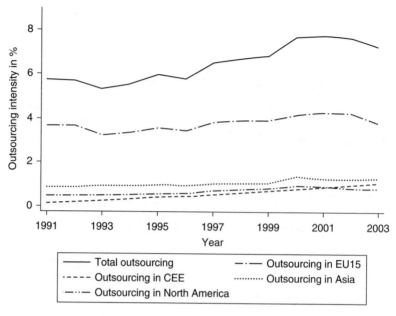

Figure 9.4: Narrow outsourcing in German manufacturing by region

9.3   Theoretical background

Given the increasing importance of international outsourcing, it has been of much concern as to what the potential implications of this are for labour market outcomes, in particular for low-skilled workers in industrialised countries. Over recent years, a number of theoretical contributions such as Feenstra and Hanson (1996), Arndt (1997, 1999), Deardorff (2001, 2002), Jones and Kierzkowski (2001) and Kohler (2004) have greatly advanced theoretical insights into the potential effects of international outsourcing for different skill groups. However, the implications of international outsourcing in terms of relative factor demand are not clear-cut.

For example, Feenstra and Hanson (1996) formulate a model of international outsourcing, which is a specific form of a Heckscher–Ohlin type model with only one final good and two countries, North and South, one specialising in high skill production and the other in low skill production. By changing relative unit costs of production, for instance due to capital flows from the North to the South or Hicks-neutral technological progress in the South, production fragments, with low skill intensity production shifting from the North to the South, which raises the average skill intensity of production in both regions. As a result, relative demand for skilled labour increases in both the North and in the South. Thus, international outsourcing has the same effects as factor biased technological change, which simultaneously occurs worldwide, i.e. in both countries.[3]

Similarly, Arndt (1997, 1999) develops a model of international outsourcing that is also based on a Heckscher–Ohlin type framework, but makes less restrictive assumptions. In his setting he considers trade between a small price-taking economy and the rest of the world, allowing for two factors of production and two final goods. If, within the model, the low skill intensive industry shifts some fragments of production abroad, this results in a productivity improvement in the low skill intensive industry and, with given world prices, ultimately in higher relative wages for low-skilled workers. Thus, the effects of outsourcing correspond to sector biased technological change.[4]

However, it is also easily conceivable that the high skill intensive industry shifts some less skill intensive fragments of production abroad. Again, this acts as technological progress in the skill intensive sector and thus raises (lowers) relative wages for high-skilled (low-skilled) workers. Both scenarios are, in principle, equally plausible, and outsourcing can therefore lead to relative wage gains or losses for low-skilled workers.

To complicate things, if one considers a Heckscher–Ohlin type model with many goods and many factors, as in Jones and Kierzkowski (2001) or Deardorff (2001), the implications of international outsourcing become even more ambiguous. Thus, depending on the models' assumptions and framework, low-skilled workers could either gain or lose from international outsourcing in terms of relative wages.

What is important to note, however, is that all of the aforementioned general equilibrium models assume that labour market adjustments are achieved by sufficiently flexible relative wages. Although this may be justifiable in the long run, in the medium and short run, especially in many European countries, relative wages might be fairly rigid. If this is the case, labour market adjustments to international outsourcing have to be achieved mainly by changes in employment. More specifically, Krugman (1995) stresses the implications of rigid relative factor prices for employment and welfare in a parsimonious two country, two factor and two sector model. With rigid relative wages, relative factor proportions (that is the ratio of skilled to unskilled workers) are also fixed in each sector. Thus, there is not sufficient scope for low-skilled workers from the low skill intensive sector to move into the high skill intensive sector. As a result reduced demand for low-skill intensive goods has to be met by unemployment of low-skilled workers. Furthermore, due to reduced employment, domestic income also falls, multiplying the immediate adverse effect.

Another important limitation of the aforementioned models that needs to be kept in mind is that they generally abstract from adjustment costs. However, as authors such as Davidson and Matusz (2004) convincingly show, if displaced workers experience spells of unemployment and in some cases have to be retrained, short-run adjustment costs can consume a significant part of the overall gains from international trade (see Chapter 2 of this volume). In terms of policy recommendations it is therefore important not only to focus on the long-run effects of international outsourcing, but also to obtain a better understanding of its immediate short-run effects.

9.4   Empirical evidence: industry level

In the last few years there has been an upsurge of empirical studies assessing the labour market impact of international outsourcing. The first strand of this literature has used industry level data and has been concerned mainly with partial equilibrium effects, as labour is implicitly or explicitly assumed to be immobile between sectors.[5] We review a number of these contributions in this section.[6]

Feenstra and Hanson (1996) provide one of the first empirical assessments of the impact of international outsourcing on the relative demand for low-skilled workers. In their study for the United States they approximate international outsourcing by the share of imports from a particular industry abroad in total domestic demand for that industry's products. Their empirical model is based on a translog cost function with capital as a quasi-fixed input. From this cost function, a cost share equation for non-production workers is derived. In order to assess the impact of outsourcing, Feenstra and Hanson extend the cost share equation to include each industry's outsourcing intensity. Following this procedure the authors report that approximately 15–33 per cent of the increase of the cost share of non-production labour over the period 1979–87 can be explained by international outsourcing. In a follow-up study, Feenstra and Hanson (1999) apply the narrow definition of international outsourcing (as discussed in Section 9.2) by focusing on imported intermediate inputs of an industry from the same industry abroad. According to this study international outsourcing can explain between 11 per cent and 15 per cent of the observed decline in the cost share of production labour in US manufacturing between 1979 and 1990.

Morrison-Paul and Siegel (2001) extend the above studies by simultaneously incorporating several trade and technology related measures that can shift relative labour demand in a system of factor demand equations. Their results suggest that international outsourcing, as well as trade and technological change, significantly lowered relative demand for low skilled labour in the US.

Kletzer (2000) follows a different approach. Instead of focusing on net labour demand effects, as in the above papers, she is concerned with industry level displacement rates and analyses the role of changes in exports, import penetration and imported intermediate goods, which arguably correspond to international outsourcing, for the US. While the author finds that overall import penetration increases industry displacement rates significantly, imports of intermediate goods have no effect. Furthermore, when she controls for industry fixed effects, even overall import penetration is rendered insignificant.

As regards evidence for European countries, a number of studies should be mentioned. In one of the first studies, Anderton and Brenton (1999) look at the case of the UK and estimate the impact of outsourcing for a panel of eleven disaggregated (low skill intensive) textile and (high skill intensive) mechanical engineering industries. The authors approximate outsourcing by industry level import penetration ratios, but distinguish between imports from low and high wage countries. While the effect of import penetration is, in general, not statistically significant for the mechanical engineering industries, in the textiles industry up to 40 per cent of the observed rise in the cost share of skilled workers between 1970 and 1983 can be explained by import penetration from low wage countries. To take account of Krugman's (1995) point that adjustment may be through unemployment rather than wages, they also examine the effect of outsourcing on the employment share of skilled relative to unskilled workers. Again, they find no statistically significant results for the engineering industry, but a positive relationship in the textile industry: import penetration can explain up to 33 per cent of the rise in the employment share of skilled relative to unskilled workers over the observed periods. Hence, for the UK, adjustment works through both the wage and employment channels. This may not be too surprising, as it has a relatively flexible labour market compared to other European countries.

Hijzen, Görg and Hine (2005) extend the work of Anderton and Brenton (1999) using data for UK manufacturing industries for 1982 to 1996.

They measure international outsourcing in a similar manner to Feenstra and Hanson (1996, 1999), as a share of imported intermediate inputs – arguably a more appropriate measure of outsourcing than the import penetration ratio used by Anderton and Brenton. Their data cover all manufacturing sectors, and they simultaneously estimate a system of four variable factor demands (skilled, semi-skilled, unskilled labour and materials) using panel data techniques. Estimating a system of variable factor demands provides more detailed information on the impact of structural change on industry level factor demands. They find strong evidence that international outsourcing reduces the demand for unskilled labour in the UK. They also estimate cost and employment share equations and, similar to Anderton and Brenton, find these effects to be present in both settings.

Turning to a European country with arguably fairly rigid labour markets (certainly compared to the UK or US), Falk and Koebel (2002) present an analysis of the effect of outsourcing on wages using industry level data for Germany. They use a Box-Cox cost function, which nests the normalised quadratic as well as the translog functional form, and estimate elasticities of substitution from a system of input-output equations. International outsourcing is implemented in the model as a flexible choice variable captured by relative prices for imported intermediate goods and purchased services. Their findings suggest that between 1978 and 1990, neither imported material inputs nor purchased services substituted for unskilled labour in German manufacturing industries.

Their approach can be criticised since the impact of international outsourcing is only captured by relative price changes for imported intermediate inputs. However, intensified international outsourcing is consistent with unchanging or even increasing observed relative prices for imported intermediate inputs. Factors such as trade liberalisation, the opening up of former communist states or new advances in communication technologies reduce the costs of outsourcing. These developments are not necessarily reflected in relative prices for intermediate goods if outsourcing costs were previously prohibitive.

In a more recent study for Germany, Geishecker (2006) uses the Feenstra and Hanson (1996, 1999) approach, measuring international outsourcing as the value of imported intermediate goods. His focus is on the impact of outsourcing (implemented as a technological shift parameter) on the relative demand for low-skilled workers in Germany during the 1990s, differentiating between the effects of outsourcing to different geographic regions. Furthermore, following authors such as

Egger and Egger (2003), he applies instrumental variable techniques to account for the endogeneity of international outsourcing using lagged outsourcing values as instruments. In this study, international outsourcing is found to be an important factor for reducing the relative demand for manual workers in German manufacturing. Distinguishing outsourcing by geographic regions, Geishecker finds that outsourcing to the European Union has no statistically significant impact. By contrast, a one percentage point increase in outsourcing towards Central and Eastern Europe lowers the wage bill share of manual workers by more than four percentage points for narrow outsourcing and by almost three percentage points for wide outsourcing. By way of assessing the economic relevance of these estimates, Geishecker (2006) demonstrates that increased international outsourcing to Central and East Europe can explain around 50 per cent of the overall decline in the wage bill share of manual workers during the 1990s. This contrasts strongly with the earlier findings of Falk and Koebel (2002) who find no significant impact of outsourcing on the relative demand for low-skilled (manual) workers.

Although the industry level studies discussed in this section have, in general, greatly advanced the understanding of the labour market effects of international outsourcing, they have some inherent shortcomings that potentially limit the applicability of their findings. First of all, the use of aggregated industry level data can seriously bias estimated coefficients as individual heterogeneity is not captured by unconditional industry means of employment and wages. Furthermore, most industry level studies assume international outsourcing to be exogenous to labour demand, an assumption that is rarely tested. If international outsourcing is, however, jointly determined with the demand for labour, estimated coefficients suffer from endogeneity bias. Authors such as Egger and Egger (2003) and Geishecker (2006) propose instrumental variable techniques to overcome this problem. However, finding valid instruments may, however, prove to be difficult in practice. Finally, aggregated industry level data typically suffer from poor skill classifications, with most studies associating non-manual workers with high skills and manual workers with low skills. Clearly, this is only a crude approximation, however, and due to limited data availability at the industry level it is hard to assess the extent to which this affects the estimation results.

9.5   Empirical evidence: micro level

More recently, a new strand of the literature has attempted to overcome these shortcomings by using firm or individual level data and assessing the impact of international outsourcing in a microeconometric framework.

The aggregation bias of industry level studies concerns the failure of such studies to control for individual heterogeneity, i.e. compositional changes within the sample. Individual labour market outcomes are determined by a wide range of characteristics such as age, marital status, education, occupation or firm size. In addition, unobserved individual characteristics play an important role. Simply calculating unconditional industry means of individual labour market outcomes neglects these heterogeneous determinants and is therefore inappropriate if the composition of the workforce changes. Moreover, even if the composition of an industry's workforce does not change, there is the possibility of a time constant selection of certain characteristics into the respective industry which could deliver biased results if, for example, firms with certain worker characteristics are more likely to outsource and also more likely to pay higher wages. Aggregation to the industry level without controlling for this process leads to an omitted variable bias as the error term is correlated with the industry's outsourcing intensity. While the latter problem of time constant selection is easy to tackle in industry level studies by allowing for an unobserved industry fixed effects, the former problem of compositional change is more difficult to address. The use of micro level data, however, allows one to control adequately for micro level observed and unobserved heterogeneity.

Despite these potential advantages, only a few studies have used firm level data to look at the labour market effects of international outsourcing. Head and Ries (2002) use Japanese firm level data to look at the effect of international outsourcing on relative labour demand at the level of the plant. They find that Japanese firms that increase employment in foreign affiliates in low income countries raise the skill intensity of employment in their headquarters (as measured by the share of non-production workers). No such effect is apparent for firms outsourcing production to high income countries.

Görg and Hanley (2005) examine the effect of international outsourcing on labour demand at the plant level using data for the Irish electronics sector. Estimating a dynamic employment equation they find that, in the short run, plant level labour demand is significantly reduced by outsourcing. In addition, they are able to separate the effects of outsourcing of materials from that of services and find that the former has a stronger impact than the latter. However, due to data limitations they cannot extend the analysis to distinguish between high- and low-skilled labour. In addition, they point out that their analysis, being concentrated on one sector only, fails to pick up overall economy-wide employment gains, because it merely captures employment losses within this one sector. Hence it fails to pick up extra-sectoral employment leakages.

Since the labour market effects of outsourcing ultimately concern individual workers, it is fruitful to examine individual worker data. However, to date, only a few studies have done so, using household panel data combined with industry level outsourcing measures. The use of this type of data arguably has some further advantages. Due to the disaggregated nature of the analysis, the potential endogeneity of industry level variables (in particular outsourcing) is considerably reduced, as individual characteristics are unlikely to affect industry level aggregates. In addition, individual level data typically provide more detailed information about individual skills than do industry or firm level data.

Geishecker and Görg (2008) look at the wage effects of international outsourcing for the years 1991–2000 using individual worker data for Germany from the German Socio-Economic Panel. This is combined with industry level information on outsourcing from input-output tables. They, thereby, extend the work by Geishecker (2006) who found, using industry level data, that there are relative wage effects of international outsourcing. Furthermore, Geishecker and Görg (2004) extend the literature by employing more accurate definitions of workers' skill levels. One definition distinguishes three skill categories that comply with the International Standard Classification of Education (ISCED), and the other applies a skill grouping that is based on required on the job skills rather than educational attainment. Utilising the more detailed micro data, Geishecker and Görg (2008) incorporate the industry's international outsourcing activity as a shift parameter in a Mincerian wage model and find that outsourcing has had a marked impact on wages. For workers in the lowest skill categories, real wages were reduced by up to 1.5 per cent while real wages for high-skilled workers grew up to 2.1 per cent.

In addition to the wage effects, Geishecker (2008) focuses on the employment effects of international outsourcing using the same database as in Geishecker and Görg (2008). Specifically, he investigates the impact of outsourcing on job security, i.e. the risk of exiting employment, capturing the risk of leaving employment within a micro-level hazard rate model.[7] The main advantage is that he can control for a wide range of person-specific observed and unobserved characteristics and, most importantly, for duration dependence. He finds that international outsourcing over the period 1991 to 2000 significantly increases the individual risk of leaving employment by 13 per cent. However, he does not find significant differences in the impact of international outsourcing on employment security for the different skill groups (low, medium and high skilled). This is an interesting result as it diverges from the findings of industry level studies that typically identify low-skilled workers as more adversely affected by international outsourcing than high-skilled workers. It is important to keep in mind, though, the finding by Geishecker and Görg (2008) that wages for unskilled workers are negatively affected by international outsourcing, while those for skilled workers are positively affected. Hence, while both types of workers face an equal level of threat of losing their jobs, high-skilled workers that are able to stay in employment gain in terms of wages, while unskilled workers that keep their job face lower wages.

Munch (2005) provides a similar study for Denmark, a country with arguably a less rigid labour market than Germany. Specifically, he analyses the impact of industry level international outsourcing on job separations using yearly data for a 10 per cent sample of the Danish population using an employment duration model. Unobserved individual heterogeneity is captured within a random effects mass point model. Estimating a single risk model, his general finding is that international outsourcing, at least when broadly defined, has a significant but small impact on individual job separation risks. Estimating a competing risk model and differentiating between exit into unemployment and changing jobs, he finds that international outsourcing increases the risk of becoming unemployed, but that the effect is only statistically significant for low-skilled workers. For high-skilled workers, international outsourcing increases the probability of changing jobs, but has no effect on the individual hazard of becoming unemployed.

In a related approach, Pfaffermayr, Egger and Weber (2007) use individual level data to focus on inter-sectoral worker flows that arise as a consequence of outsourcing. They calculate the transition probabilities of employment, using a worker flow framework similar to that pioneered by Kletzer (2000). Utilising a random sample from Austrian social security data, the authors estimate a transition model for multiple states, i.e. employment in the service sector, the trade sector, the manufacturing sector, unemployment and out of the labour force.[8] Their results suggest that international outsourcing significantly reduces the probability of transition into manufacturing employment, at least into that part of manufacturing that has a revealed comparative disadvantage and, thus, is more affected by international competition.[9]

9.6 Conclusions and policy implications

Broadly speaking, there is evidence from the EU and other countries that international outsourcing leads to a shift in relative demand for labour, and that this can have implications for the wage bill as well as the employment prospects of high- versus low-skilled labour. What are the policy implications of these findings? First of all, it is important to stress that the crucial issues for policy-makers are the medium and long-run effects of international outsourcing. However, empirical studies generally deal with partial equilibrium (short-run) effects. Thus, factor movements between sectors or long-run competitiveness effects due to outsourcing are not taken into account. However, the partial equilibrium results give some indication of the direction in which the labour market adjustment in response to international outsourcing seems to go.

A common conclusion of most theoretical contributions is that international outsourcing generally improves welfare as it yields substantial efficiency gains.[10] However, welfare gains are not conclusive if some of the standard assumptions of general equilibrium models are altered. Krugman (1995) shows that only with sufficiently flexible factor prices can potential gains from trade be realised. In addition, Davidson and Matusz (2004) demonstrate that, although welfare gains dominate, adjustment costs can consume a substantial part of these gains if workers experience unemployment or have to be retrained. Thus, policies that foster wage flexibility and lower adjustment costs can certainly increase the ability to reap gains from international outsourcing (and trade more generally).

Even if international outsourcing does indeed lead to welfare gains, the question is whether the potential losers ought to be compensated. As the analysis showed, it is in particular low-skilled workers who feel the pressure from international outsourcing. Hence, as a reaction, it may be essential for workers to either obtain higher qualifications or to find new employment opportunities in other sectors of the economy. However, changing industry most likely results in substantial losses in terms of post-displacement earnings (e.g. Burda and Mertens, 2001; Haynes et al., 2002) which is a significant obstacle for such transitions. Insurance schemes that partly compensate workers for their potentially lower post-displacement earnings, as discussed in Kletzer (2004), are therefore a particularly interesting policy which might help the transition between sectors. However, crowding-out and windfall effects may significantly limit the scope of action for policy-makers.

Data appendix

Industry level data on international outsourcing were constructed by combining input-use tables from input-output statistics (for Germany: Tables 1.1.1991–1.1.1999 in Statistisches Bundesamt, 2002, and Table 1.1 in Statistisches Bundesamt, 2004; for the UK: Input-Output Supply and Use Tables, 1992–2000, Combined Use matrix, intermediate demand, provided by Office for National Statistics, 2002).

Although for Germany use tables for imported goods are available this is not the case for the UK. Accordingly, in order to ensure the highest possible level of comparability, we only use combined use tables capturing domestic production and imports.

Constructed use shares Ω_{i*it} were carried forward and backward to fill in values for 1991 and 2001, 2002, 2003.

Import data were obtained from the OECD International Trade by Commodity statistics. Disaggregated trade data, which complies with the five digit Standard International Trade Classification (SITC Rev. 3), was aggregated to two digit industries applying a concordance table between SITC Rev. 3 and the International Standard Industrial Classification of All Economic Activities (ISIC Rev. 3).

Notes

1. The data used to construct these figures are described in the appendix.
2. Outsourcing in CEE, EU15, Asia and North America does not fully add up to total outsourcing. CEE includes: Bulgaria, Czech Republic, Estonia, Hungary, Latvia, Lithuania, Poland, Romania, Slovakia, Slovenia.
3. This implies that there is a problem of identification in empirical studies, which need to make sure that they are able to control for technological change in order to identify the effect of outsourcing. This is done, for example, in Machin and Van Reenen (1998) and Hijzen et al. (2005) by including industry level R&D intensity as a control variable to capture the impact of changes in technology on relative labour demand. Feenstra and Hanson (1996, 1999) represent technical change in the form of expenditures on high-technology capital such as computers.
4. Accordingly, in a scenario in which world prices are not given, changes in relative factor prices depend on the elasticity of world demand.
5. Contributions that empirically assess the labour market impact of international outsourcing in general equilibrium include Hijzen (2007), Tombazos (2003), Harrigan (2000), Harrigan and Balaban (1999) and Feenstra and Hanson (1999).
6. Our review does not claim to be exhaustive, but focuses on the evidence for the US, UK and Germany. See Feenstra and Hanson (2001) for a more comprehensive review, covering also studies for other countries.
7. This study is therefore related to the industry level displacement studies by authors such as Kletzer (2000) and Davidson and Matusz (2004).

8. To control for unobserved individual heterogeneity the authors chose a fixed effects specification. Although such a fixed effects specifying has the clear advantage that no assumptions about the correlation between the unobserved component and the individual time varying variables have to be made, the estimator used does not allow computing the probabilities of the transition matrix as no constant can be estimated.

9. However, Pfaffermayr et al. (2007) do not address the issue of duration dependence and the potentially different impact of international outsourcing for employment transitions of different skill groups.

10. In line with this, studies such as Görg, Hanley and Strobl (2007) and Amiti and Wei (2006) show that international outsourcing is associated with higher productivity at the firm or industry level in the short run. An important exception in the theoretical literature is Kohler (2004) who points to the possibility of welfare losses due to outsourcing under certain conditions.

References

Amiti, M. and Wei, S.-J. (2006). 'Service Offshoring and Productivity: Evidence from the United States', NBER Working Paper 11926.

Anderton, B. and Brenton, P. (1999). 'Outsourcing and Low-Skilled Workers in the UK', *Bulletin of Economic Research*, Vol. 51, 4, pp. 267–85.

Arndt, S. W. (1997). 'Globalization and the Open Economy', *North American Journal of Economics and Finance*, Vol. 8, 1, pp. 71–9.

Arndt, S. W. (1999). 'Globalization and Economic Development', *Journal of International Trade and Economic Development*, Vol. 8, 3, pp. 309–18.

Berman, E., Bound, J. and Machin, S. (1998). 'Implications of Skill-Biased Technological Change: International Evidence', *Quarterly Journal of Economics*, Vol. 113, 4, pp. 1245–80.

Burda, M. and Mertens, A. (2001). 'Estimating Wage Losses of Displaced Workers in Germany', *Labour Economics*, Vol. 8, pp. 15–41.

Campa, J. and Goldberg, L. (1997). 'The Evolving External Orientation of Manufacturing Industries: Evidence from Four Countries', *Federal Reserve Bank of New York Economic Policy Review*, Vol. 3, 2, pp. 53–81.

Davidson, C. and Matusz, S. J. (2004). 'Should Policy Makers be Concerned About Adjustment Costs?', in A. Panagariya and D. Mitra (eds), *The Political Economy of Trade, Aid and Foreign Investment Policies: Essays in Honor of Ed Tower*. Amsterdam: Elsevier.

Deardorff, A. V. (2001). 'Fragmentation Across Cones' in Henryk Kierzkowski and Sven W. Arndt, eds, *Fragmentation: New Production Patterns in the World Economy*. Oxford: Oxford University Press, pp. 35–51.

Deardorff, A. V. (2002). 'Fragmentation in Simple Trade Models', *North American Journal of Economics and Finance*, Vol. 12, 1, pp. 121–37.

Egger, H. and Egger, P. (2001). 'Cross-border Sourcing and Outward Processing in EU Manufacturing', *North American Journal of Economics and Finance*, Vol. 12, pp. 243–56.

Egger, H. and Egger, P. (2003). 'Outsourcing and Skill-specific Employment in a Small Economy: Austria after the Fall of the Iron Curtain', *Oxford Economic Papers*, Vol. 55, 4, pp. 525–643.

Falk, M. and Koebel, B. M. (2002). 'Outsourcing, Imports and Labour Demand', *Scandinavian Journal of Economics*, Vol. 104, 4, pp. 567–86.

Feenstra, R. C. and Hanson, G. H. (1996). 'Foreign Direct Investment, Outsourcing and Relative Wages', in Robert C. Feenstra, Gene M. Grossman and D. A. Irwin (eds), *The Political Economy of Trade Policy: Papers in Honor of Jagdish Bhagwati*. Cambridge, MA: MIT Press, pp. 89–127.

Feenstra, R. C. and Hanson, G. H. (1999). 'The Impact of Outsourcing and High-technology Capital on Wages: Estimates for the United States, 1979–1990', *Quarterly Journal of Economics*, Vol. 114, 3, pp. 907–40.

Feenstra, R. C. and Hanson, G. H. (2001). 'Global Production Sharing and Rising Inequality: a Survey of Trade and Wages', NBER Working Paper 8372.

Fitzenberger, B. (1999). 'International Trade and the Skill Structure of Wages and Employment in West Germany', *Jahrbucher für Nationalokonomie und Statistik*, Vol. 219, pp. 67–89.

Geishecker, I. (2006). 'Does Outsourcing to Central and Eastern Europe Really Threaten Manual Workers' Jobs in Germany?', *The World Economy*, Vol. 29, 5, pp. 559–83.

Geishecker, I. (2008). 'The Impact of International Outsourcing on Individual Employment Security: a Micro-level Analysis', *Labour Economics*, forthcoming.

Geishecker, I. and Görg, H. (2008). 'International Outsourcing and Wages: Winners and Losers', *Canadian Journal of Economics*, forthcoming.

Görg, H. (2000). 'Fragmentation and Trade: US Inward Processing Trade in the EU', *Weltwirtschaftliches Archiv*, Vol. 136, 3, pp. 403–22.

Görg, H. and Hanley, A. (2005). 'Labour Demand Effects of International Out-sourcing: Evidence from Plant-Level Data', *International Review of Economics and Finance*, Vol. 14, pp. 365–76.

Görg, H., Hanley, A. and Strobl, E. (2007). 'Productivity Effects of International Outsourcing: Evidence from Plant Level Data', *Canadian Journal of Economics*, forthcoming.

Harrigan, J. (2000). 'International Trade and American Wages in General Equilibrium, 1967–1995', in R. C. Feenstra (ed.), *The Impact of International Trade on Wages*. Chicago: University of Chicago Press.

Harrigan, J. and Balaban, R. (1999). 'US Wages in General Equilibrium: the Effect of Prices, Technology, and Factor Supplies, 1963–1991', NBER Working Paper 6981.

Haynes, M., Upward, R. and Wright, P. (2002). 'Estimating the Wage Costs of Inter- and Intra-sectoral Adjustment', *Weltwirtschaftliches Archiv*, Vol. 138, pp. 229–53.

Head, K. and Ries, J. (2002). 'Offshore Production and Skill Upgrading by Japanese Manufacturing Firms', *Journal of International Economics*, Vol. 58, 1, pp. 81–105.

Hijzen, A. (2007). 'International Outsourcing, Technological Change and Wage Inequality', *Review of International Economics*, Vol. 15, 1, pp. 188–205.

Hijzen, A., Görg, H. and Hine, R. C. (2005). 'Outsourcing and the Skill Structure of Labour Demand in the United Kingdom', *Economic Journal*, Vol. 115, 506, pp. 861–79.

Hummels, D., Ishii, J. and Yi, K.-M. (2001). 'The Nature and Growth of Vertical Specialization in World Trade', *Journal of International Economics*, Vol. 54, 1, pp. 75–96.

Jones, R. W. and Kierzkowski, H. (2001). 'A Framework for Fragmentation', in Sven W. Arndt and Henryk Kierzkowski (eds), *Fragmentation: New Production Patterns in the World Economy*. Oxford: Oxford University Press, pp. 17–34.

Kletzer, L. G. (2000). 'Trade and Job Loss in US Manufacturing, 1979–1994', in Robert Feenstra (ed.), *The Impact of International Trade on Wages*. Chicago: University of Chicago Press.

Kletzer, L. G. (2004). 'Trade-related Job Loss and Wage Insurance: a Synthetic Review', *Review of International Economics*, Vol. 12, 5, pp. 724–48.

Kohler, W. (2004). 'International Outsourcing and Factor Prices With Multistage Production', *Economic Journal*, Vol. 114, 494, pp. C166–C185.

Krugman, P. (1995). 'Growing World Trade: Causes and Consequences', *Brookings Papers on Economic Activity*, Vol. 1, pp. 327–77.

Machin, S. and Van Reenen, J. (1998). 'Technology and Changes in Skill Structure: Evidence from Seven OECD Countries', *Quarterly Journal of Economics*, Vol. 113, 4, pp. 1215–44.

Morrison-Paul, C. J. and Siegel, D. S. (2001). 'The Impacts of Technology, Trade and Outsourcing on Employment and Labor Composition', *Scandinavian Journal of Economics*, Vol. 103, 2, pp. 241–64.

Munch, J. R. (2005). 'International Outsourcing and Individual Job Separations', mimeo, University of Copenhagen.

Office for National Statistics, online database, 2002: http://www.statistics.gov.uk/about/methodology_by_theme/inputoutput/

Pfaffermayr, M., Egger, P. and Weber, A. (2007). 'Sectoral Adjustment of Employment to Shifts in Outsourcing and Trade: Evidence from a Dynamic Fixed Effects Multinomial Logit Model', *Journal of Applied Econometrics*, Vol. 22, 3, pp. 559–80.

Reinberg, A. and Hummel, M. (2005). 'Höhere Bildung schützt auch in der Krise vor Arbeitslosigkeit', *IAB Kurzbericht*, No. 9.

Statistisches Bundesamt (2002). 'Volkswirtschaftliche Gesamtrechnung-Input-Output-Tabellen in jeweiligen Preisen 1991–2000', *Technical Report*.

Statistisches Bundesamt (2004). 'Volkswirtschaftliche Gesamtrechnung-Input-Output-Rechnung 2000', *Fachserie 18*, Reihe 2.

Tombazos, C. G. (2003). 'A Production Theory Approach to the Imports and Wage Inequality Nexus', *Economic Inquiry*, Vol. 41, 1, pp. 42–61.

Yeats, A. J. (2001). 'Just How Big is Global Production Sharing?', in Henryk Kierzkowski and Sven W. Arndt, eds, *Fragmentation: New Production Patterns in the World Economy*. New York: Oxford University Press, pp. 108–43.

10
Immigration and Labour Market Adjustment

Alexander Hijzen and Douglas Nelson

10.1 Introduction

Unlike international trade policy, on which economists display a truly impressive level of agreement, immigration policy divides. International trade liberalisation is expected to have distributional effects – in fact, in the standard model, distributional effects are increasing in gains from trade. Many economists find this to be an argument for redistributive policies that turn the potential Pareto improvement into an actual Pareto improvement, but not an argument against trade liberalisation.[1] By contrast, at least some economists seem to argue that the presence of such redistributive effects do constitute an objection to a liberal immigration policy.[2] Perhaps more surprisingly, these arguments are made in the face of substantial empirical evidence that such redistributive effects are rather small. This survey focuses on this empirical evidence. However, before proceeding to a survey of these results, we begin with a short overview of the theoretical frameworks that have been used to organise and evaluate this research.

10.2 Basic theoretical frameworks

This section introduces the main analytical framework that lies behind most of the empirical work reviewed in Section 10.3. In addition, we also consider a number of extensions of that framework and alternative frameworks that might account for the seemingly small estimates of the effects of immigration on wages and unemployment.

10.2.1 The partial equilibrium labour-market adjustment model

For most economists, like most citizens, our primary intuition comes from the partial equilibrium model – a model of a single market in

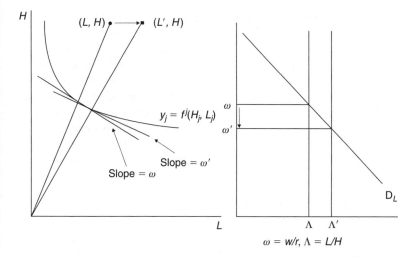

Figure 10.1: Basic PE model

isolation from others. To derive this framework, suppose that output is derived from inputs of skilled (H) and unskilled (L) labour according to a production function which is strictly quasi-concave and characterised by constant returns to scale: $Y = f(H, L)$.[3] If we assume perfect competition in factor and output markets, that there is perfect mobility between Y-producing firms, and that there is no preference for leisure, we will have that all factors are fully employed and paid a wage (w for unskilled labour, r for skilled labour) equal to the value of their marginal product. In the left hand side of Figure 10.1 we have graphed an isoquant (level set) of this production function. It can be shown that the slope at any point gives the ratio of marginal physical products of L to H and, under the maintained institutional and technological assumptions, in equilibrium this will be equal to $\omega = w/r$, i.e. the inverse of the skill premium. In this case, it is easy to see that an increase in the relative endowment of unskilled to skilled labour will result in a fall in ω (i.e. the slope is lower). That is, the skill premium rises.

From this, and the strict quasi-concavity of the production function, we can derive the more standard representation of w/r ratio as a negative function of the relative endowment of labour – shown in the right hand side of Figure 10.1. Since the relative endowment of unskilled labour ($\Lambda = L/H$) is fixed, this appears as a vertical line. The intersection of relative supply and relative demand picks out the equilibrium wage.

Thus, an increase in the relative endowment of unskilled labour as a result of immigration is expected to put downward pressure on ω.

As we shall see in Section 10.3, this framework more or less explicitly underlies the great majority of empirical work on the labour market effects of immigration. Perhaps more importantly, as we have already noted, it is the main source of intuition on those effects. Since, as we shall see, the estimated effects of even sizeable immigration shocks are rather small, it is worthwhile considering what sorts of factors might interfere with that inference. We will start with factors that operate within the basic model and then consider more significant departures from the basic model.

10.2.2   Things that interfere with inference in the partial equilibrium model

Without moving away from the partial equilibrium framework, there are at least two major factors that could affect the results: changes in endowments of other factors of production; and technological change. With respect to the first, there is considerable evidence of skill-upgrading of native populations in OECD countries over time, as well as sizeable immigration of skilled foreigners. Both of these will reduce the effect of the immigration shock considered by itself. It is very easy to introduce these considerations into the simple framework introduced in Figure 10.1. In the LHS of Figure 10.2 this is illustrated by shifting the endowment point from $z = (L, H)$ to $z' = (L', H)$, with the effect that the new equilibrium ω approaches the initial ω, thus undoing the effect of the initial shock. In the right hand side of Figure 10.2 we see this as a shift Λ' back toward Λ and a shift along the relative demand curve toward the initial equilibrium and, thus, equilibrium relative wages.[4]

Technological change in the one-sector case is, again, straightforward to illustrate. A neutral innovation would be shown by a shift towards the origin along the expansion path given by the initial prices. With a fixed endowment, ω would be unchanged, as would the relative demand curve. Thus, an immigration shock would have the same qualitative effect in this case. Factor-biased technological change involves a shift in the orientation of the isoquant such that, at unchanged factor-prices, equilibrium production would involve increased employment of the factor toward whose use the change is biased. With a fixed endowment, this implies that the relative return to the factor in higher demand must rise. We illustrate the case of unskilled labour biased technological change in Figure 10.3. It is easy to see, in this case, that, relative to the initial situation, for any given endowment of factors, equilibrium ω is higher.

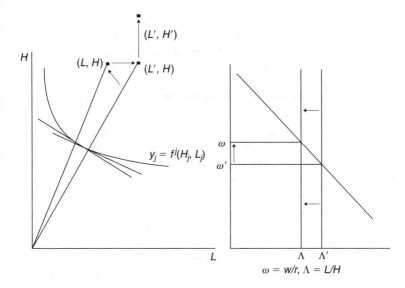

Figure 10.2: Changes in other factors

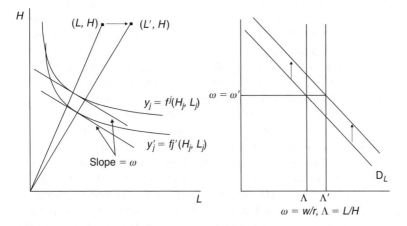

Figure 10.3: Technological change

In terms of the diagram on the right hand side, this is an upward shift in the relative demand for unskilled labour curve. Figure 10.3 is drawn such that the shift just offsets the increase in the endowment of unskilled labour. Unfortunately, at least from the perspective of accounting for the effects of immigrant inflows in the one-sector model, most researchers who have considered the bias of technological change in the 1980s have concluded that such change is *skill*-biased. That is, if this technological change is not accounted for, we should observe *increased* effects of immigration on relative wages.

10.2.3 Things that interfere with inference in the general equilibrium model

The standard model is partial equilibrium in at least two important ways. Even within the context of the one-sector model, a general equilibrium analysis would evaluate the interaction between immigrant labour and native labour, and between immigrant labour and capital. Beyond this, extending the model to include multiple sectors has additional effects.

Greenwood, Hunt and Kohli (1996, 1997) and Ottaviano and Peri (2006) show that allowing immigrant labour to be differentiated from domestic labour permits a more nuanced analysis of the relationship between immigrant and domestic labour. These authors argue persuasively that, for a variety of reasons, immigrants may be imperfect substitutes for native workers within any given education/experience category. By permitting such imperfect substitutability, they allow the data to determine the magnitude of these interactions.[5] In addition, Ottaviano and Peri argue that capital should be treated as if it adjusts endogenously to the immigration shock so as to retain the fixed rate of return found in the data.

A different set of general equilibrium issues are raised by moving from a one-sector to a many-sector model. Once the number of sectors rises beyond unity, some of the adjustment to an immigration shock occurs on the output margin, rather than falling entirely on the wage margin. In fact, as long as there are at least as many commodities as factors of production (which would seem to be the natural assumption), and as long as all the other assumptions of the partial equilibrium model are retained (including constant returns to scale, perfect competition in all markets, perfect factor mobility, and fixed commodity prices), we have the surprising result that *all adjustment occurs on the output margin, and there is no change in relative factor prices*. Leamer (1995) calls this striking result the *factor-price insensitivity theorem*. Consider the left hand side of Figure 10.4, where we graph two unit-value isoquants. For both commodities to be produced in equilibrium, they must be tangent to a common (unit value) isocost constraint. The expansion paths consistent with the equilibrium relative factor-prices define a cone in input-space. As long as the endowment point for the economy remains in this cone, the economy adjusts to any change in endowment by adjusting output

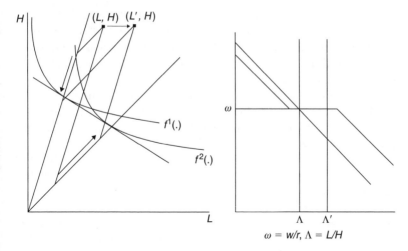

Figure 10.4: Two-sector GE model

along the fixed expansion paths. Thus, the increase in the endowment of unskilled labour shown by the shift from z to z' results in an increase in the output of the unskilled labour intensive good and a decrease in the output of the skilled labour intensive good.[6] Note the implication for the relative demand curve for unskilled labour on the right hand side of Figure 10.4: now there is a flat portion in the curve over the range in which the economy continues to produce both commodities. It is important to understand that this does not say that the relative labour demand curve is flat over its entire range, but only over some range. For a sufficiently large change in Λ (or, alternatively, z), the curve will slope downward. Like the partial equilibrium framework, this is intended to be a long-run analysis. However, for a variety of reasons, this schedule might well not be strictly flat in the relevant range. The issue here is presumption. The one-sector, partial equilibrium presumption is that this curve must slope downward everywhere, implying that immigration shocks composed of unskilled labour must always cause a deterioration in the return to unskilled labour. By contrast, the general equilibrium presumption is that adjustment occurs on the output margin. Choosing between presumptions is a tricky business, but in this case it seems rather easy: the sole difference between the two interpretive frameworks is dimensionality. It is hard not to choose the framework whose sole difference seems broadly more consistent with reality. The fact that this produces a presumption (no relative wage effect) that is broadly consistent with the data is an additional benefit.

Factor-price insensitivity is a one-country result. The more well-known multi-country result is called *factor-price equalisation (FPE)*. This theorem asserts that, two countries sharing the same technologies, under the same technological and institutional assumptions that we have maintained to this point, producing the same commodities, and facing the same commodity prices, must also have the same factor-prices. The logic can be illustrated in Figure 10.4. Instead of a migration shock, suppose that z and z' are two national endowments. The common technology and prices fix the location of the unit value isoquants, so that the only way both countries can produce both goods is for them to share the same relative factor-prices (i.e. those given by the slope of the isocost line tangent to the two unit value isoquants). Under the maintained assumptions of the model to this point, as long as countries remain in the same cone of diversification, it should be clear that trade in goods and factor mobility are perfect substitutes (Mundell, 1957). Thus, if there is free trade between countries with sufficiently similar production structure, there should be no incentive for migration (e.g. if there is even a modest social or cultural preference for staying home); alternatively, if countries seek to maintain different commodity prices, say by using protectionist instruments, factor mobility can undo this.

This result raises a number of interesting issues with respect to the empirical literature presented in the next section of this chapter. Much of the empirical literature on labour market effects of migration uses data on local labour markets to identify those effects. If we are to maintain the assumptions common to labour and trade economists, the presence of such differences is only possible if factor mobility is very imperfect and local labour markets (between which there is presumably free trade) produce different mixes of goods (i.e. they are in different cones). Loosely speaking, the multi-cone nature of production seems plausible: Northern and Southern California seem to produce different mixes of goods, which support very different wage structures. However, factor mobility is surely very free between these two. This is the same problem as between the US and Puerto Rico – free trade, free factor mobility, different factor-price structures. From a theoretical perspective this is not problematic: it is well known that factor-price equalisation, and substitutability between commodity and factor flows, are sensitive to assumptions (e.g. Markusen, 1983; Markusen and Svensson, 1985; Wong, 1986; Norman and Venables, 1995). The problem has to do with interpreting the results of empirical analysis derived in the context of models which imply such equalisation, but rely on differences for their results.

10.3 Empirical evidence

10.3.1 Wages (partial equilibrium)

Two approaches have dominated empirical research on immigration and wages: the 'local labour market' approach and the 'aggregate factor proportions' approach. Both approaches are typically presented in the context of a single-good economy and therefore share the same theoretical predictions. The crucial difference between the two approaches relates to the appropriate definition of the labour market. The local labour market approach defines labour markets at the regional or city level, whereas the factor proportions approach defines labour markets nationally.

The local labour-market approach

Early local labour-market studies can be classified into three categories on the basis of the method adopted: structural studies; econometric studies; and natural experiments. More recent studies tend to combine elements of different methods.

The pioneering work by Grossman (1982) falls in the category of studies that rely on structural estimation. The econometric specification is explicitly derived from a production function framework. The approximation of the production function by a flexible functional form allows one to estimate the cross-price in addition to the own-price elasticities. The latter can be used to make inferences regarding the degree of substitutability between immigrants and domestic factors of production.

An interesting feature in Grossman's study is that she distinguishes between the long- and short-run impacts of immigration. It is assumed that in the long run labour markets clear so that labour market adjustment fully occurs to changes in wages, whereas in the short run it is assumed that wages are downwardly inflexible. Grossman finds that a 10 per cent inflow of immigrants reduces native employment by 0.8 per cent in the short run and reduces native earnings by 0.1 per cent in the long run. Thus, she concludes that even sizeable inflows of immigrants do not pose a serious threat to the economic fortunes of natives. Subsequent research using the structural approach has concentrated on the role of functional form and curvature restrictions implied by economic theory without challenging the main conclusions reached by Grossman.[7]

The main weakness of early studies that adopted a structural approach is that they rely for the identification of the causal effect of immigration on theoretical assumptions. For example, it is assumed that factor supplies, including the supply of migrant workers, may be considered exogenous. In reality, however, migrants may self-select into those local labour markets where economic conditions are more favourable. As a result, the variation of migrant supplies across local labour markets is not exogenous. The resulting positive correlation between immigration and unaccounted demand conditions across local labour markets will lead to an upward bias of the estimated impact of migration on the economic outcomes of natives. The small effects obtained from structural estimation may thus reflect correlations rather than causal relationships.

This concern motivated a more pragmatic approach, which also exploits the regional variation in immigration inflows to identify its impact on native wages, but without imposing much economic structure. This is sometimes referred to as the spatial correlations approach. The main challenge is to appropriately define the unobserved counterfactual, i.e. the economic outcomes that would have occurred in the absence of immigration inflows. Econometric studies rely on various econometric techniques for the identification of the causal effect of immigration, whereas natural experiments exploit specific events in the source country that give rise to exogenous immigration inflows.

An early study of the econometric type is presented by Altonji and Card (1991), who analyse the relationship between immigration and the economic outcomes of low-skilled natives using US Census data for 1970 and 1980. They account for the possible correlation between immigrant inflows and local demand conditions in two ways. First, they estimate the model in first-differences to control for any time-invariant differences across regions that may be correlated with immigration. However, first-difference estimates may still be biased when the location choices of migrants are sensitive to *changes* in local economic conditions. They therefore combine first-differences with instrumental variable (IV) estimation. They use the stock of foreign-born individuals by country of origin and region in 1970 to predict the change in the population of foreign-born individuals. The instrument is based on Bartel's (1989) insight that immigrants tend to locate in regions with large populations of previous immigrants from the same country of origin. Although Altonji and Card's estimates appear to be large, as Friedberg and Hunt (1995: 34) point out, to compare the magnitudes in this study to those in others these results need to be converted to elasticities. When this is done, the 'large and negative' effects imply that a 10 per cent increase in the percentage of foreign-born in a local labour market implies a minuscule 0.86 per cent reduction in wages.[8] In addition, Altonji and Card find essentially zero effect on unemployment.

Perhaps most striking are the results from studies that make use of a natural experiment. Card (1990) analyses the effect of the Mariel boatlift on the Miami labour market, when 125 000 Cuban nationals arrived in the US port of Mariel on 20 April 1980. The boatlift resulted in a 7 per cent increase in the Miami labour force and a 20 per cent increase in the number of Cuban workers in Miami. Due to the political events in Cuba the Mariel boatlift provides an exogenous source of variation to study the effects of immigration on the labour market. Even though many Cubans making the boatlift may have been motivated by economic considerations, the timing and the destination are likely to have been exogenous. Strikingly, Card finds 'essentially no effect on the wages or employment outcomes of non-Cuban workers in the Miami labour market ... and no strong effect on the wage of other Cubans' (Card, 1990: 255). Card explains the apparent ease with which Mariel immigrants were absorbed into the Miami labour market by pointing out that the industrial structure of Miami was characterised by predominantly unskilled intensive activities and that the net migration rate of natives into Miami slowed down in the aftermath of the Mariel boatlift relative to the rest of Florida.[9]

One problem with the local labour-market studies discussed above is that, irrespective of the specific method used, they do not provide a complete picture of the effects of immigration. To the extent that immigration worsens local labour-market conditions it provides an incentive for natives to move elsewhere. The subsequent increase in the labour force due to native inflows elsewhere implies that the effect of immigration of native wages is spread across different local labour markets. As a result local labour-market studies may suffer from omitted variable bias if native inflows and outflows and immigrant inflows are correlated. More precisely, when immigrant inflows displace natives, local labour-market studies will tend to underestimate the true factor price elasticity with respect to factor supplies. The remainder of this section surveys recent local labour-market studies that attempt to control for internal migration. A detailed discussion of the relationship between international and internal migration is provided in Section 10.3.2 which explicitly concentrates on the role of internal labour mobility as an alternative mechanism of labour-market adjustment.

Card (2001) provides the first study of local wage effects of immigrant inflows whilst controlling for the role of internal migration. A further important contribution of his study is that, in contrast to most of the previous literature, which treats immigrants as a homogeneous group, he takes account of immigrant heterogeneity. This is important because immigrants are likely to exhibit substantial differences in terms of their skills. Controlling for the skill composition of immigrants and natives is complicated due to measurement problems associated with skills that are acquired in different countries.

In order to account for immigrant heterogeneity Card stratifies the national labour market along occupational lines. Using the individual-specific occupational probabilities, which are estimated from a multinomial logit model for six occupational categories, he constructs a measure for the number of people that would be expected to work in a certain occupation and region in the absence of any distortions due to local demand and supply conditions. This method allows one to bypass classification problems that are likely to arise when assigning immigrants and natives to specific skill categories.

The regression analysis proceeds in two steps. In the first step, Card estimates the impact of immigration inflows during the period 1985–90 on population shares in 1990. In the second step, he regresses population shares on labour market outcomes. OLS estimates suggest that a 10 per cent rise in the population share of an occupational group depresses employment and wages in that group by about 0.5 per cent. Instrumental variable estimation is used to net out the exogenous supply-push component of immigration. The IV estimates suggest that the impact of immigration is three to four times larger in the case of employment, but still not very large. He does not find any robust effects for wages. Card concludes that even after controlling for the role of local demand conditions as well as the possibility that immigrants displace natives, the results suggest that the impact of immigration on natives is relatively small, and limited to employment.

Dustmann, Fabbri and Preston (2005) provide a recent application of the local labour-markets approach for the United Kingdom for the period 1983–2000.[10] In contrast to immigration to the US, immigrants that entered the UK during the 1990s are not significantly different from natives in terms of skills and educational attainment. The authors, however, note that this does not necessarily mean that labour-market effects are small as the distribution of immigrants across UK regions is far from uniform.[11]

Rather than adopting the two-step procedure as in Card (2001) they directly control for the size of the native population in their econometric model in order to control for changes in the labour supply due to movements of natives between regions. Furthermore, the use of panel data allows them to control for time-invariant differences in demand across regions and nationwide differences in demand over time, by including region and time fixed effects. The use of panel data further allows them to employ generalised methods of moments (GMM) techniques in order to control for the potential correlation between immigration inflows and unobservables.[12]

They find a positive effect of immigration inflows on wages using OLS, but the sign becomes negative when they turn to GMM. With GMM, a 10 per cent increase in immigration leads to a decrease of 0.7 per cent in native employment. For unemployment, labour force participation and wages the estimated effects of a 10 per cent increase in immigration inflows are 0.07 per cent, −0.04 per cent and 0.91 per cent respectively. However, none of these estimates is statistically significant. If there is any negative effect, then it is for the group with intermediate qualifications.

In a recent study, Kugler and Yuksel (2006) exploit the natural experiment provided by Hurricane Mitch, which displaced 1.5 million people in Central America in October 1998. It has been widely acknowledged that a large proportion of the displaced responded by moving north in an attempt to start a new life in the United States. Kugler and Yuksel exploit this exogenous variation by looking at the inflows of immigrants from Central America across US states. In order to purge any remaining demand-driven immigration they use the distance from Honduras as an instrument. They find that unskilled migration tends to raise the wage of skilled natives without finding much of an effect for unskilled natives. They explain their findings by pointing out that unskilled immigrants are likely to act as complements to skilled natives (Borjas, 1995).

The aggregate factor proportions approach

In contrast to the local labour-markets approach which utilises the variation in immigration across local labour markets, the national labour markets or factor proportions approach assumes that labour markets are integrated nationally, but are segmented across skill groups. Thus, it is assumed that any wage differences across regions for certain skill groups are likely to be short-lived due to worker mobility, whereas wage differences across skill groups are expected to persist over time.[13]

The early contributions that adopted the factor proportions approach typically proceeded in two stages (Borjas, Freeman and Katz, 1992, 1996, 1997). First, one evaluates the effect of immigration on the national supply of workers with equivalent skills. Second, one assumes a certain elasticity of substitution to simulate the wage effects of immigration. Borjas et al. find that immigration had a moderate impact on the rise in wage inequality in the US during the 1980s. The main problem with this approach is that it operates too mechanically by assuming the relevant elasticities of substitution. Consequently, one might argue that these studies also assume the wage effects of immigration.[14]

Borjas (2003) makes an important methodological contribution that allows one to directly estimate the wage effects of immigration without making assumptions on the elasticity of substitution. The principal idea is that one can exploit the independent variation in immigration across skill groups by noting that individuals in the same educational category, but with different levels of experience, are imperfect substitutes.

As with the local labour-market studies, self-selection of individuals into high wage cells may bias results. In the long run, individuals may move to skill groups that are associated with higher wages by investing in education and experience. The independent variation in immigration is therefore used as an instrument for changes in the group size of the different skill categories. 'In other words, the immigrant influx into particular skill groups provides the supply shifter required to identify the labour demand function' (Borjas, 2003: 1362).[15]

The empirical model is derived from a structural model in the spirit of the early work by Grossman (1982), which allows one to consider the cross-wage effects of immigrants in addition to the direct effects on individuals in the same skill group. In order to ensure that the model can be identified in the presence of 32 factors of production he derives his model from a nested three-level CES production function. The obvious advantage is that the technology can be summarised in terms of three elasticities of substitution. The disadvantage is that it greatly restricts the substitution possibilities across factors of production.[16]

Borjas (2003) uses decadal data obtained from micro-samples for the period 1960–2000. He considers 32 skill groups on the basis of 4 education groups and annual differences in experience. Borjas obtains an own-price elasticity in the range of −0.3 and −0.4. Accordingly, the observed influx of immigrants during the period 1980–2000 (which increased male labour supply by 11 per cent) reduced the wage of the average native by 3.2 per cent. However, there are some important differences across education groups. The average wage of high school dropouts was depressed by 8.9 per cent, that of high school graduates by 2.6 per cent. There was no significant effect on individuals with some college education and the wage of college graduates was reduced by 4.9 per cent.

Borjas also employs an informal version of the model which is similar to the spatial correlation studies discussed earlier, which allows him to estimate the model at different levels of geographical aggregation. At the national level, his results are in line with his results from the structural model. However, when reducing the level of geographical aggregation, he finds smaller effects of immigration on native wages. He concludes that ignoring the potential for 'spatial arbitrage' due to internal labour mobility, as is typically the case in local labour market studies, effectively cuts the national estimate by two-thirds.[17]

The main problem with the study presented by Borjas (2003) is that it lacks a clear counterfactual. As a result, Borjas relies on assumptions on the role of other factors relevant to the structure of wages, such as capital accumulation and skill-biased technological change. Capital does not feature explicitly in the model. Instead it is assumed that the capital stock is fixed and the elasticity of substitution between capital and labour is unity. Moreover, given the CES technology, this elasticity is the same for all types of workers. This clearly goes against the conventional wisdom that capital and skilled workers are complements, whereas capital acts as a substitute to unskilled workers. Furthermore, it is assumed that demand shifters such as skilled biased technological change (SBTC) can be appropriately controlled for using an education-group-specific linear time trend.

An important recent paper by Ottaviano and Peri (2006) adopts the same structure and specification as Borjas (2003) with two extensions: immigrants are allowed to be imperfect substitutes for native workers; and capital is assumed to adjust endogenously to maintain a fixed rate of return. The result is striking: immigration significantly *increases* the average wage of US workers (by over 1 per cent). This increase is composed of increases for all native workers with at least a high school degree (88 per cent of the native workforce in 2000) and a reduction of 1 per cent for high school dropouts.

Friedberg (2001) studies the wage effects of the Russian immigration into Israel during the period 1989–94 by exploiting the cross-sectional variation of immigration across occupations. The mass immigration of Russian Jews to Israel provides an interesting case for the study of immigration for at least four reasons. First, similar to the Mariel boatlift, the inflow of Russian immigrants into Israel was triggered by political events in the country of origin. Second, the Russian immigration was massive by historical standards. In 1990, Russian immigration increased the Israeli population by 4 per cent. Total population growth due to Russian immigration amounted to 12 per cent during 1990–4. Third, in contrast to mass immigration observed in Europe and the United States, Russian immigrants tend to be rather skilled. Finally, Israel is both relatively small and relatively open.

While Friedberg argues that the immigrants are less likely to sort into high (or low) wage occupations than into high wage regions, self-selection may still be an issue when employers sort immigrants into specific occupations with certain wage characteristics. The estimations are conducted in first differences in order to remove the potential correlation between immigration and unobserved fixed effects. To account for the possibility that immigrant inflows are correlated with unobserved time-varying characteristics, instrumental variable estimation is employed. The previous occupation of immigrants in Russia is used as an instrument, which is unlikely to be related to changes in pay conditions in Israel.[18]

Generally, the results do not suggest that the influx of Russian immigrants adversely affected the wage growth of natives. Interestingly, the results change signs from negative with OLS to positive with IV, which suggests that Russian migrants tend to sort into *low* wage occupations. Consequently, OLS tends to *overestimate* the negative effect of immigration inflows on the wage growth of natives. While migrants may sort into high wage cities, they tend to sort into low wage jobs. The positive and significant effect on natives' wage growth in the IV estimations suggests that Russian immigrants complement native workers.

Bonin (2005) applies the skill-correlation approach to West Germany for the period 1975–1997,[19] but finds no significant effect on employment and a small negative effect on wages.[20] Carrasco, Jimeno and Ortega (2006) analyse the impact of immigration across gender-education-experience groups in Spain, but generally do not find statistically significant employment effects. Cohen-Goldner and Paserman (2005) provide an interesting study for Israel in which the elasticity of substitution between immigrants and natives is allowed to change as immigrants assimilate and the economy adjusts. They find a negative effect of immigrant inflows on native wages in the short run. However, this effect dissolves after 4 to 7 years.

Discussion

In our view, the literature on immigration and native wages faces two main challenges. First of all, one has to address the issue of immigrant heterogeneity. Only when the skill composition of immigrants differs from that of the domestic labour force may one expect any wage effects. Even when data on both the skills of immigrants and natives are available, these may not be readily comparable when work experience and qualifications are obtained in different countries. An appropriate alternative may be to use occupational groupings as does Friedberg (2001). The drawback of using occupation relative to skills may be that individuals more easily sort into occupations than into skill groups. Friedberg

(2001) remedies this problem by using a convincing instrument of the exogenous variation of immigrant inflows across occupation by using the occupation in the country of origin. However, this kind of information is unlikely to be available in most cases.[21] At a minimum, it seems important to permit immigrants to be imperfect substitutes for native workers as in Greenwood, Hunt and Kohli (1996, 1997) and Ottaviano and Peri (2006).

The second main challenge is to appropriately define the counterfactual, i.e. what would have happened to native wages in the absence of immigrant inflows. Several creative solutions based on econometric techniques and natural experiments have been employed. In our view, local labour market studies typically do a better job in identifying the causal effects of immigration by netting out any common changes in the skill structure of wages across regions due to skill-biased technological change and capital accumulation. To the extent that immigrants are predominantly unskilled, immigrant inflows may be negatively correlated with factors not controlled for in national labour market studies and thus overestimate the negative effect of immigrants on native wages.

While substantial progress has been made in accounting for immigrant heterogeneity and defining the appropriate counterfactual, measurement error problems and omitted variable bias are likely to explain to an important extent the variability of the results across studies and specifications. In spite of these problems, we can conclude that the local labour-market effects of immigration are relatively small. As Gaston and Nelson put it: 'The overwhelming majority of empirical studies conclude that there is essentially no statistically significant effect of immigration on labour market outcomes, with the possible exception of the least skilled domestic workers' (Gaston and Nelson, 2002: 202).

10.3.2 Inter-regional mobility

We now turn to the issue of inter-regional mobility as a channel of labour-market adjustment. Almost all studies that address this question have concentrated on the United Sates. A number of early studies find that internal migration acts as an important channel to absorb immigrants (Filer, 1992; Frey, 1995a, 1995b). Frey (1995a, 1995b) suggested that immigrant inflows may induce a 'demographic balkanisation' of the United States. Other studies, however, which typically use very similar data, did not find any significant outflows of natives in response to immigration inflows (Butcher and Card, 1991). Again, the sensitivity of the results can be attributed to an important extent to the way the counterfactual is defined across studies. The definition of the counterfactual matters to the extent that immigration inflows are correlated with unobserved economic conditions that are not controlled for in the regression analysis.

Borjas et al. (1997) provide an interesting example of a relatively early study that finds that internal migration plays an important role in absorbing foreign migrants. In their baseline specification they find a weak positive correlation between migrant inflows and aggregate labour supply at the state level. As it is implicitly assumed that native population growth would be zero in the absence of international migration, differences in native growth rates are entirely attributed to migration inflows. They attempt to control for the growth in the population of natives which would have occurred in the absence of immigration inflows by taking double differences, i.e. by focusing on the change in the growth rate. Consequently, the implicit assumption about the counterfactual is that in the absence of migrant inflows the growth rate in the population of natives is stable so that any change in the growth rate of the native population can be attributed to the change in the growth rate of migrant inflows. Using double differences they find a strong negative relationship between foreign inflows and native outflows.[22] They conclude that immigration has hardly any effect on the aggregate labour supply within states.

They next assess to what extent relative factor proportions of immigrant inflows match that of native outflows. An advantage of distinguishing between different skill groups is that one can control for skill and state fixed effects in addition to taking double differences. Double differences allow one to concentrate on deviations from the stable growth paths within state and skill groups, while fixed effects control for differences in the stable growth paths across states and skill groups. Fixed effects thus help to further refine the counterfactual.

They find that migration inflows significantly change factor proportions. However, once they control for the initial conditions of factor proportions in 1950 this effect entirely disappears. According to the authors, the initial conditions variable is needed to capture the convergence in the skill distribution across states which is independent of migration. Controlling for initial conditions allows factor proportions to grow more quickly in states with relatively low amounts of skilled labour in the absence of immigration inflows (adjusting the counterfactual). To the extent that migrants move to states with relatively large concentrations of unskilled workers this lowers the estimated coefficient on migrant inflows.

While Borjas et al. (1997) make a considerable contribution to the literature the results may still be deemed inconclusive.[23] Amongst others, one may wonder whether it is reasonable to assume that the growth rate of the native population is stable in the absence of migration. Wright, Ellis and Reibel (1997) argue that this is not the case. They argue that the significant negative relationship in some studies between immigration inflows and native outflows is due to the failure to properly control for the determinants of urban centres. While large urban centres did attract large inflows of immigrants, the loss of natives was related to industrial restructuring which took place independently from the competition from immigrant workers.

Card and Di Nardo (2000) and Card (2001) both analyse the impact of immigration on local labour supply while accounting for the heterogeneity of immigrants. Card (2001) finds that in the absence of any further controls a 1 per cent increase in the rate of immigration will result in a more than proportional increase in the net population growth of 1.6 per cent. These results, however, are likely to be biased due to the role of local demand conditions. After including city and occupation fixed effects the estimated effect falls to 1.3 per cent, still significantly larger than unity. City fixed effects are included to control for local demand conditions that affect all occupations equally; occupation fixed effects capture nationwide demand shifts (technological change). In order to take account of the role of time-varying differences in local demand conditions that vary across occupations and regions, Card employs IV estimation to single out the exogenous supply-push component of immigration using historic immigration patterns by US region and country of origin. However, the IV estimates are not significantly different from the OLS estimates with city and occupation fixed effects. Card and Di Nardo (2000) provide very similar results when looking at longer time differences. Thus, it is concluded that immigrants do not cause outflows of native workers. If anything, immigrant inflows tend to be associated with net population growth. 'The local labour market impacts of unskilled immigration are mitigated by other avenues of adjustment, such as endogenous shifts in industry structure, rather than by rapid adjustment in the native population' (Card and Di Nardo, 2000: 366).[24]

Hatton and Tani (2005) analyse the role of inter-regional mobility in the context of migration of the United Kingdom. As such, this is the only study that does not concentrate on the United States.[25] They construct an annual panel for the period 1981–2000 for eleven UK regions. A drawback of their data is that they cannot distinguish between individuals with different skills.

The analysis differs in three important ways from the work by Card (2001). First, they focus on net bilateral flows of natives between regions. Second, given the longitudinal nature of their data, they control for time and bilateral region fixed effects. The former capture economy-wide changes in conditions that affect regional mobility, while the latter capture relative differences in economic conditions that are constant over time. Third, Hatton and Tani explicitly control for differences in the economic conditions across regions and over time. Instead of using IV methods to account for the endogeneity of migrants due to demand-pull factors, they directly control for economic conditions in their model on top of region and time fixed effects.

In all specifications they find a positive relationship between immigrant inflows and native outflows; however, this relationship is not always statistically significant. When they do not explicitly control for economic conditions, but simply include a full set of region and time dummies, they do not find any significant effects. The results are stronger when they concentrate only on the six southern regions. Hatton and Tani conclude that, although more research is needed, inter-regional mobility may be an important channel in absorbing immigrants into the economy.[26]

Borjas (2005) theoretically and empirically analyses the relationship between wages in local labour markets and native migration decisions. Regional deviations from the (national) equilibrium wage are ascribed to differences in relative factor proportions across regions. He uses his model to show explicitly how failing to account for internal migration at the local level may lead to underestimates of the wage effect of immigration nationally. His empirical results suggest that, in line with his theoretical model, immigration is associated with a decline in the population growth of natives, which mitigates its wage effect locally by spreading it out over the national economy. In gross terms immigration is also found to be associated with higher outflows and lower inflows of natives. As one would expect, the displacement effects of immigration become smaller the larger the geographic units used for the analysis.

Discussion

The literature on the link between international and internal migration does not provide a conclusive answer to the question as to whether internal migration may account for the different findings from the local labour markets and aggregate factor proportions approach. These inconsistencies across studies, most of which are for the same country, are again likely to be related to immigrant heterogeneity and the defini-tion of the counterfactual. Even when a strong correlation between international and internal migration exists it is not clear whether this is a causal relationship, i.e. immigrants displace natives, or whether natives and immigrants sort into different regions related to their socio-economic class.

In our view, the absence of a strong positive relationship between immigrant inflows and native outflows suggests that internal migration is unlikely to undo the labour supply shock due to migration inflows. In fact, Card (2005: 307) states that 'all studies that have looked at the relative supply impacts of immigration find very large effects on local labour markets'. Moreover, there does not seem to be a good reason why immigration would be undone by native outflows immediately, given that regional differences in economic conditions tend to persist over time (Blanchard and Katz, 1992). Even when factor price equalisa-tion holds in the long run this may be more likely to result from trade in goods and services, capital mobility and technology transfer. Each of those channels seems to be more fluid than that of labour mobility. Thus, we conclude that internal migration does not appear to be the pre-dominant factor explaining the small wage effects in small open labour markets.

More fundamentally, the above studies, as well as those in the previous section, have a tendency to assume implicitly or explicitly that labour demand is relatively inelastic, i.e. the labour demand curve is downward-sloping. If this is indeed the case then the only way to explain the small wage effects in small open economies as evidenced in the previous sec-tion is that labour supply is very elastic. The evidence in this section, however, suggests that labour supply is relatively inelastic. It therefore seems plausible that the assumption underlying a large part of the litera-ture on the elasticity of labour demand may be inappropriate. Indeed, if labour demand is relatively elastic, then migration may also have a small effect on native employment even though the native labour sup-ply reacts strongly to wages (Hatton and Tani, 2005). An elastic labour demand curve may reflect the role of trade which allows the economy to adjust in response to changes in factor supplies through changes in the output mix. Capital mobility and endogenous skill-biased technological change are also consistent with elastic labour demand. In order to analyse the role of these channels, one has to exchange the partial equilibrium framework, which implicitly or explicitly underlies most of the studies reviewed so far, for a general equilibrium framework. We do this in the next section.

10.3.3 Wages, specialisation and technological change

In this section we survey the literature that analyses labour market adjustment in response to immigration (or shocks in relative factor supply more generally) in general equilibrium, by explicitly allowing for the presence of different sectors between which factors of production may be allocated. As discussed in the theory section, in a small open economy any changes in relative factor supplies are fully absorbed through changes in the output mix, so relative factor prices remain unaffected. In fact, factor prices will be equalised across all countries/region in the same cone of diversification.[27]

The first approach we discuss tests whether factor price equalisation holds across local labour markets. We subsequently turn to studies that use informal decomposition methods to approximate the relative importance of labour market adjustment through changes in the output mix and changes in the input mix. The role of region-specific SBTC has recently been proposed as an alternative to changes in the output mix. Thus, we will discuss studies that have explicitly focused on the relationship between changes in relative factor supplies and SBTC. While, strictly speaking, models of endogenous skill-biased technological change are one-sector (partial equilibrium) models, the presence of alternative production technologies to produce the same good gives the model a general equilibrium interpretation similar to that of the traditional Heckscher–Ohlin model. We conclude this section by discussing a number of studies that have attempted to analyse the effects of immigration using a structural approach based on a multi-sector production-theoretic framework.

In order to get a first idea of whether one should expect adjustment in response to immigration to take place through changes in relative factor prices, or through other channels of labour market adjustment, we will briefly review the evidence in favour of FPE across local labour markets.

Hanson and Slaughter (2002) test whether FPE holds across fourteen US states using data for 1980 and 1990. Rather than directly comparing factor prices across states they compare input coefficients in forty different industries. For equal factor prices, input coefficients should be identical. However, even when factor prices may be the same across states, input coefficients may differ as a result of factor-specific productivity differences across states due to, for example, scale effects, externalities, or differences in underlying technology. They control for productivity differences by including a fixed effect dummy for each state-pair, factor type and year combination.[28] They find that in their data, productivity-adjusted FPE may indeed hold which suggests that 'regional openness to flows of factors, goods, and technology may be sufficient to ensure that state-specific factor-supply shocks tend to trigger common state relative wage responses' (Hanson and Slaughter, 2002: 5).

Bernard et al. (2005a) develop an alternative method for testing factor price equality. Their method is characterised by two main features. First of all, they focus on relative factor price equality (RFPE) rather than absolute FPE. This effectively represents a difference-in-differences specification that allows them to take account of (i) region-specific differences common to both skilled and unskilled labour such as total factor productivity and the cost of living; (ii) industry-specific differences in relative factor rewards common across regions due to industry features of the production technology and labour market institutions. Second, they focus on the relative wage bill rather than relative wages or relative inputs. By combining observed factor prices and observed factor quantities into the wage bill one can control for any unobserved variation in factor quality across industries and regions.

Bernard et al. (2005a) apply their methodology to data for the United States for 181 regions for the period 1972–92. Bernard et al. (2005b) provide results for the United Kingdom using data for the period 1978–93. According to both studies the null of RFPE is rejected. More specifically, they find that (i) skill-abundant regions exhibit lower skill premia than skill-scarce regions, and (ii) skill-abundant regions have a higher concentration of skill-intensive industries than skill-scarce regions. Thus, differences in factor endowments appear to generate differences in factor prices and consequently differences in industrial structure. In terms of neoclassical trade theory this implies that both the US and the UK are characterised by multiple cones.

An interesting implication of these two papers is that regional specialisation creates a differential susceptibility to competition from low-wage countries across regions. This is also borne out by the data. Of course, the same would be true for consequences of unskilled migration. The message for policy-makers is that regional development policies are likely to be more successful when trying to change comparative factor endowments rather than targeting certain industries directly.

Debaere (2004) considers the question whether regions are 'lumpy', i.e. sufficiently different within countries in order to induce specialisation. He does this using the 'lens condition' which states that 'regions have equal factor prices and produce the same goods if and only if the regional endowment lens ... lies inside the goods lens' (Debaere, 2004: 488).[29]

Using data for Japan, the UK and India, Debaere concludes that, when taking regional factor endowments as given, regions are typically not sufficiently different to induce specialisation. Debaere does not conclude, though, that this necessarily implies that FPE holds within those countries, but merely that regional differences in relative factor endowments are typically not sufficiently large to invalidate FPE if all other assumptions required for FPE hold. Thus, if indeed FPE fails for the UK as suggested by Bernard et al. (2005b) this is unlikely to be the primary result of differences in relative factor endowments across countries.

In sum, the empirical evidence does not provide any conclusive answer to the question whether factor price equalisation is likely to hold across regions. While Hanson and Slaughter (2002) find that FPE may hold for local labour markets in Japan and the US respectively, Bernard et al. (2005a, 2005b) reject the null hypothesis of FPE across regions both for the US and the UK. Indeed, they suggest that differences in factor endowments across regions induce differences in factor prices and therefore industrial structure. Debaere (2004), however, suggests that regional differences in relative factor endowments for India, Japan and the UK are not sufficiently large to induce specialisation. We now turn to studies that have directly explored the relevance of product specialisation and technological change as channels of labour-market adjustment.

Hanson and Slaughter (2002) are the first to look at the role of the output mix as a channel of labour-market adjustment. They decompose regional employment by skill groups into changes in the regional output mix, national changes in the industry input mix, and regional changes in the input mix. Their results suggest that both the changes in the output mix and the national input mix provide important channels through which changes in factor supplies can be absorbed. In other words, open-economy adjustment mechanisms do suppress region-specific wage adjustment to region-specific labour supply shocks.

Gandal et al. (2004) analyse the role of changes in global production technology and changes in the national output mix in absorbing the influx of Russian migrant workers into Israel. The role of SBTC in the wage inequality literature has often been interpreted as global SBTC that originated in the US and then spread out abroad. This view has been most elegantly expressed in Krugman (2000). The spread of global SBTC to Israel may have reduced the effective supply of skilled labour and thus helped to absorb the influx of skilled migrants. Both global SBTC and changes in output mix are likely to be particularly relevant in the context of Israel, as this is clearly a small open economy.

Using a similar methodology as Hanson and Slaughter (2002) they find that (i) global SBTC more than offset the influx of skilled migrants; (ii) changes in the output mix were not important in absorbing the excess supply of skilled labour; (iii) local Israel-specific changes in production techniques (skill upgrading) along with the rise in the skill premium are consistent with local SBTC, but not with factor supply driven changes in the wage structure.[30]

Lewis (2003) conducts a similar exercise, but is particularly interested in the role of region-specific technological change as a channel of labour-market adjustment.[31] This idea is based on the conjecture by Acemoglu (2002) that SBTC may have been in part an endogenous response to changes in the structure of labour supply, rather than an exogenous force driving the changes in the skill structure of wages during the last twenty-five years. According to this view, the use of computer technology became more attractive for profit-maximising firms as the labour force became more skilled. Beaudry and Green (2005) examine changes in the US wage structure during the period 1970–96. They find that, rather than SBTC, the ratio of skilled workers to physical capital drive the observed changes in the skill structure of wages over their sample period. They explain their findings through a model of endogenous technological change in which factor supplies determine the choice between an old and a new general purpose technology which drives the increase in the skill premium.

In order to analyse the role of endogenous region-specific SBTC, Lewis (2003) starts off with a variant of the familiar between and within decomposition. However, in contrast to previous studies, he carefully takes account of the counterfactual by netting out any technological change and employment growth that would have occurred in the absence of any changes in factor supply.

In a first step, he conducts the between and within decomposition for a sample of cities that experienced high inflows of unskilled immigrants, along with a sample of cities that did not experience such inflows, but were very similar in terms of their industrial structure and labour market conditions in the base year. In the treatment cities the dropout labour force increased on average by 7 per cent, while it declined by 44 per cent in the control cities. However, despite the differences in changes in relative labour supplies and the similarity of their initial conditions, the observed differences in the change of wages and employment across the treatment and control cities are extremely small. The decomposition exercise suggests that changes in the output played no role in absorbing the excess supply of low-skilled immigrants in the treatment cities (the between component). Practically, all the workers are absorbed through increases in the drop-intensities within industries in the treatment cities (the within component).[32]

In a second step, he retrieves the within and between components and uses regression techniques to estimate for the full sample how changes in factor supplies affect the extent of within-industry and between-industry absorption. A full set of skill and city dummies is included to account for city-wide changes in total output, and country-wide changes in relative factor use. The main advantage of the regression specification, however, is that one can control for the role of demand shocks by accounting for the endogeneity of immigrant inflows using IV estimation as in Card (2001). Again, Lewis finds that practically all immigrants are absorbed through city-specific changes in the input mix within industries, while city-specific changes in the output mix do not play a role.[33]

In order to explore the role of city-specific technological change as a channel of labour market adjustment, Lewis (2003) also presents some simple correlations between computer use and changes in relative factor supplies. They indicate, in line with the conjecture by Acemoglu (2002), that computer use is positively correlated with the skill upgrading of the labour force across cities.

Lewis (2005) analyses the relationship between technology choice and local input supplies in more detail by exploring the relationship between the rate of plant automation and the change in the relative supply of high school dropouts. Using plant level data for 1988–93, he finds that plant automation occurred more slowly in cities where the relative supply of high school dropouts grew more quickly. IV estimation, based on the historical pattern of low-skilled immigrants, further strengthens the negative relationship.

Finally, a different but related literature has used a structural approach based on the GNP function to shed light on the relative importance of wages, the output mix and SBTC. The GNP function approach, similar to early structural studies on migration such as Grossman (1982), represents a production-theoretic framework but, in contrast to those early studies, they explicitly distinguish between different sectors. Consequently, this approach allows one to study adjustment through changes in relative factor prices, whilst allowing for adjustment through changes in the output mix. National welfare is maximised with respect to the vector of output prices and the vector of factor endowments for a given technology. The GNP function implies factor prices and output supplies, which are determined endogenously. As factors are assumed to be perfectly mobile across sectors (not countries or regions) the analysis is necessarily conducted at the national (or regional) level.

The GNP function has been applied mainly in the context of the trade and wages debate (Harrigan, 2000; Tombazos, 2003), but has received little attention in the context of the debate on migration where it is arguably most suitable. Exceptions are recent studies by Kohli (1999, 2002) of the Swiss economy and Hijzen and Wright (2005) of the United Kingdom.

Kohli (1999, 2002) explicitly treats both migrants and imports as inputs into the production process and examines the relationship between them. He concludes that higher migration leads to higher levels of imports and lower levels of exports. Further, higher immigration lowers the income of domestic workers, or causes severe displacement effects if wages do not adjust downwards. Owners of capital, on the other hand, benefit.

Hijzen and Wright (2005) provide an application of the GNP function approach to analyse the effects of immigration for the United Kingdom during the period 1975–96.[34] This approach allows them, in line with the recent debate on immigration and labour-market adjustment, to simultaneously study adjustment through changes in relative factor prices and adjustment through changes in the factor mix. They extend the work by Kohli (1999) by also examining how migration affects the relative returns of skilled domestic labour relative to unskilled domestic labour.

They find that an increase in the number of unskilled migrants reduces the wages of unskilled domestic workers. However, the quantitative impact of immigration is small. No discernible impact of migration is found for skilled native workers. Moreover, they find some suggestive evidence that changes in the output mix help alleviate the potentially adverse effects of immigration on the structure of wages in an open economy. The results also suggest that unskilled migrant workers and imports are substitutes in production, whilst skilled migrant workers and imports are complements.

In sum, it appears that open-economy mechanisms are important in absorbing changes in relative factor supplies. However, contrary to the expectations of most trade economists, the evidence does not suggest a large role for adjustment on the output margin. Instead, it appears that local factor supply shocks result in some combination of endogenous changes in technology in production and in the reallocation of factors across firms within industries. In other words, technological change and firm heterogeneity need to be taken into account in order to gain a more complete understanding of the way local economies adjust in response to changes in relative factor supplies.

10.4 Conclusions

Taking the literature we have considered here as a whole, it is hard to avoid the conclusion that, at present levels of immigration, the econometrically identifiable labour-market effects of that immigration are small in aggregate and fall most heavily on other immigrants with similar labour-market traits. Why this is so, however, is a matter of considerable dispute. We have seen a number of plausible accounts for these small effects: local labour-market studies miss the effect of immigration on the circulation of natives; immigrant competition with natives is imperfect; firms adjust on the technology margin; economies adjust on the output margin; and so on. However, each of these claims is at least as controversial as the claim of small effects. There will clearly be much more research on this topic.

It is, however, important to understand what this conclusion does not say: that *any* level of immigration would have only modest effects. It also does not say that the only policy-relevant effects of immigration are labour-market effects. In the construction of policy, both of these caveats must be taken into account.

Notes

1. There is also a sizeable literature on the political economy of trade policy which seeks to explain why policies are adopted that interfere with the welfare optimal policy of free trade.
2. Note that we are not arguing that, in a policy environment characterised by a large redistributive state, a liberal immigration policy is optimal. We are agnostic on that issue in this chapter. Rather, we are suggesting that basing such an argument on redistributive effects that work through the labour market is both inconsistent with widely held positions on similar policies and with the state of empirical research on the effects in question.
3. The assumption of 2 inputs is adopted for graphical convenience. All of the empirical studies assume a fairly large number of inputs: $Y = f(z)$, where z is a vector of inputs/endowments of various types of labour (and sometimes capital). Labour inputs are described by: skill level (education or job classification); years in the labour market; age; gender; and, often, immigrant status or country of origin. Details of this analysis can be found in Hammermesh (1993) and Johnson (1998). In contrast, as we shall see below, the assumption of a single sector is not simply a convenience, it is essential to the framework.

4. It is easiest to visualise the multidimensional case using the isoquant diagram. In that case, given our technological assumptions, the isoquant is a hyper bowl and, from any shift induced by the immigration shock, a move back towards the initial expansion path will produce a shift towards the initial structure of relative wages. In this context, it is also worth considering the role of capital. If it is treated as a fixed endowment, the other side of the fall in the return to labour is an increase in the relative return to fixed capital. As Ottaviano and Peri (2006) argue, such an increase in the return to capital is counterfactual, with the implication that capital adjusts endogenously.

5. By contrast, the widely cited recent work of Borjas (2003) assumes that natives and immigrants with the same (effective) labour market characteristics are perfect substitutes.

6. The illustration relies on full-employment and applies elementary vector-addition.

7. See, for example, Greenwood and Hunt (1995) and Greenwood et al. (1996, 1997).

8. Winter-Ebmer and Zweimuller (1996) and Pischke and Velling (1997) employ a similar methodology using data for Austria and Germany respectively. They find relatively small wage effects, if any at all.

9. Similar results are found in other 'natural experiment' papers on France (Hunt, 1992), Portugal (Carrington and di Lima, 1996), and Israel (Friedberg, 2001).

10. Using data from the British Labour Force Survey (LFS) they analyse the effects of immigration across seventeen UK regions in terms of employment, labour force participation, unemployment and wages. For the latter the sample period had to be restricted to 1992–2000 due to data limitations.

11. In contrast to most previous studies they explicitly frame predictions in both partial and general equilibrium.

12. As well as measurement problems due to small sample size of the LFS.

13. Of course, factor price equalisation could also result from changes in the output mix across regions without assuming factor mobility.

14. Borjas et al. emphasise that immigration and international trade are likely to be interdependent. Consequently, in order to get the complete picture the effects of immigration and international trade are analysed jointly.

15. The variation in immigration into different skill groups only provides a valid instrument when immigration is independent of the wage associated with them. To the extent that immigrants self-select into skill groups that are associated with higher wages the estimated coefficients will tend to understate the true effects associated with immigration. Similarly, if, as seems more plausible, immigrants select into lower-wage skill groups, the estimated coefficients would be overestimates.

16. The elasticity of substitution does not depend on the relative difference in terms of either experience or education.

17. Attenuation bias from the measurement error that arises when calculating the immigrant supply shock at more detailed levels of disaggregation may also account for the relatively small effect in local labour studies (Borjas, 2003: 1354). However, it is impossible to evaluate the importance of this mechanism.

18. In contrast to previous studies, Friedberg (2001) conducts her estimations at the level of the individual worker instead of occupational group (or region) which enhances the efficiency of the estimations. However, the results at the individual level and the occupational level are qualitatively similar.

19. In contrast to Anglo-Saxon studies that use country of birth to define immigrants, the German data define immigrants according to their country of citizenship.

20. Thus, perhaps surprisingly for the case of Germany, in this study, if anything labour markets appear to adjust through changes in wages rather than through changes in employment. Bonin (2005) further notes that the small labour-market effects of immigration do not mean that the labour demand curve is not downward sloping in Germany, 'it rather indicates that foreigners and natives even with the same level of measured skill are working in different segments of the labor market and therefore complement each other' (Bonin, 2005: 18).

21. Instead of using the observed occupations of individuals, Card (2001) uses the probability of having a certain occupation. While this may solve the problem of self-selection it is subject to the same criticism as studies that use observable skills.

22. In fact, their estimate is not significantly different from minus one.

23. For example, in his comment on Borjas, Freeman and Katz (1997), Di Nardo observes that half of their specifications do not suggest any offsetting effects whatsoever. In other words, as in the case of immigration and wages, priors continue to play an important role.

24. Kugler and Yuksel (2006) control in the study of Hurricane Mitch for the possibility that immigrants from Central America affect the internal migration of earlier migrants and natives, but also do not find any evidence that this is indeed the case.

25. A key difference between migration into the US and that into the UK is that migrants to the UK do not exhibit lower or very different levels of skills than that of the native population (Borjas, 1999 for the US; Dustmann et al., 2005 for the UK).

26. Similar to Borjas et al. (1997) the analysis may be deemed not truly local.

27. Though we note that the conditions for international factor-price *equalisation* are considerably more demanding than national factor-price *insensitivity*.

28. 'In testing for equal production techniques across states we are then testing for equal factor prices and for sufficiently similar production technologies' (Hanson and Slaughter, 2002: 9).

29. This is only a necessary condition (Demiroglu and Yun, 1999).

30. They acknowledge the potential role of capital accumulation, but do not explicitly address this issue.

31. Hanson and Slaughter (2002) look at productivity adjusted FPE, that is, using fixed effects they control for industry-neutral region-specific productivity differences. Lewis (2003) looks into the fixed effects, i.e. the industry changes in production techniques not common across regions.

32. The remainder is 'absorbed' through an increase in the unemployment rate.

33. Similar to Hanson and Slaughter (2002) he accounts for the fact that adjustments in output mix are only expected to occur in traded sectors.

34. The United Kingdom provides an interesting application for a number of reasons. First, and foremost, the UK is generally considered to be a relatively flexible economy. Consequently, we would expect that the channels through which foreign workers are absorbed into the labour market to operate more strongly. One of the underlying assumptions of the GNP function is indeed that markets operate perfectly. Second, the United Kingdom, in contrast to the United States for which most work on migration has been conducted, may be deemed a small open economy.

References

Acemoglu, D. (2002). 'Technical Change, Inequality, and the Labor Market', *Journal of Economic Literature*, Vol. 40, pp. 7–72.

Altonji, J. and Card, D. (1991). 'The Effects of Immigration on the Labor Market Outcomes of Less-skilled Natives', in J. Abowd and R. Freeman (eds), *Immigration, Trade and the Labor Market*. Chicago: University of Chicago Press/NBER, pp. 201–34.

Bartel, A. (1989). 'Where Do the New US Immigrants Live?', *Journal of Labor Economics*, Vol. 7, 4, pp. 371–91.

Beaudry, P. and Green, D. A. (2005). 'Changes in US Wages, 1976–2000: Ongoing Skill Bias or Major Technological Change?', *Journal of Labor Economics*, Vol. 23, pp. 609–48.

Bernard, A., Redding, S. and Schott, P. K. (2005a). 'Factor Price Equality and the Economies of the United States', CEPR Discussion Paper, No. 5111.

Bernard, A., Redding, S., Schott, P. K. and Simpson, H. (2005b). 'Relative Wage Variation and Industry Location in the United Kingdom', mimeo.

Blanchard, O. and Katz, L. (1992). 'Regional Evolutions', *Brookings Papers on Economic Activity*, No. 1, pp. 1–75.

Bonin, H. (2005). 'Wage and Employment Effects of Immigration to Germany: Evidence from a Skill Group Approach', IZA Discussion Paper, No. 1875.

Borjas, G. J. (1995). 'The Economic Benefits from Immigration', *Journal of Economic Perspectives*, Vol. 9, 2, pp. 3–22.

Borjas, G. J. (1999). *Heaven's Door: Immigration Policy and the American Economy*. Princeton: Princeton University Press.

Borjas, G. J. (2003). 'The Labor Demand Curve is Downward Sloping: Re-examining the Impact of Immigration on the Labor Market', *Quarterly Journal of Economics*, Vol. 118, 4, pp. 1335–74.

Borjas, G. J. (2005). 'Native Internal Migration and the Labor Market Impact of Immigration', NBER Working Paper, No. 11610.

Borjas, G. J., Freeman, R. B. and Katz, L. R. (1992). 'On the Labor Market Effects of Immigration and Trade', in G. J. Borjas and R. B. Freeman (eds), *Immigration and the Workforce*. Chicago: University of Chicago Press/NBER, pp. 213–44.

Borjas, G. J., Freeman, R. B. and Katz, L. R. (1996). 'Searching for the Effect of Immigration on the Labor Market', *American Economic Review*, Vol. 86, 2, pp. 246–51.

Borjas, G. J., Freeman, R. B. and Katz, L. R. (1997). 'How Much Do Immigration and Trade Affect Labor Market Outcomes?', *Brookings Papers on Economic Activity*, No. 1, pp. 1–67.

Butcher, K. and Card, D. (1991). 'Immigration and Wages: Evidence from the 1980s', *American Economic Review*, Vol. 81, 2, pp. 292–6.

Card, D. (1990). 'The Impact of the Mariel Boatlift on the Miami Labor Market', *Industrial and Labor Relations Review*, Vol. 43, 2, pp. 245–57.

Card, D. (2001). 'Immigrant Inflows, Native Outflows, and the Local Labor Market Impacts of Higher Immigration', *Journal of Labor Economics*, Vol. 19, 1, pp. 22–64.

Card, D. (2005). 'Is the New Immigration Really So Bad?', *Economic Journal*, Vol. 115, pp. F300–F323.

Card, D. and Di Nardo, J. (2000). 'Do Immigrant Inflows Lead to Native Outflows?', *American Economic Review*, Vol. 90, 2, pp. 360–7.

Carrasco, R., Jimeno, J. F. and Ortega, A. C. (2006). 'The Effect of Immigration on the Employment Opportunities of Native-Born Workers: Some Evidence for Spain', *Journal of Population Economics*, forthcoming.

Carrington, W. and de Lima, P. (1996). 'The Impact of 1970s Repatriates from Africa on the Portuguese Labor Market', *ILR Review*, Vol. 49, 2, pp. 330–47.

Cohen-Goldner, S. and Paserman, D. (2005). 'The Dynamic Impact of Immigration of Natives' Labor Market Outcomes: Evidence from Israel', mimeo.

Debaere, P. (2004). 'Does Lumpiness Matter in an Open Economy? Studying International Economics with Regional Data', *Journal of International Economics*, Vol. 64, 2, pp. 485–501.

Demiroglu, U. and Yun, K. K. (1999). 'The Lens Condition for Factor Price Equalization', *Journal of International Economics*, Vol. 47, 2, pp. 449–56.

Dustmann, C., Fabbri, F. and Preston, I. (2005). 'The Impact of Immigration on the British Labour Market', *Economic Journal*, Vol. 115, pp. F324–F341.

Filer, R. (1992). 'The Effect of Immigrant Arrivals on Migratory Patterns of Native Workers', in G. J. Borjas and R. B. Freeman (eds), *Immigration and the Work Force*. Chicago: University of Chicago Press/NBER, pp. 245–69.

Frey, W. (1995a). 'Immigration and Internal Migration "Flight" from US Metropolitan Areas: Toward a New Demographic Balkanisation', *Urban Studies*, Vol. 32, 4/5, pp. 733–57.

Frey, W. (1995b). 'Immigration and Internal Migration "Flight": a California Case Study', *Population and Environment*, Vol. 16, 4, pp. 353–75.

Friedberg, R. (2001). 'The Impact of Mass Migration on the Israeli Labor Market', *Quarterly Journal of Economics*, Vol. 116, 4, pp. 1373–1408.

Friedberg, R. and Hunt, J. (1995). 'The Impact of Immigrants on Host Country Wages, Employment and Growth', *Journal of Economic Perspectives*, Vol. 9, 2, pp. 23–44.

Gandal, N., Hanson, G. and Slaughter, M. (2004). 'Technology, Trade, and Adjustment to Immigration in Israel', *European Economic Review*, Vol. 48, pp. 403–28.

Gaston, N. and Nelson, N. (2002). 'The Wage and Employment Effects of Immigration: Trade and Labour Economics Perspectives', in D. Greenaway, R. Upward and K. Wakelin (eds), *Trade, Investment, Migration and Labour Market Adjustment*. Basingstoke: Palgrave Macmillan, pp. 201–35.

Greenwood, M. and Hunt, G. (1995). 'Economic Effects of Immigrants on Native and Foreign-Born Workers: Complementarity, Substitutability, and Other Channels of Influence', *Southern Economic Journal*, Vol. 61, 4, pp. 1076–97.

Greenwood, M., Hunt, G. and Kohli, U. (1996). 'The Short-Run and Long-Run Factor-Market Consequences of Immigration to the United States', *Journal of Regional Science*, Vol. 36, 1, pp. 43–66.

Greenwood, M., Hunt, G. and Kohli, U. (1997). 'The Factor-market Consequences of Unskilled Immigration to the United States', *Labour Economics*, Vol. 4, 1, pp. 1–28.

Grossman, J. (1982). 'The Substitutability of Natives and Immigrants in Production', *Review of Economics and Statistics*, Vol. 64, 4, pp. 596–603.

Hammermesh, D. (1993). *Labor Demand*. Princeton: Princeton University Press.

Hanson, G. and Slaughter, M. J. (2002). 'Labor-Market Adjustment in Open Economies: Evidence from US States', *Journal of International Economics*, Vol. 57, pp. 3–29.

Harrigan, J. (2000). 'International Trade and American Wages in General Equilibrium, 1967–1995', in R. C. Feenstra (ed.), *The Impact of International Trade on Wages*. Chicago: University of Chicago Press.

Hatton, T. J. and Tani, M. (2005). 'Immigration and Inter-Regional Mobility in the UK, 1982–2000', *Economic Journal*, Vol. 115, pp. F342–F358.

Hijzen, A. and Wright, P. (2005). 'Migration, Trade and Wages', GEP Research Paper 2005/11.

Hunt, J. (1992). 'The Impact of the 1962 Repatriates from Algeria on the French Labor Market', *ILR Review*, Vol. 45, 3, pp. 556–72.

Johnson, G. (1998). 'The Impact of Immigration on Income Distribution Among Minorities', in D. Hammermesh and F. Bean (eds), *Help or Hindrance? The Economic Implications of Immigration for African Americans*. New York: Russell Sage Foundation, pp. 17–50.

Kohli, U. (1999). 'Trade and Migration: a Production Theory Approach', in R. Faini, J. de Melo and K. F. Zimmermann (eds), *Migration: the Controversies and the Evidence*. Cambridge: Cambridge University Press.

Kohli, U. (2002). 'Migration and Foreign Trade: Further Results', *Journal of Population Economics*, Vol. 15, pp. 381–7.

Krugman, P. R. (2000). 'Technology, Trade and Factor Prices', *Journal of International Economics*, Vol. 50, pp. 51–71.

Kugler, A. and Yuksel, M. (2006). 'Effects of Low Skilled Immigration on US Natives: Evidence from Hurricane Mitch', mimeo.

Leamer, E. (1995). 'The Heckscher–Ohlin Model in Theory and Practice', *Princeton Studies in International Finance*, Vol. 77.

Lewis, E. (2003). 'Local Open Economies Within the US: How Do Industries Respond to Immigration?', FRBP Working Paper.

Lewis, E. (2005). 'Immigration, Skill-Mix and the Choice of Technique', FRBP Working Paper.

Markusen, J. (1983). 'Factor Movements and Commodity Trade as Complements', *Journal of International Economics*, Vol. 14, 3/4, pp. 341–56.

Markusen, J. and Svensson, L. (1985). 'Trade in Goods and Factors with International Differences in Technology', *International Economic Review*, Vol. 26, 1, pp. 175–92.

Mundell, R. (1957). 'International Trade and Factor Mobility', *American Economic Review*, Vol. 47, 3, pp. 321–35.

Norman, V. and Venables, A. (1995). 'International Trade, Factor Mobility, and Trade Costs', *Economic Journal*, Vol. 105, pp. 1488–1504.

Ottaviano, G. I. P. and Peri, G. (2006). 'Rethinking the Gains from Immigration: Theory and Evidence from the US', University of California-Davis.

Pischke, J.-S. and Velling, J. (1997). 'Employment Effects of Immigration to Germany: an Analysis Based on Local Labor Markets', *Review of Economics and Statistics*, Vol. 79, 4, pp. 594–604.

Tombazos, C. G. (2003). 'A Production Theory Approach to the Imports and Wage Inequality Nexus', *Economic Inquiry*, Vol. 41, 1, pp. 42–61.

Winter-Ebmer, R. and Zweimuller, J. (1996). 'Immigration and the Earnings of Young Native Workers', *Oxford Economic Papers*, Vol. 48, pp. 473–91.

Wong, K. Y. (1986). 'Are International Trade and Factor Mobility Substitutes?', *Journal of International Economics*, Vol. 21, 1/2, pp. 25–43.

Wright, R., Ellis, M. and Reibel, M. (1997). 'The Linkage between Immigration and Internal Migration in Large Metropolitan Areas in the US', *Economic Geography*, Vol. 73, 2, pp. 234–54.

Index

NB: Page numbers in bold refer to figures and tables